THE
POWER
OF THE
POPPY

"Kenaz Filan's well-researched compilation of Poppy's history, uses, constituents, derivatives, and personal accounts will more than inform you about this powerful plant—it will invite you to deeply consider the price one pays for such a potent ally."

PAM MONTGOMERY, HERBALIST
AND AUTHOR OF *PLANT SPIRIT HEALING*

"Like cannabis, the poppy is an ancient medicinal plant, both revered and maligned. Kenaz Filan performs a crucial service in educating us about its history, both agricultural and cultural, and examining its potential for healing and harm. Most importantly, the author offers hope and heart to those struggling with addiction."

JULIE HOLLAND, EDITOR OF *ECSTASY: THE COMPLETE GUIDE*
AND *THE POT BOOK: A COMPLETE GUIDE TO CANNABIS*

"*The Power of the Poppy* offers a frank and precise analysis of the mystical, chemical, and social aspects of a plant that has fascinated humans for millennia. Readers will gain the data they need to make informed decisions."

ELIZABETH BARRETTE, AUTHOR OF *COMPOSING MAGIC*

THE
POWER
OF THE
POPPY

Harnessing Nature's
Most Dangerous Plant Ally

KENAZ FILAN

Park Street Press
Rochester, Vermont • Toronto, Canada

Park Street Press
One Park Street
Rochester, Vermont 05767
www.ParkStPress.com

Text paper is SFI certified

Park Street Press is a division of Inner Traditions International

Library of Congress Cataloging-in-Publication Data

Filan, Kenaz.
  The power of the poppy : harnessing nature's most dangerous plant ally / Kenaz
Filan.
      p. cm.
  Includes bibliographical references and index.
  Summary: "A comprehensive look at the inspiring, healing, and addictive
powers of the Opium Poppy and its derivatives throughout history"—Provided by
publisher.
  ISBN 978-1-59477-399-0
  1. Opium. 2. Opium poppy. 3. Opioids. I. Title.
  RS165.O6F55 2011
  615'.7822—dc22

                                                              2010045566

Printed and bound in the United States by Lake Book Manufacturing
The text paper is SFI certified. The Sustainable Forestry Initiative® program
promotes sustainable forest management.

10   9   8   7   6   5   4   3   2   1

Text design and layout by Priscilla Baker
This book was typeset in Garamond Premier Pro with Bembo and Myriad Pro
used as display typefaces

To send correspondence to the author of this book, mail a first-class letter to the
author c/o Inner Traditions • Bear & Company, One Park Street, Rochester, VT
05767, and we will forward the communication.

I would like to thank my wife, editor, and supporter, Kathy Latzoni, for all her assistance in this and in all my writing.

Thanks to Jon Graham, acquisitions editor at Inner Traditions, for seeing this project to press.

A shout-out to the fine (if sometimes dysfunctional) folks at Bluelight (www.bluelight.ru), one of the Internet's best harm-reduction boards. It is good to learn from your mistakes; it's generally less painful to learn from the mistakes of others.

This book is dedicated to the memory of Paul Hulabek.
I conquered my demons and got sober. I'm sorry you couldn't. Rest in peace, old friend. See you on the other side.

CONTENTS

INTRODUCTION

Before ingesting a magical or medicinal plant, shamans might spend hours talking with it. They might provide it with offerings of food or drink; they might decorate its branches or sing songs in its honor. Only after propitiating the plant and becoming acquainted with its spirit would they work with it as a teacher and ally. Even then their dealings would be tempered with a good bit of caution, respect, and healthy fear. If treated disrespectfully, an ally could become a terrible, even a lethal, enemy.

Today most scientists would consider this behavior the height of folly. Instead of talking to a plant, they would rather uproot it and subject its remains to biochemical analysis. The idea that plants might communicate with humans is laughable. Accepting that plants might have an innate intelligence would mean that their existence might have some meaning outside of that which humans assign to it. Instead of viewing plants as the sturdy base of the food pyramid, we might have to see them as fellow travelers on planet Earth. This is, of course, sheer superstition. Why, next we'll be saying that chemicals and elements have their own spirits!

For thousands of years shamans have followed these "silly" and "superstitious" beliefs. Rather than reserving intelligence, will, and volition for a chosen few life-forms, they have found it all around them. Instead of a model where a Most High Being manipulates things like pawns on a very large chessboard, they imagined a world where plants and animals communicated with each other and where mountains, rocks, and rivers were not inanimate objects but wise and powerful beings. The alchemists who followed their lead believed that sulfur, mercury, and the other substances they used were living beings and that their work could proceed only if their spirits were properly treated.

Our modern chemical and pharmaceutical industries have created many substances that alchemists would have considered miraculous blessings. But they have also given us some terrible toxins. Many of their creations fall into both categories. Among the most infamous of these are the various drugs that have been derived from *Papaver somniferum,* better known as the opium poppy.

We have spent untold amounts of money trying to control the illegal distribution and abuse of opiates. We have sent millions of addicts to prison or involuntary treatment programs. Every year we burn hectares of poppy fields and intercept tons of heroin and billions of stolen pills. And yet despite our best efforts, the scourge of addiction continues to grow and thrive. Our "War on Drugs" has to date been a one-sided rout. We keep saying "no" to drugs, but they refuse to listen.

Perhaps the problem lies not in our approach but in our outlook. So long as we see poppies as mere flowers and opiates as mere chemicals, we will have no chance of controlling them. Only when we recognize that *Papaver somniferum* and its derivates are sentient beings will we have a chance of understanding their attraction. We must learn once again to approach them with the respect due powerful and potentially hazardous allies. Until we do that, we will never be able to reap their full benefits and avoid their worst dangers.

Shamans trained for years at the feet of their teachers. There they learned the legends and stories of their ally. They heard tales of the ancestors who had first spoken to the plant, along with warnings about those who had treated their ally carelessly or disrespectfully and paid a terrible price for their arrogance. They were taught the secret ways by which poison could be transmuted into medicine, and they were provided with an introduction to the ally's spirit as well as its body.

Understanding the allure of opiates requires far more than a simple knowledge of biology and chemistry. We must learn what they mean to Western culture and what they have meant to others. We must study the example of those who have worshipped at the altar of Morpheus and learn from their triumphs and tragedies. We must explore the ways we have used and abused the poppy and understand why all our attempts to "control" it have failed so miserably. Only then will we be ready to approach this most powerful and most dangerous ally.

You may be interested in using opiates recreationally. Lots of people do. Many of them are even capable of doing so on an occasional basis without becoming physically or psychologically addicted. Others are not so fortunate. They either become hooked or run afoul of law enforcement in their quest for euphoria. If you learn from their example, you may be able to avoid their mistakes. Or you may decide the risks are greater than the potential reward and choose other, safer indulgences.

PART ONE

HISTORY

If we are going to seek Poppy's counsel, we must learn from those who came before us. Thankfully, this is not difficult. Few plant allies have such a long and well-documented history as *Papaver somniferum*. Its usage dates back to the earliest agricultural period and continues to this day. Innumerable scribes have written down the details of its cultivation, preparation, and usage. Poppies have played an important role in medicine for as long as there have been physicians.

Any shaman knows that when you learn the history of your ally, you cannot help but learn about your tribe. In studying opium poppies, we learn the ways we have interacted with them. Those stories contain great wisdom for those who can understand. They allow us to learn from the mistakes of others. Secrets are hidden here in plain sight; those who have ears will hear and understand.

1

IN THE BEGINNING

Neolithic and Mesolithic archaeologists are at a distinct disadvantage. No written records remain of the people they are studying; any legends of their traditions and cultures have long since been forgotten, buried under multiple waves of cultural invasions and counterinvasions. While tribes may have built stone megaliths, they generally resided in wooden huts or longhouses that were ill-suited for surviving for millennia in the moist European clime. We have only the most scattered and fragmentary evidence left to us, and piecing it together to find any kind of definitive answer is challenging in the extreme. The best we can hope for is educated guesswork and enlightened speculation—which must, of course, be colored by the prejudices and preconceptions of those who are left to interpret these puzzles.

The Dawn of Poppy Cultivation

Approximately 7,500 years ago agricultural communities began to develop along the basin of the Danube River. Within less than two hundred years they had spread to what would become Belgium and northern France in the west and Ukraine in the east. Where their ancestors had foraged and hunted for a living, these people (called *linearbandkeramik,* or LBK, for their distinctive pottery) worked the land for their food. They took cues—and seeds—from the Near East, where farming had been taking place for millennia. Among the charred remains of their fires, archaeologists have found traces of *emmer* and *einkorn* wheat, linseed (flax), lentils, and peas, crops that originated in modern-day Turkey, Syria, Israel, and Iran.[1] But amid all those eastern seeds was one other nonnative plant that came not from the east but from the southwest—*Papaver somniferum,* otherwise known as the opium poppy.

Today most botanists believe *P. somniferum* descends from *Papaver setigerum,* a wild poppy growing in the western Mediterranean. *P. setigerum* is found in Italy, northern Africa, eastern Spain, the Mediterranean coast of France, and the Canary Islands. *P. setigerum* is slightly smaller than *P. somniferum;* its leaves are thinner, with long, jagged teeth tipped with a bristle that is not found on *P. somniferum* leaves. They also lack *P. somniferum*'s waxy coating. Like its domesticated cousin, *P. setigerum* contains morphine alkaloids; indeed, the two poppies are so similar that some botanists believe them to be the same species.[2]

It has been suggested that poppies were introduced to LBK agriculture through trade with the La Hoguette culture, a group known primarily by its distinctive bone-tempered pottery. The La Hoguette culture is believed to have originated in southern and southwestern France. They descended from an earlier impressed ware culture that resided on the shores of the Mediterranean. La Hoguette and LBK pottery has been found together at many sites east and west of the Rhine, suggesting that contact and trade took place between the two cultures.

From there, poppies continued on their journey northward. A dig at Raunds, a site in rural Northamptonshire, England, uncovered eight opium poppy seeds dated from the early Neolithic period (5,800–5,600 years ago). While opium poppies can grow as weeds, the lack of other weeds in the ditch and the absence of cereal remains suggest this plant may have been a crop in its own right.[3] While Neolithic civilization has traditionally been envisioned as scattered collections of hunter-gatherers who supplemented their foraging with primitive agriculture, the Raunds poppy seeds reveal trade routes between Britain and the Continent. They also suggest that the people of Raunds held poppies in high regard—high enough, at least, to carry seeds across the English Channel, then haul them into the East Midlands and plant them.

At Cuevo de los Murciélagos (Cave of the Bats, a Neolithic burial site located in Albuñol, Granada, in southern Spain) we find still more evidence of poppy usage. Thanks to the cave's arid conditions, the round, woven grass bags that were buried with the dead have been preserved, along with their contents—large numbers of poppy capsules, which have been shown by carbon dating to be more than six thousand years old. Given the somnolence caused by ingestion of poppies, it seems clear that even at this early date they were associated with death and, presumably, with shamanic journeying.

Excavations at Egolzwil, an archaeological site located in Switzerland's Lucerne canton, have revealed signs of poppy cultivation dating back more than six thousand years, including poppy seed cakes and poppy heads. These may have been used to feed their cattle in emergencies (cattle generally dislike foraging on bitter-tasting poppies and will eat them only if no better food is available), but these farmers would certainly have known that poppies can produce intoxication and even death in cattle if too many are given. Yet evidence suggests that poppies were the most common crop at Egolzwil, more common than club wheat, barley, or flax.[4]

Even earlier evidence of opium poppy use comes from recent underwater archaeological work at La Marmotta, a site in Lake Bracciano, Italy (northwest of Rome). La Marmotta was occupied by a Neolithic farming community for about five hundred years before it was abandoned, then submerged by water some 7,700 years ago. Based on the sophisticated artifacts found at the La Marmotta site—and the paucity of evidence for any other contemporaneous cities or villages in the area—archaeologists believe this was a colony from another civilization in Greece or the Near East. And given the model boats (along with a well-preserved longboat found buried in the mud), it seems likely that there was considerable water traffic between the La Marmotta colony and traders from other civilizations.

"This was not an ordinary village," says Maria Antonietta Fugazzola Delpino, director of the La Marmotta expedition. "The people were in touch with other communities in the Mediterranean. We picture it as a kind of highway—there were many ships coming and going."[5] Organic remains preserved beneath three meters of limestone included poppy seeds, presumably cultivated for food, oil, medicine, and possibly for religious use. It may be here that poppies and their seeds were first brought eastward from Europe. Two thousand years later they would be seen again in the kingdom of Sumeria (see chapter 2).

Exploring the Archaeological Record

Most of what we know of the LBK and La Hoguette cultures comes from shards of their pottery and scraps gleaned from long-buried campfire sites where they cooked their meals. We do not know whether they encountered each other through trade, through warfare, or (as seems likely, given what we know of posthistoric humankind) through some combination thereof. We do not know whether the LBK culture consisted of colonists moving in via the Balkans (as some theorize) or whether it sprung up among the indigenous people after they were exposed to pottery, agriculture, and other accoutrements of the "Neolithic Revolution."

If we know little about LBK culture, we know even less about the La Hoguette peoples. Their sites show evidence that they, like contemporaneous Mediterranean cultures, had domesticated sheep and goats but not cattle or pigs. Their pottery also shows evidence of Mediterranean influence, but the stone tools recovered at their sites are very similar to those used by earlier regional Mesolithic cultures. And while we believe that the LBK culture acquired poppies from the La Hoguette people, thanks to *P. setigerum*'s distribution, we cannot say for certain. While wild poppies grow in the region of the La Hoguette culture, to date no seeds have been found at the few La Hoguette sites that have been excavated.

It is difficult to distinguish between the carbonized seeds of wild and domesticated poppies. Furthermore, their small size means that only a very few poppy seeds have been found at LBK sites. This makes it difficult to determine how extensive the cultivation of poppies was among Neolithic farmers, especially since cultivated poppies can quickly spread and become weeds given the proper soil and climate. As a result, some archaeologists have tried to downplay poppy cultivation among Central Europe's Neolithic and Mesolithic peoples, claiming that all evidence of poppies at their sites comes from wild poppies growing in the area. (This, of course, begs the question of how these wild poppies came to Central Europe in the first place.)

An artifact found in Meinling, Germany, however, suggests that poppies were of some considerable importance. This pot is more than six thousand years old and was made from clay tempered (mixed) with poppy seeds. While it is common for potters to temper clay with inert matter like straw or sand, poppy seeds are oily and not particularly suitable for use as a temper.[6] Their usage in this context suggests this pot had some special purpose. Given the role of poppies in other cultures, we can speculate that it had some religious significance and may have been used as a sacramental vessel.

Furthermore, we should note that much early agriculture among hunter-gatherers involved "prestige" crops rather than staples. Early agriculture was laborious, backbreaking work. Forests were cleared with flint rocks chipped to produce an edge. Straight sticks were used to dig roots out of the ground, forked sticks to till the dirt, and sharpened stones to harvest wild-growing and cultivated grains. With such inefficient tools, it was difficult to produce large-scale food crops, especially in the moist, heavy soil of the LBK region. Hence, it is likely that many of the earliest crops were grown not to support the population but for ceremonial purposes. Many believe that grains were first grown to produce not bread but beer, or, as one archaeologist put it, "Thirst rather than hunger may have been the stimulus behind the origin of small grain agriculture."[7]

Poppies produced oil that could be used in lamps—but animal fat provided by abundant herds and game would serve a similar purpose. Poppy seed provided a food source—but so did the hazelnuts that grew wild throughout the region. It is most unlikely that primitive farmers expended so much effort to establish poppies while remaining unaware of their psychoactive properties.

The Religion of Hunter-Gatherers

We limit the role of religion to "spiritual" questions, and we draw hard and fast lines between facts and myths. This is a very recent development, and one that is still controversial in many quarters. So too is our idea that the "soul" is something unique to humankind, not to mention our separation of this world from the heavenly realms. Among hunter-gatherer cultures, these distinctions are meaningless. They live in a world where the spiritual is immanent, where they have social relationships not only with their family and clan but also with the animals they hunt, the springs from which they draw water, and the plants that provide them with roots and berries.

The specific nature of this life force is envisioned differently among different groups. The hunter-gatherer Mbuti pygmies of the Congo envision the forest as father and mother. They sing to it while going about their daily affairs; in times of trouble they call on it by blowing their *molimo* trumpets and singing special songs to ensure it "awakens happy."[8] To Australian Aborigines the "eternal" is present in daily life and temporal space, even if it sometimes becomes obscured in the day-to-day rhythms of an individual's existence; the spirit world presents itself in the rocks, trees, dances, songs, and experiences of the living.[9] But the overarching theme remains: the life force that animates humans also animates other beings; they are as much a part of the community as the children and ancestors.

Because these "objects" are part of the community, they are treated as such. They are not only spoken to, but spoken *with*. They share their bodies and provide nourishment for the community, but they also share their wisdom and provide counsel and encouragement. Alternately, they may be hostile to the clan and treated with fear and healthy respect. The hunter-gatherer lifestyle has little to do with the idyllic but fictitious world of the "noble savage"—they live in a world where disease, starvation, and injury are ever-present dangers and where those outside the clan are generally seen either as threats or as potential prey. But whether friend or foe, they are recognized as sentient and capable of communication.

Many world myths connect the development of agriculture to the gods. Dionysus taught Hellenics the secrets of viniculture while Athena gave the olive tree to the citizens of her namesake city. Various Native American tribes speak of how Corn Maiden took pity upon hungry humankind and gave them the gift of maize, while many Egyptologists connect the death and resurrection of Osiris with the sowing and harvesting of wheat. We see these stories as "creation myths" and "archetypal representations." But suppose we look at them from the hunter-gatherer viewpoint—as literal truths?

If a species wished to propagate itself (and what species doesn't?), hitching its wagon to the fortunes of Neolithic humans would be a superb way of doing so. By communicating their likes and dislikes to the people who gathered their fruits, they could establish a partnership with carriers who would take their seeds farther than wind, water, or the vagaries of chance. They could ensure their offspring would be placed in fitting soil with proper drainage and light, not just scattered about randomly. They could take advantage of humankind's mobility and tool-making skills to spread their range farther. Today some people talk to their plants. Could it be that our hunter-gatherer ancestors learned how to farm by listening to theirs?

One of the first plants to share its secrets was the poppy. In a time when dysentery and stomach illnesses frequently proved fatal, the poppy provided potent medicine against diarrhea. In a world where those who made it to thirty were old and arthritis was commonplace, poppy provided relief from pain and allowed those who consumed it to continue serving the clan as productive hunters and foragers. Those who wished to explore alternate realities through the use of plant allies found Poppy to be invaluable. By drinking poppy tea or consuming poppy pods, they could induce hypnagogic states and vivid dream-visions.

As it cemented its symbiotic relationship with humankind, Poppy began developing higher concentrations of the alkaloids that were the secret of its power. In return, those whom it served returned the favor, and soon *P. somniferum* was spreading across Europe and into Asia.

2

THE BRONZE AGE WORLD

When hunter-gatherers become farmers, their relationship with their world changes. They must now clear fields to plant their crops and graze their flocks. As the cultigen plants drive other plant species away, they introduce a new dichotomy to their human symbiotes—the distinction between tame and wild. The village becomes a place of safety and security; the area beyond is now a place of danger. In time it becomes a place where exiles and outsiders roam. The shaman who goes into the bush in search of healing herbs and sacred wisdom is overshadowed by the witch wandering through the briars in search of curses and poisons. This dichotomy ensures that the cultivated territory grows and the cultigens prosper.

In time the relationship between many cultigens and their cultivators becomes one of *obligate symbiosis*. Without planters to prepare the land for them, most modern-day food crops and farm animals would soon become extinct. Without agriculture, human populations would decline dramatically after widespread famine. (The preagricultural population of Great Britain has been estimated at between five thousand and ten thousand; today, Britain is home to more than sixty million people.)[1]

In the struggle to establish this relationship, the opium poppy is at a decided disadvantage. While its seeds can provide a nutritious, protein-filled meal, it is not so efficient a food crop as wheat, soybeans, or lentils. But when it increased the size of its psychoactive capsules, it lost the ability to self-seed; its pods no longer split of their own accord, even when dried. To ensure its continued cultivation and survival, *P. somniferum* had to adapt itself to meet other needs. And one of humankind's strongest drives—stronger, in many cases, than the instincts for procreation, security, or even self-preservation—is the urge to seek pleasure.

Mesopotamia and the "Joy Plant"

Early in the morning old women, boys and girls collect the juice, scraping it off the notches (of the poppy capsule), and place it within a clay receptacle.
SUMERIAN TABLET, FOURTH MILLENNIUM BCE[2]

Before the rise of the Sumerians, this region between the Tigris and Euphrates Rivers was a patchwork of arid steppe and reed-choked marshes. The earliest records credit Enki, god of wisdom and fresh water, with creating the irrigation systems and canals that allowed farmers to take full advantage of the fertile soil. Nomadic herders settled down in houses made of bricks baked from the clay that provided them with abundant crops of barley, wheat, flax, and grapes. With these they traded for copper and tin to make bronze farm tools and weapons. Skilled professions arose, with weavers, smiths, bakers, brewers, and other artisans selling their services and their wares. And one of those wares was the dried juice of sliced poppy capsules—what the Greeks would later name "opium."

When the unripe pods of an opium poppy are cut or sliced, the plant exudes a thick, milky white sap. This sap is a latex, a collection of polymers suspended in water. Extruded latex acts as a bandage over the wound, protecting the plant from bacterial or fungal infections. Because it is very bitter, it discourages browsing animals and insects from consuming it. And because it contains a significant quantity of psychoactive alkaloids—10% or more morphine by weight—it has long been popular with those enamored of poppy's recreational potential. The Sumerians referred to poppies with the ideogram *Hul Gil,* or "joy plant." A fragment from a Sumerian vessel dated between 2400 and 2250 BCE features a figure who may be Nisaba, goddess of grains and brewers, with dates in her hand and poppy pods growing from her shoulders.[3]

The process of opium gathering described in the Sumerian tablets is still used today. Approximately two weeks after the poppy flowers bloom, their petals drop off, leaving behind the pods. Harvesters watch the gray band at the top of the capsule where the petals were attached. When it has become almost black (fourteen to twenty days later) the pod is fully ripe and the opium is ready to harvest.

At that time workers go through with special tools, wooden handles fitted with small sharp pieces of metal or glass. With these they make incisions, which must be neither too shallow nor too deep. If the cut is too shallow, not enough juice will be produced; too deep and the latex will flow into the pod, causing the whole yield to be lost. As soon as the cut is made, small drops of milky white juice begin flowing. These are left exposed to the air to solidify and grow darker. At dawn the next day these solidified drops of latex are removed from the capsule with a blunt knife, then collected in a vessel. Each pod can produce 20 to 100 milligrams of opium. Most poppies produce three to five pods per plant.

After the Sumerians came the Assyrians. They too knew of poppy juice, which they called *arat-pa-pal* (this may be the etymological origin of the Latin word for poppy, *papaver*). Among the surviving tablets of the temple of the Assyrian king Assurbanipal (685–627 BCE), poppies are mentioned forty-two times.[4] An Assyrian fertility seal shows Ashera (the Mesopotamian Ishtar) with two priests, two demons, and a "magical plant," which is likely a poppy, given Ishtar's connections to dream divination.[5]

Assyria was strategically located along the Spice Route (also known as the Silk Route) between Asia and Egypt. As one of the great trading powers of their day, it is likely that the Assyrians played a role in the eastern distribution of poppies. By the sixth century BCE poppies were grown in Persia, where opium was known as *theriac*.[6] Theriac was considered a great balm against snakebites and other illnesses. Many drug salesmen named their cure-alls "theriac" and, as would be the case with patent medicines millennia later, many of their preparations included liberal doses of opium.

Poppies in Egypt

The Ebers Papyrus, dated from about 1552 BCE, contains 876 magical formulas and folk remedies for afflictions ranging from crocodile bite to toenail pain. One of the five hundred substances used to make these remedies was opium poppy. It was to be mixed with fly dung, then given to crying children, who would immediately be calmed. *P. somniferum* pods are found in tomb paintings of the early dynasties and are quite common by the Eighteenth Dynasty (1550–1292 BCE).[7]

Some Egyptologists believe the poppies mentioned in these texts were actually *Papaver rhoeas*, the corn poppy. While corn poppies do not contain morphine or generate opium, their petals contain the alkaloid rhoeadine, a mild sedative and antitussive (cough suppressant). Tests on jars and pots found in early Egyptian tombs have been inconclusive. In 1937 a *P. somniferum* pod was found in a storage jar at Deir el-Medina, a workman's village dating from the Eighteenth to the Twentieth Dynasties (1550–1069 BCE). Some controversy exists as to whether it was placed there during the Pharaonic era or in the fourth century CE, when Coptic monks used these ruins as a hermitage.[8]

It is difficult to believe that dynastic Egypt had no knowledge of opium, given its close proximity to Crete, the Mediterranean's largest opium trading center, and the number of poppy-head figurines imported from there. Whatever the case, it is clear that by the Classical era (see chapter 3), Egypt was not only importing opium but also producing it as well. The poppies grown at Thebes produced the well-regarded *opium thebaicum,* from which the alkaloid thebaine derives its name.

Poppies in the Mediterranean

In July 1959 excavations at Gazi, a small village on Crete, revealed five twelfth century BCE figurines representing the Minoan goddess. The first and largest bears on her head three movable pins that resemble *P. somniferum* pods. She was named by Professor Spyridon Marinatos, leader of the exhibition, "the Poppy Goddess, Patroness of Healing."[9]

The Poppy Goddess smiles vacantly, her lips parted and her eyes closed, fixed on a place between dream and waking. Even more telling, her poppy-head pins are decorated with vertical slits that have been darkened to represent the color of dried opium latex. Near the goddess was a tubular vase with a hole on one side, which bore a remarkable resemblance to Javanese tools for the inhalation of opium vapors. Alongside her statue (which was found in a doorless, windowless room that could only be approached from above) was a heap of coal.[10]

There is little evidence that the Minoans had any sort of standing army but much evidence that they supported themselves through trade and mercantile activities. Based on the finds of Marinatos and others, it seems clear that poppies, along with copper and tin, were a major part of their business. Another major opium center was located on the island of Cyprus. Cypriot vases and tiny containers designed to look like cut poppy heads have been found in tombs and excavated settlements throughout the Middle East, and traces of opium have been found in some. Other interesting artifacts include a Cypriot necklace of multi-colored glass beads, with one bead notched like a poppy capsule, and a considerable number of brooches that have been identified as pomegranates but may actually be poppy capsules.[11]

Concurrent with the Minoan civilization on Crete, the Mycenaean culture ruled over much of mainland Greece. A fifteenth century BCE gold ring found in the Acropolis at Mycenae (about 90 km north of modern-day Athens) shows a vegetation goddess receiving her followers. In her hands she holds three poppy heads; above her floats the double-headed axe that symbolizes the Minoan great goddess.[12] A royal tomb at Mycenae also revealed poppy pod–shaped amulets and brooches, as well as very long pins. Some archaeologists believe these pins are unsuited for use as hairpins or clothing pins. They may have been heated, then applied to opium to vaporize it for inhalation. A similar technique is used among opium smokers to this day.

According to Hesiod's *Theogony,* written in the eighth century BCE, Prometheus first taught how to sacrifice ox bones (rather than the more valuable meat) at Mekone (the "Place of Poppies"). While this resulted in immediate benefit for humankind, it had horrible consequences. As a result of Prometheus's trickery, Zeus sent Pandora—and a whole host of evils, including death, disease, war, and madness—to humankind.

Mekone was located in Sikyon, a small city in Corinth with a site sacred to the goddesses Demeter and Persephone. Demeter (who many believe to be a survival of the Minoan mother-goddess into the later Hellenic era) was intimately connected with poppies. She was often depicted with stems of poppy, along with barley and wheat, in her hands and on her headdress. After her daughter was kidnapped by Hades, she was said to ease her grief and seek sleep by eating poppies. And it is possible that aspirants were prepared for the Eleusinian Mysteries by draughts of poppy tea or opium preparations.

Possibilities for the *kykeon,* the hallucinogenic sacramental substance given to candidates, have included ergot fungus and psychedelic mushrooms. Given the connection between Demeter and poppies—not to mention poppies and deathlike hypnotic sleep—it seems probable that *P. somniferum* would be one of the ingredients. In the proper setting, the visions induced by poppies could certainly cause, as one ancient diarist noted, "intensive psychic changes, which cleared their souls, and made them accept death not so much as harm as a blessing."[13]

Evidence suggests that ingestion of the kykeon was a pleasant and euphoric experience, since there were no reports of "bad trips" or terror—

something we would expect from concoctions containing ergotine or *Amanita muscaria* (fly agaric mushrooms). Indeed, Athenian rogue and bad boy Alcibiades (450–404 BCE) got in trouble for stealing a batch of kykeon and sharing it with his friends at a party.

In Homer's eighth century BCE saga the *Odyssey*, Helen drugs the wine of her company with the opium-like drug *nepenthe*,

> an herb that banishes all care, sorrow, and ill humour. Whoever drinks wine thus drugged cannot shed a single tear all the rest of the day, not even though his father and mother both of them drop down dead, or he sees a brother or a son hewn in pieces before his very eyes. This drug, of such sovereign power and virtue, had been given to Helen by Polydamna wife of Thon, a woman of Egypt, where there grow all sorts of herbs, some good to put into the mixing-bowl and others poisonous.[14]

In Homer's *Iliad* two powerful metaphors show that the Greeks were already familiar with cultivated poppies.

> The arrow hit Priam's brave son Gorgythion in the breast . . . and now he bowed his head as a garden poppy in full bloom when it is weighed down by showers in spring—even thus heavy bowed his head beneath the weight of his helmet.[15]
> . . . Peneleos then drew his sword and smote him on the neck, so that both head and helmet came tumbling down to the ground with the spear still sticking in the eye; he then held up the head, as though it had been a poppy-head, and showed it to the Trojans, vaunting over them as he did so.[16]

When speaking of Greek healing gods, we cannot neglect Asclepius (Asklepios). From his main sanctuary in the port city of Epidauros, Asclepius came to Athens in 420 BCE and from there his cult spread rapidly throughout the Greek, and later the Roman, world. His sacred snake, *Zamenis longissimus* (the Aesculapian snake) can today be found throughout southern and central Europe after being brought to his temples. Patients came to his shrines, called *asklepions* to seek his counsel in dreams. They would take a sleeping draught and then lie down near his altar. There his sacred snakes would supposedly come in and whisper in the sleepers' ears. While the contents of the sleeping draught were a closely guarded secret, it is worth noting that the columns of his temple at Epidauros were decorated with poppy motifs.[16]

Hippocrates (460–370 BCE) and Aristotle (384–322 BCE) both discussed the hypnotic and medicinal properties of poppy preparations. But not every philosopher was so enthusiastic about the substance. Diagoras of Melos (third century BCE) wrote, "It is better to suffer pain than to become dependent upon opium," while Eristratus (fifth century BCE) advocated the complete eschewal of opium.[17] Their warnings would be echoed centuries later among the philosophers and physicians of Rome.

3

ROME

Around 753 BCE a number of agrarian Italic tribes founded a city on seven hills east of the Tiber. It took the Romans nearly five hundred years to cement their rule over the entire Italian peninsula (265 BCE), but after that their expansion proceeded at a rapid pace. By 201 BCE they had gained ascendancy over the mighty Carthaginian Empire and control of its holdings in North Africa and Iberia (modern-day Spain). Thirty years later Roman armies conquered Greece and the remains of Alexander the Great's kingdom. What had begun as a provincial backwater run by small farmers was now a wealthy world power; over the next five hundred years it would only continue to grow.

Self-conscious about their humble beginnings, the Romans were quick to appropriate the culture of their foreign subjects. Rome made the gods of the Hellenic world their own; they imported Greek statues and artwork to decorate their homes and temples, and appropriated Greek treasure to fill their coffers. Along with Greek art, gold, and religion, they also imported many Greek physicians and scholars, both as slaves and full citizens. These would leave an indelible mark on Roman history, so much so that many today speak of "Greco-Roman culture."

But as with many provincials, Romans had a deep moralistic streak. Even as they recognized the superiority of Greek culture, they distrusted its "soft" and "womanish" elements. Many of the most titillating stories of Roman excess were exaggerated accounts by outraged conservatives trying to smear their opponents or warning impressionable youths of the dangers of decadence. While they would happily take advantage of inexpensive commodities from far-flung regions, they would also trumpet the superiority of simple, austere Roman living.

This tension would continue throughout Rome's history, as more foreigners became Roman citizens and the lines between Roman and barbarian became increasingly blurred. We can gain a clearer view of these fault lines by exploring the ways Roman culture dealt with poppies and their products—and since much of Western culture was directly or indirectly inspired by Roman ideals, we can learn a great deal about ourselves in the process.

Virgil's *Aeneid*

Although his family was able to provide him with a first-rate education, Virgil (70–19 BCE) came from humble stock. His father was an artisan potter or laborer who acquired his fortune through a combination of hard work, smart investment, and marrying his master's daughter. While Virgil's coarse features and swarthy complexion betrayed his peasant roots, his ability with verse showed an unparalleled intelligence and command of Latin.

His poems also showed that, despite his shy and retiring nature, he had inherited his father's ambition. His poems frequently included references to contemporary political figures and dedications to wealthy and powerful men. The fourth book of his *Georgics* (a long didactic poem on farming) praised Gallus Asinius, son of his patron Asinius Pollio. Later, when Gallus was arrested and killed on suspicion of conspiracy against Caesar Augustus, Virgil rewrote this section and replaced it with the story of Aristeus.[1]

Virgil's *Aeneid,* written between 29 and 19 BCE, originated at the request of Augustus, who wished to create an epic that celebrated Roman history and his lineage. Having come to power after twenty years of civil war and internecine strife, Augustus wished to legitimize his reign as Rome's first emperor. He knew all too well that many viewed him as a tyrant who had seized power by force. By taking advantage of Virgil's considerable poetic talents, he hoped to leave a memorial to his reign and justify the blood he shed in assuming the throne.

Taking his cue from the Homeric epics and from old legends that claimed Rome had been settled by Trojan refugees seeking a new home after the Fall of Troy, Virgil gave us the tale of Aeneas. A model of Roman virtue, Aeneas is willing to sacrifice everything to fulfill his deity-proclaimed destiny and found a new city that would one day rule the world. To that end, nothing could stand in his way, not even love.

Dido, queen of Carthage, is one of the obstacles he must overcome. Although sworn to chastity after her husband's death, she finds herself falling madly in love with the handsome Trojan. They make love in a cave, and Aeneas is tempted to stay but ultimately leaves to do his duty. Heartbroken, Dido builds a pyre to burn all of the things Aeneas has left behind, including herself. To justify her plan, she tells her sister that this is part of a love spell she learned from

> *a priestess, of Massylian* race, there*
> *a keeper of the temple of the Hesperides, who gave*
> *the dragon its food, and guarded the holy branches of the*
> *   tree,*
> *scattering the honeydew and sleep-inducing poppies.*
> *With her incantations she promises to set free*
> *what hearts she wishes, but bring cruel pain to others:*
> *to stop the rivers flowing, and turn back the stars:*
> *she wakes nocturnal Spirits: you'll see earth yawn*
> *under your feet, and the ash trees march from the hills.*[2]

Unlike the rational, disciplined Aeneas, Dido is lustful and violent. This is in keeping with the Roman view of Carthaginians as uncivilized

---

*Massilia is modern-day Marseille, France, a city within the original native range of *P. somniferum* and one that would later become famous for its role in the heroin trade.

savages. Aeneas ultimately chooses duty over love; contemporary readers would have recognized the distinction between this idealized Roman and Augustus's old adversary Marc Antony, whose dalliance with the African queen Cleopatra had tragic results. And her dying curse that there would ever be enmity between her kingdom and Aeneas's descendants would be a reminder of the enemy who had nearly defeated them.

For the Romans of Virgil's time, Carthage was remembered as a fearsome adversary. Their brilliant general Hannibal had nearly beaten the Roman armies in the Second Punic War (218–201 BCE). Only in 146 BCE did Rome finally defeat Carthage once and for all by sacking the city and enslaving its citizens. As rulers of the Mediterranean sea trade, Carthaginians would have been intimately familiar with opium. Indeed, Roman historians claimed that drugs were the reason for Rome winning the Second Punic War. After the Carthaginians landed in Capua, an Italian province that sided with Carthage against Rome, they were seduced by the drugs readily available in the region, which was "frequented by gilded youths with dandified manners."[3] As a result they became soft and corrupt and were ultimately defeated by the more disciplined Roman forces.

Although Virgil was willing to link poppies with decadent Carthage, he also recognized their importance to the Italian economy. The first book of his *Georgics* explains that poppies "filled with Lethean sleep"[4] exhaust the soil and spoke of sowing poppies after the autumn equinox—advice that is still followed by poppy farmers today. In book four, Aristaeus hopes to cure his sick bees by an offering to Orpheus.

> *Then when the ninth dawn shows her light*
> *send funeral gifts of Lethean poppies to Orpheus,*
> *and sacrifice a black ewe, and revisit the grove:*
> *worship Eurydice, placate her with the death of a calf.*[5]

While poppy was still grown for seeds (and poppy tea remained a popular folk remedy for a number of conditions), Greece and Italia produced little or no opium. Several hundred years after Cyprus and Minos grew wealthy on the opium trade, the balance of production shifted to Egypt. It was now easier to import Egyptian opium than to produce it at home—a situation that would lead, centuries later, to the decline of opium use in formerly Roman Europe.

Hecate in Greece and Rome

In Hesiod's *Theogony,* a poem composed around 700 BCE, Hekate is described as the one Zeus the son of Cronos honored above all. He gave her splendid gifts to have a share of the earth and the unfruitful sea. She received honor also in starry heaven and was honored exceedingly by the deathless gods.[6]

In the Homeric hymn to Demeter, composed around the same time, Hekate assists Demeter in finding her kidnapped daughter Persephone and ultimately is declared Persephone's attendant and substitute queen. But as time went on, her offices became different, and darker. In the *Argonautica* she is the patron of the powerful sorceress Medea. In Rome her transformation continued. She became Hecate (the Latinized version of her name), the goddess of crossroads, wild dogs, and tombs. In the eighth satire of Horace's first book of satires (written in 35 BCE) we see her as a patroness of the most vile black magic.

> They began to claw up the earth with their nails, and to tear a black ewe-lamb to pieces with their teeth. The blood was poured into a ditch, that thence they might charm out the shades of the dead, ghosts that were to give them answers. There was a woolen effigy too, another of wax: the woolen one larger, which was to inflict punishment on the little one. The waxen stood in a suppliant posture, as ready to perish in a servile manner. One of the hags invokes Hecate, and the other fell Tisiphone. Then might you see serpents and infernal bitches wander about, and the moon with blushes hiding behind the lofty monuments, that she might not be a witness to these doings.[7]

As Demeter had been connected with poppies, so too was Hecate. But where Demeter's devotees praised the poppies for their ability to bring relief from suffering, those who sought Hecate's help were more interested in opium's power to kill. Along with wolfsbane or aconite (called *hekaitis* by the Greeks), hemlock, mandragora, and belladonna, Hecate became patroness of opium poppies. In his *Natural History* (77 CE), Pliny the Elder mentions how opium is frequently used by the elderly and infirm to end their lives. By rubbing her breast with opium, a mother could rid herself of an unwanted nursing baby. When Agrippina wanted to ensure her son Nero's succession to the throne in 50 CE, she arranged a lethal dose of hemlock and opium for her stepson Britannicus. (And yet one of the most common remedies against poisoning was theriac, a concoction that generally contained a good deal of opium!)

Later Hecate would become connected with Eastern cults. It was not uncommon to find wealthy Romans in the late empire dedicated to the Phrygian Magna Mater and Attis, the Egyptian Isis and Serapis, and the Persian Mithras, along with Hecate. As Christianity became increasingly popular, a "Pagan resurgence" sought to revive the pre-Christian practices—but because many of the old Roman traditions had fallen into decay by that time, it was necessary to re-create them from surviving non-Roman cults. It is interesting to note that Hecate, in her guise as queen of witchcraft, poison, and sorcery, was remembered when many more benevolent gods had been forgotten.

Ovid's Land of Sleep

In the *Fasti* of Ovid (43 BCE–18 CE), when Demeter (or, as the Romans called her, Ceres) wishes to make the child Triptolemus immortal, she

> *gave to the boy*
> *Poppy seeds in warm milk to make him sleep.*
> *It was midnight: silent in peaceful slumber,*
> *The goddess took Triptolemus on her lap,*

Caressed him with her hand three times, and spoke
Three spells, not to be sounded by mortal tongue,
And she covered the boy's body with live embers
On the hearth, so the fire would purge his mortal
burden.[8]

Alas, Triptolemus's mother awakens and yanks the baby from the fire, thereby depriving him of the gift of eternal life.

In his *Metamorphoses,* Ovid describes the land of sleep.

Beneath the cave the flow of Lethe's waters
Calls out to sleep in sleep that sleeps forever.
And it is where dream-haunted poppies grow,
Hanging their heads above wet ferns and grasses,
Where mossy herbs distill sleep-gathering wines,
Breathing their fragrance to the night-filled land,
And weighted lids close each day to darkness.[9]

Statues of Somnus, the god of sleep, frequently portrayed him as a child stretched on a couch sleeping. In one hand he holds a bunch of poppies, which also serve for a pillow; in the other he holds a horn of the type used to this day in the collection of opium. He brings sleep to mortals by sprinkling drops of poppy juice on them. When those drops are mixed with water from the infernal rivers, they bring troubled sleep and nightmares. His son Morpheus, ruler of dreams, was also frequently represented holding an opium horn and bunches of poppies in his hand.[10]

Morpheus's name means, literally, "he who shapes," for Morpheus can transform himself into any form when he appears in a dream. Although his name is derived from the Greek "morphe," or form, he first appears in Ovid's *Metamorphoses.* The Greeks credited dreams to the *Oneiroi,* black-winged demons who were sons of Nyx, or night. It is unclear whether Morpheus was ever seen by the Romans as a god or merely as a poetic invention. But there is no doubt that he exerted a profound fascination on those who came after the Romans. Centuries later, Friedrich Sertürner would give his name to the substance he derived from opium, morphium (see chapter 8).

Galen and Marcus Aurelius

Opium resists poison and venomous bites, cures chronic headache, vertigo, deafness, epilepsy, apoplexy, dimness of sight, loss of voice, asthma, coughs of all kinds, spitting of blood, tightness of breath, colic, the iliac poison, jaundice, hardness of the spleen, stone, urinary complaints, fevers, dropsies, leprosies, and the troubles to which women are subject, melancholy and all pestilences.

GALEN OF PERGAMON, SECOND CENTURY[11]

According to Galen (130/131 to 199/201), he was studying philosophy at his father's request when he was visited in a dream by Asclepius, god of healing, and told he should instead study medicine. He wisely chose to follow his vision. By 161 he left his Greco-Roman provincial city for Rome, where he soon became physician to the new emperor, Marcus Aurelius, and other important Roman aristocrats. Among the most useful substances in his pharmacological toolkit was opium thebaicum, opium harvested in the fields around the Egyptian city of Thebes and distributed throughout the Roman Empire.

To protect himself from poisoning—a very real threat to any powerful Roman—Marcus Aurelius consumed regular doses of theriac compounded by Galen. These offered him some surcease from the rigors of his imperial duty and a deep melancholia, which can be seen in passages from his *Meditations*.

What is the nature of all sensible things, and particularly those which attract with the bait of pleasure or terrify by pain, or are noised abroad by vapoury fame; how worthless, and contemptible, and sordid, and perishable, and dead they are—all this it is the part of the intellectual faculty to observe.[12]

Ever the devoted leader, Marcus discovered that the dosages he was taking during a winter campaign on the Danube River made him drowsy and unable to fulfill his duties. He then had Galen remix the theriac without opium—but then found himself unable to sleep, a condition that Galen attributed to his inherently "dry humours" but that opiate addicts will recognize as one of the most troublesome signs of withdrawal. To counteract this, Galen reported that Marcus "was obliged to have recourse again to the compound which contained poppy-juice, since this was now habitual with him."[13]

Marcus's death in 180 marked the beginning of what Edward Gibbon famously called "the decline and fall of the Roman Empire." While most scholars today recognize that Europe's purported fall into barbarism and superstition was overstated, there is no question that Rome's rule over its provinces became increasingly tenuous. By 330, Constantine, ruler over the Eastern Roman Empire, moved his center of government to Byzantium and renamed it Constantinople, marking the beginning of Byzantium as a major power. (The Western Roman Empire had already moved its operations to Milan in 285.) In 395, Theodosius I, ruler of the Eastern and Western Empires, died. The Roman Empire was now divided between the Greek-speaking East and the Latin-speaking West, which within one hundred years would be in the hands of the "barbarians."

As the Roman Empire fell, so did the trade routes. Imported goods like opium became increasingly scarce and costly. The drugs that had been readily available in Roman cities were now forgotten in most parts of Europe. But in the East, the poppy was finding other devotees with the rise of new empires—and a new religion.

4

THE ISLAMIC WORLD

The Islamic message was a simple one: there is no god but Allah, and Muhammad is his prophet. Those willing to accept it could become full citizens in the *umma,* the community of Muslims. While the early Muslims had a strongly pro-Arab bias (and study of the Q'uran required at least proficiency in Arabic), the caliphate included Persian, Turkic, Black African, and Indian peoples in prominent military and government positions. And as the umma grew in size and power, so did the opportunities available to an ambitious convert to the faith. Islam also offered protection against the various marauding armies that were now making their way into Europe. The Avars, Slavs, Goths, and other tribal confederations found the armed might of the new caliphate every bit as intimidating as the Roman Empire in its glory days. Much of the world now found itself living under the banner of Islam, in a far-flung political and economic network that promised far more tangible benefit than the Christian rulers could offer.

Even those Christians and Jews who wished to hold to their ancestral faiths had little reason to rebel. While they were taxed more heavily than Muslim subjects and certain offices were not open to them, they had a great deal of liberty under the caliph's government. So long as they kept civil peace and refrained from trying to convert Muslims, they were free to live as fellow "People of the Book." (For their part, and despite the legends, Muslim rulers generally refrained from converting them "by the sword," because the *jizya* tax on non-Muslim subjects was an important source of income.)[1]

As a result, within thirty years after the prophet Muhammad's death in 632, his followers' rule stretched over three continents. A movement that began in an impoverished land of deserts and nomadic tribes now held sway over the lands of Persia's Sassanid Dynasty and more than half of the Byzantine Empire's holdings. As the Western Empire's roads and ports fell into disrepair and the Roman bureaucracy was replaced by various local strongmen, the Muslims gained control of the old Asian and African trade routes. Silk from China and spices from India were brought by Muslim merchants to Islamic holdings in Sicily, Corsica, and Andalusia (modern-day Spain). In return they shipped European goods throughout the realm—and among those goods were poppies and their juice.

Greece, Rome, and the Umma

While civilizations overrun by the barbarians were usually plundered and left in ruins, those brought under Islamic rule were generally left administratively and intellectually intact. Islamic leaders translated Persian, Indian, Chinese, Greek, and Latin works into Arabic, the language of the Q'uran and the lingua franca of the new empire and its trade.

One of the important technologies that soon spread throughout the empire was the Chinese process of making paper. In the mid-eighth century, papermaking arrived at the empire's eastern border in the central Asian city of Samarkand. The labor-intensive process of preparing parchment and papyrus was soon replaced by the mass production of paper from pulped rags, hemp, and bark. Libraries (public and private) grew at an astounding rate. From India they imported Arabic numerals, which are still in use today, replacing the cumbersome Roman numeric system. This allowed for new mathematical advances. Meanwhile, a growing bureaucracy required ever more literate clerks and employees— all trained in the *madrassahs* (public schools) that Muhammad had also required.[2]

Baghdad, home base of the Abbasid Caliphate, became the capital of the scientific and intellectual world. By the tenth century the essential writings of Galen, Hippocrates, and other Greek and Roman physicians had been translated into Arabic and distributed throughout the empire. But where the few European doctors who were acquainted with the classical physicians took their words as holy writ, the Islamic world used them as the starting point for further study and experimentation. A quote from Abu Bakr al-Razi (865–930), considered one of the Islamic world's greatest physicians, shows this spirit of skepticism and trial by experimentation.

I have heard amazing accounts, amongst which is the following: the physician of . . . prescribed for gout a potion prepared with two mithqals (4.5 g) of colchicum, half a dirham (1.5 g) of opium and three dirhams (9 g) of sugar. The drug is said to be effective within the hour, but I need to verify this.[3]

Physicians in the Islamic world prescribed opium for a number of conditions. Thābit ibn Qurra, a Kurdish hermeticist and gnostic, claimed "eating poppy with syrup of rose-water and syrup of grapes is useful for colds."[4] (One of poppy's active alkaloids, codeine [see chapter 9], is still used as a powerful cough suppressant.) Al-Razi described a "very remarkable" ointment for anal fissures consisting of camphor, to which opium is added when the pain is severe. (Opioid suppositories are still used today.) Al-Razi also introduced the usage of opium as a sedative and anesthetic before performing surgery.[5]

Another proponent of opium usage was the great Persian physician and philosopher Abū 'Alī al-Husayn ibn Sina (980–1037), better known in the Western world as Avicenna. An avid scholar and prolific writer, Ibn Sina produced more than 450 works on various subjects, 240 of which survive today. Among them is a treatise on opium, calling it the most powerful of narcotics and recommending it for diarrhea and diseases of the eyes. He also advised, "If a child does not sleep properly, mix some poppy with his food"[6]—a recommendation that the makers of patent medicines would take to heart centuries later.

Like many of his fellow citizens of Bukhara, Ibn Sina consumed opium for its recreational effects. He was well known as a libertine who enjoyed the company of concubines and, despite the Q'uranic prohibitions against drinking, the fruits of the vine. When his colleagues recommended he slow down, he reportedly said, "I prefer a short life with width to a narrow one with length."[7] His death in 1037 was reportedly due to an overdose of opium dissolved in wine.*

Poppies Come to India

Before the rise of Islam, the spice trade involved local merchants who worked exclusively in their local area. Spices were transported from one carrier to another, without any singular group making the entire journey. Islamic traders, by contrast, frequently traveled the entire length of the trade route personally, without relying on intermediaries. The Indian luxury goods that had been in demand in the Roman Empire were now attracting newly wealthy consumers in Baghdad and Damascus. Journeying by sea in their *dhows* (longboats) or over land by caravan, they brought with them goods they could easily sell. Opium was a particular favorite; it was compact, valuable, and did not degrade easily. And as they spread the faith, so too did they spread the poppy and its fruits.

Although one myth claims that poppies were originally intro-

---

*It should also be noted that Ibn Sina suffered from severe colic—what we today call irritable bowel syndrome or Crohn's disease. He may have been taking opium and wine to relieve pain, a use that the vast majority of Islamic authorities then and now would consider acceptable.

duced to India by Alexander the Great, no references to opium appear in the *Vedas, Puranas,* or early Indian medical texts. But the early thirteenth-century ayurvedic guides *Dhanwantari Nighantu* and *Sodhala's Gadanigraha* describe the properties, actions, and medical indications of *ahiphena,* a Sanskrit word that shows the influence of the Arabic word for opium, *afiyun.* (Chinese records from the same period speak of *ya pien* and *a-fou-yong.*)[8]

In ayurvedic medicine, preparations including opium are generally used for the treatment of diarrhea and insomnia. One preparation, *kaminividravana rasa,* is used in cases of premature ejaculation. Because many opiate users report an inability to orgasm, it is conceivable that small doses of opium could help someone troubled with this condition. (Overdoing it would likely lead to a lack of interest in sex and impotence, another problem common to opiate addicts.) Poppy seeds (*khas-khas*) are also used to treat thirst, fever, inflammation, and stomach upset and are added to many tasty curry preparations.

For centuries India relied on the opium produced in Egypt, then it began growing and harvesting its own. By 1511 Portuguese explorer Duarte Barbosa noted poppy farming on the Malabar coast. In 1516 the Portuguese historian Pyres wrote of "the opium of Egypt and Bengal," and by 1590 Sheik Ab'ul Fazal described poppies as a major crop in Agra, Oud, and Allahabad.[9] Indian opium would become a major product in centuries to come, sparking several wars and providing finance to yet another empire. The rearing of poppies would also move farther north to Afghanistan, which is today one of the world's biggest producers of opium for illicit heroin production.

An Indian folktale describes the origin of the poppy thusly:

On the banks of the river Ganges lived a *Rishi* (holy sage) who shared his small palm-leaved hut with a small mouse. One day the mouse asked the Rishi for a boon. "I am always being chased by cats. Please make me a cat so that I am their equal." The Rishi sprinkled some water on the mouse and it turned into a cat which bounded off happily. But a few days later the cat returned, its fur torn. It asked the Rishi to change it into a dog so it could fight its new enemy. The Rishi obliged. Later, the dog was transformed into a monkey, then a boar, then an elephant, then, finally, the beautiful maiden Postomoni. Postomoni wound up married to the king of a nearby kingdom, then fell in a well and died. Broken-hearted, the king went to the Rishi for counsel.

"Do not grieve, King," he said. "The queen was born a mouse who became a cat, a dog, a monkey, a boar, an elephant and finally your wife. Now I will make her immortal. Let her body remain in the well. Fill up the well with mud. A plant will grow from her flesh and bones and it will be called Posto or Poppy. This flower will produce opium. Men will take it greedily. Whosoever partakes of it will have one quality of each of these animals into which Postomoni was transformed. He will be as mischievous as a mouse, as fond of milk as a cat, as quarrelsome as a dog, as unclean as a monkey, as savage as a boar, as strong as an elephant and as spirited as a queen."

The king went back and did as the sage had said. In time a tall plant with delicate white leaves grew. The king looked after Postomoni. Every year he planted her seeds in the fields around, as his children, so that by the time he died, there were poppy flowers all over the kingdom.[10]

Poppies in the Islamic Republic of Iran

Opium is used mainly as a painkiller or medicine. But heroin helps you to run away from the truth, from the facts. Youth wants something that helps us run away from the reality of everyday life, and that's heroin.

FARIBOORZ KOOCHEKI, 29,
TEHRAN HEROIN ADDICT, 2005[11]

A number of contemporary movements are striving to re-create the world of the early Islamic empires. Rather than Enlightenment-era philosophy or Marxist economic theory, they look to the Q'uran and Islamic jurisprudence for guidance. One of the most famous examples is Iran, a country whose laws are based on the tenets of Shi'a Islam and the writings of Ayatollah Ruhollah Khomeini. Today they seek to apply Q'uranic wisdom to a modern manifestation of a very old problem that threatens the foundations of their Islamic republic.

Iran shares nearly six hundred miles of its eastern border with Afghanistan, producer of more than 90% of the world's illicit opium. Most of that area consists of rugged mountains, bleak deserts, and swampy marshes—ideal country for smugglers. The Balochi tribesmen who live on both sides of the border have been taking advantage of the remote terrain for centuries. Many are armed with cell phones, night-vision goggles, Kalashnikovs, rocket launchers, and even United States–made Stinger missiles left over from the Russian war. And to make matters worse, as one Iranian army officer puts it: "Unfortunately Iran is on the shortest route from the producers in Afghanistan to European consumers. The Central Asian states of the former Soviet Union have split into separate countries, with many borders to cross. Via Iran, there are only two."[12]

As a result, at least half the drugs leaving Afghanistan pass through the Islamic Republic of Iran, flooding the country with cheap opium and heroin. After the 1979 revolution, Iran quickly eradicated the growing of opium poppies. Today no opium is produced in Iran, but despite this, the country has the world's highest rate of addiction. According to the *2005 World Drug Report,* issued by the United Nations, 2.8% of Iran's population over age fifteen is addicted to heroin or opium. Of a population of about seventy million, some government agencies put the number of regular users at close to four million.[13]

Iran has more than thirty thousand troops guarding its border areas. In 2000 they seized more than 250 tons of narcotics; in 2007 they con-fiscated approximately 900 tons.[14] Iran has erected concrete walls across mountain passes, dug trenches in deserts, and raised hundreds of watch towers. In the past two decades more than 3,500 law enforcement personnel have been killed in armed clashes with drug traffickers.[15] The United States refuses to give money to the UN to support Iran's antidrug efforts, while in 1999 the UK parliament had to pass a special law to allow bulletproof vests to be exported to Iranian antinarcotics forces.[16]

> *If Iran let the drugs through, our soldiers wouldn't get killed and less heroin would stop here. The West, which is the biggest consumer, does little to help. Probably because it doesn't like us.*
>
> ALI, WHO RUNS A RADIO STATION FOR AFTAB,
> AN IRANIAN NGO SPECIALIZING
> IN HELPING ADDICTS, 2002[17]

After the mullahs came to power in 1979, they tried to attack drug addiction through a zero-tolerance program. Hundreds of thousands of addicts were jailed, and thousands of narcotics traffickers executed. Today, in the face of an exploding AIDS crisis, they have begun taking a more pragmatic approach. Needles are available without a prescription and subsidized by the government, so they cost less than five cents each; free methadone (chapter 13) is available to addicts who wish to stop injecting. Azarakhsh Mokri, director of the Iranian National Center for Addiction Studies, has recommended that Iran renew its poppy cultivation to provide itself with "a strategic reserve of narcotics" and advocates a program to dispense opium tinctures in addition to methadone.[18]

While this may seem surprising given Iran's spotty record of tolerance and liberalism, we must view it in a cultural perspective. In the 1920s Iran supplied around one hundred tons of opium a year to internal and external markets. It has been estimated that by 1949 more than one in ten adults in Iran were using drugs; there were 1.3 million regular opium users, and Tehran contained five hundred opium dens.[19] And while the Q'uran prohibits the use of alcohol, it does not specifically condemn the usage of opium or other psychoactive substances. This has given the religious leaders more leeway to approach the issue as a social problem that must be addressed rather than as sinful behavior that must be eradicated.

But there is still reason to fear that these reforms will not last. In January 2009 physicians Arash and Kamyar Alaei, two brothers who won international acclaim for their HIV/AIDS treatment and prevention programs aimed at drug addicts, prostitutes, and other high-risk groups, were sentenced to three to six years in prison for allegedly taking part in a U.S.-backed plot to overthrow Iran's ruling establishment by creating a social crisis and stirring up street demonstrations and ethnic disputes.[20] As in any other autocratic country, support for these programs could end at any time based on the whims of a few ruling officials.

5

THE RETURN TO EUROPE

As the twelfth century loomed, Europe was steadily descending into chaos. The prelates of Rome and Constantinople struggled for control of Christiandom after excommunicating each other. After the decline and fall of Charlemagne's Carolingian Empire, the countryside split into numerous fiefdoms ruled by squabbling strongmen. Meanwhile, the birthrate expanded at a speed that would triple Central, Western, and Eastern Europe's population by the beginning of the fourteenth century.[1] Impoverished, overtaxed peasants lived with constant malnutrition interspersed with periods of famine and crop failure. The only thing that could bring unity to this chaos was a common enemy—and Islam provided that threat.

Between 1096 and 1099, more than 40,000 (some say as many as 130,000) peasants, paupers, petty nobles, and ambitious feudal lords made their way to the Holy Land. For the next two centuries Crusaders would maintain a tenuous hold on an area that encompassed much of modern-day Israel and southern Lebanon. Their brief, tumultuous stay introduced Europeans to Islamic delicacies like sugar, saffron, jasmine, and coffee. It reintroduced them to Greek and Roman philosophers who were all but forgotten in the West through Arabic translations of their work. And it revolutionized medieval medicine by adding drugs like camphor, aloes, and laudanum to its pharmacological toolkit.

In Acre, the port city that was home to the Knights Templar, the Roman Catholic bishop complained that second- and third-generation Franks indulged in "baths, fine clothes, sex and magical practices, which they find more important than fighting. Furthermore, they make alliances with the Arabs, accept their ideas, and are soft and effeminate."[2] While devout Christians (and, later, the Templars' enemies) might be outraged at this fascination with Islamic culture, there was no resisting temptation. Much as the Romans simultaneously condemned and emulated the Greeks, the Crusaders fought the Muslims while appropriating as much of their wisdom—and treasure—as they could carry home.

Islam Meets Medieval Medicine

In his mid-thirteenth century *Chirurgia,* Theodoric Borgononi provided a recipe for an anesthetic sponge similar to one that had been used centuries earlier by Baghdad surgeons.

> Take of opium and the juice of unripe mulberry, hyoscyamus, the juice of spurge flax, the juice of leaves of mandragora, juice of ivy, juice of climbing ivy, of lettuce seed and of the seed of lapathum which has hard round berries and of the shrub hemlock, one ounce of each. Mix these altogether in a brazen vessel then put into it a new sponge. Boil all together out under the sun until all is consumed and cooked down onto the sponge. As often as there is need, you may put this sponge into hot water for an hour and apply it to the nostrils until the subject falls asleep. Then the surgery may be performed.[3]

But usage of opium remained limited. As an imported spice, opium was a luxury only the wealthiest patients could afford. Shipped from Persia through Acre (or Venice and Genoa, where trade with the Muslim world continued after the Holy Land returned to Islamic control), opium shipments had to pass through several intermediaries before reaching physicians. Each would be tempted to adulterate the substance with sugar, with cheaper gums, or with lead pellets hidden in the bricks; each transaction would increase the market price.

As a result, most soldiers and injured peasants faced operations, sickness, and recovery with no anesthesia at all. If they were lucky, they might receive a concoction made with mandrake (*Mandragora* spp.) or henbane (*Hyoscyamus* spp.), plants containing high concentrations of the dissociative deliriants hyoscyamine and atropine. Those with a bit more money might be treated with medicinal distilled elixirs like brandy and whiskey, products that also owed their existence to Islamic ingenuity but used more readily available ingredients. (This was not entirely unfortunate, as those who could afford opium as an anesthetic not infrequently died from overdose. Opium's strength could vary widely from batch to batch. A dosage that alleviated suffering one day could prove fatal the next. To make things more complicated, the line between a dose that causes unconsciousness and one that kills is very slender.)

Still, opium's fame spread with tales from returning Crusaders. They told stories of the Old Man of the Mountains who spurred on his assassins (*hashishins*) with concoctions of poppy juice and hemp. They described Turkish soldiers who were capable of superhuman feats of strength after eating opium and of the ecstasies and visions that the rare drugs of the East could bring to those who dared to indulge in them. Their high price and danger only added to their allure. This may have been one of the things that recommended opium to a Swiss physician, surgeon, and ardent self-promoter who has gone down in history as one of the leading figures of Renaissance medicine.

Paracelsus and His Disciples

From the middle of this age the Monarchy of all the Arts has been at length derived and conferred on me, Theophrastus Paracelsus, Prince of Philosophy and of Medicine. For this purpose I have been chosen by God to extinguish and

blot out all the phantasies of elaborate and false works,
of delusive and presumptuous words, be they the words of
Aristotle, Galen, Avicenna, Mesva, or the dogmas of any
among their followers.

PARACELSUS, *THE BOOK CONCERNING*
THE TINCTURE OF THE PHILOSOPHERS,
SIXTEENTH CENTURY (FIRST
PUBLISHED 1603)[4]

Nobody could accuse Philippus Theophrastus Aureolus Bombastus von Hohenheim of modesty. His 1527 appointment to the chair of medicine at the University of Basel was cut short soon after he made a bonfire with the books of Galen and other old masters of medicine. Later that year he was forced to flee the city after losing a lawsuit, then criticizing the judges as corrupt and incompetent. Even his self-chosen title, Paracelsus, indicated that he felt he was equal to or greater than the famous first-century Roman author and physician Aulus Cornelius Celsus.

But neither could they accuse him of being a charlatan. From his father (also a physician) he learned the fundamentals of medicine and the basics of alchemy, a blend of Arabic chemistry (*al-chymia*), Hermeticism, and mysticism. His work as a military surgeon gave him practical clinical experience. So too did his contacts with the folk healers, herbalists, and midwives whom no self-respecting academic would deign to consult. And while they might mock his stutter or his penchant for extended drinking binges, few could question his success at treating patients. As one admiring student described him:

In curing intestinal ulcers he did miracles where others had given up. He never forbade his patients to eat as much food and drink as much as they liked. On the contrary, he frequently stayed all night in their company feasting with them. He said he cured them most quickly when their stomachs were full. He had pills which he called *laudanum*, which looked like mouse shit but which he used only in extreme cases. He claimed that with these pills he could wake up the dead.[5]

According to Paracelsus, his laudanum pills were made of one-quarter opium compounded with henbane, crushed pearls and coral, amber, musk, and other ingredients including bezoar stones from a cow's intestine, unicorn horn, and stag's heart.[6] While the opium and henbane are pharmacologically active, the other substances were likely added to justify the prices Paracelsus charged for his services and to make his treatment seem more impressive. Paracelsus was frequently prone to exaggeration; while he claimed at various times to have studied at a number of prestigious universities, contemporary records provide no record of his attendance. He was also fond of expensive clothing and luxurious living, and not averse to charging what the market would bear for his services. But those suffering from stomach pain and colic in a world with few other alternatives might well think the relief from opium worth whatever price Paracelsus wished to charge.

Despite his many personal quirks, Paracelsus had an enormous impact on the practice of medicine. His introduction of chemistry to medical practice would add new drugs to the standard pharmacopeias. His willingness to learn from folk healers and nonacademic sources, not to mention his insistence on lecturing in German rather than Latin, helped to break down the divide between academic physicians and working-class doctors. He would become the first European doctor in centuries to influence Islamic medicine—a popular tract titled *New Chemical Medicine Invented by Paracelsus* was written by Salih ibn Nasrallah ibn Sallum in or around 1640.[7]

Meanwhile, his legendary laudanum pills would inspire generations of quacks to offer their own formulations. The disciples of Paracelsus enthusiastically recommended opium. In 1600 Platerus of Basle widely promoted its usage, while Dutch physician Sylvius de la Boe stated he was unable to practice medicine without it. A Belgian doctor (and addict) called vanHelmont prescribed it so frequently that he was nicknamed "Doctor Opiatus." Traveling along a caravan route in 1546, French naturalist Pierre Belon saw fifty camels loaded exclusively with opium bound for Europe.[8] And as early as 1603 Shakespeare was familiar with opium remedies, as witnessed in *Othello,* when Iago says:

> *Not poppy, nor mandragora,*
> *Nor all the drowsy syrups of the world,*
> *Shall ever medicine thee to that sweet sleep*
> *Which thou owedst yesterday.*[9]

As trade with the Islamic world increased, opium became more widely available. So too did tales from travelers who had spent time in Egypt, India, Persia, and Asia Minor. Belon reported, "There is no Turk who would not buy opium with his last penny; he carries it on him in war and in peace."[10] In 1592 Spanish physician Cristóbal Acosta wrote that in the East Indies opium was used both as medicine and food and consumed "as a worker eats his bread."[11] He also reported the condemnation of opium by Indian, Persian, Turkish, Chinese, Malay, Arabic, and Malabar physicians who decried the risk of addiction and added, "Though opium is condemned by reason, it is used so extensively that it is the most general and familiar remedy of degraded débauchés."[12]

Sydenham's Laudanum and Dover's Powders

While Paracelsus first used the term *laudanum* for his pills, the formulation that goes by that name today comes to us from Thomas Sydenham, also known as "the English Hippocrates." Born in 1624, Sydenham came of age during the English Civil Wars and spent several years fighting in Cromwell's army. As a result, his education was limited. He was a mere licensate of the College of Physicians, only receiving his Doctor of Medicine degree in 1676, when he was already the leading physician in London. This spotty education would label him a controversial figure in the medical community, but his approach to medicine would also make him an effective healer. At a time when many doctors relied on astrology or uroscopy (inspection of the urine), Sydenham based his diagnoses on careful examination of the patient, keeping meticulous records of signs and symptoms, as well as treatments and effects.

One of his most effective treatments was a cordial that he named, after Paracelsus, "laudanum." It consisted of 2 ounces of opium, 1 ounce of saffron, and $1/16$ ounce each of cloves and cinnamon, dissolved in a pint of Canary wine or sherry and then simmered for several days. According to Sydenham,

> So necessary an instrument is opium in the hands of a skillful man, that medicine would be a cripple without it; and whosoever understands it well, will do more with it alone than he could well hope to do with any single medicine. To know it only as a means of procuring sleep, or of allaying pain, or of checking diorrhea, is to know it only by halves. Like a Delphic sword, it can be used for many purposes besides. Of cordials, it is the best that has hitherto been discovered in nature.[13]

Sydenham was a careful physician who was conservative in his usage of medicine. He was wont to say that in many cases the best thing he could do for his patient was nothing at all. Knowing opium's reputation for toxicity and addiction, he was especially cautious with laudanum. Yet he was also willing to use it, in moderation, to alleviate suffering. Afflicted with gout, Sydenham was all too familiar with chronic pain, as can be seen in this description of an attack.

> The pain starts moderately at the junction of the big toe and foot and gradually becomes more intense. As it does so, the chills and shivers begin. After half an hour or an hour the pain reaches its peak. It spreads like hot irons buried under the skin to the metatarsus and tarsus [the foot and heel], attacking bones and ligaments as well as the flesh. It varies constantly. Now it is a gnawing, now a pressure, now a burning.[14]

But where Sydenham was temperate in his prescriptions, others were not so cautious. Pharmacies throughout Europe did a brisk business selling substances that claimed to cure melancholy, increase sexual vigor, alleviate pain, and act as panaceas against any illness. As the popularity of these various "medicines" grew, so did the demand for opium and the potential for abuse.

Thomas Dover became famous for his Dover's Powder. A buccaneer and ship's doctor who was involved in the rescue of marooned sailor Alexander Selkirk (the inspiration for Daniel Defoe's *Robinson Crusoe*), Dover trained with Syndenham. While his prescriptions for mercury (frequently an ounce or more a day as a blood purifier!) raised eyebrows even then and earned him the derisive nickname "the quicksilver doctor," his Dover's Powder helped to ensure temperance in the usage of opium. First produced in 1732, Dover's recipe involved

> Opium one ounce, Salt-Petre and Tartar vitriolated each four ounces, Ipecacuana one ounce, Liquorish one ounce. Put the Salt Petre and Tartar into a red hot mortar, stirring them with a spoon until they have done flaming. Then powder them very fine; after that slice your opium, grind them into powder, and then mix the other powders with these. Dose from forty to sixty or seventy grains in a glass of white wine Posset going to bed, covering up warm and drinking a quart or three pints of the Posset—Drink while sweating.[15]

Ipecacuana (the active ingredient in the famous emetic Syrup of Ipecac) ensured that only small amounts of the powder could be taken. Patients who tried taking more would quickly vomit their dose. Dover's Powder was the first of many preparations that would attempt to take advantage of opium's therapeutic properties while discouraging abuse. Alas, Dover's Powder was but one of many opiated medicines available at any pharmacist, and so those who were less inclined to judicious opium usage had little problem finding other medications. Demand for opium—as tonic and recreation—grew apace, especially as the colonial era increased its supply and decreased its cost.

6

THE COLONIAL ERA
1500–1900

In June of 1511 Afonso de Albuquerque arrived at the port of Malacca with fourteen ships and one thousand men. There he demanded the immediate release of twenty Portuguese prisoners who had been held since a failed 1509 expedition. Sultan Mahmud, who had two thousand guns and twenty thousand men guarding his capital city, refused. On July 25, Albuquerque's forces attacked. Forty days of pitched battle followed, with heat, famine, and disease claiming many on both sides. Finally, on August 24, the sultan and his forces retreated. After sacking the city, Albuquerque proceeded to build a mint, an intimidating fortress named A Famosa, and a chapel dedicated to the Virgin.

Albuquerque's 1509 victory at Hormuz opened trade with the Persians; his 1510 triumph at Goa provided Portugal with a base to gain control of the routes linking India to the East. Now, with the fall of Malacca, he had access to the lucrative Chinese markets. The Portuguese were now in a position to seize power over a route stretching from Europe to the Far East. By setting up a line of heavily armed fortresses along the way, they hoped to monopolize the European trade in cinnamon, nutmeg, black pepper, indigo, cloves, and other Asian luxuries. But Albuquerque was not content to stop there. He hoped to take charge of the commerce between the various Asian powers and principalities.

One of the most profitable "spices" (a term used for a variety of culinary and medicinal substances and herbs) in the Malacca markets was *afyum,* or opium thebaicum, from Egypt. Albuquerque recognized the demand for afyum among Chinese and Indian physicians and recommended, in a letter to King Manuel I:

> If Your Highness would believe me, I would order poppies of the Açores to be sown in all the fields of Portugal and command afyam to be made, which is the best merchandise that obtains in these places and by which much money is made. . . . Afyam is nothing else, Senhor, but the milk of the poppy. From Cayro, whence it used to come, none comes now from Aden; therefore, Senhor, I would have you order them to be sown and cultivated, because a shipload would be used yearly in India, and the people of India are lost without it, if they do not eat it; and set this fact in order, for I do not write to Your Highness an insignificant thing.[1]

Albuquerque's scheme to make Portugal a poppy-growing center, like his plan to divert the Nile and turn the world's largest Muslim kingdom into a desert, didn't work out. However, the Portuguese merchants took advantage of Indian poppy farming (see chapter 4) and began exporting opium to China in direct competition with the Indian and Arab merchants who had long controlled the trade.

As they struggled for command of the opium market, the Portuguese also exchanged Brazilian tobacco for Chinese silks. This market also failed to produce the demands they expected. As the demand increased, the Chinese began growing their own tobacco. But the method of ingestion introduced along with the tobacco—smoking (see chapter 29)—led to a booming market in opium.

As recreational opium smoking spread across China, Indian opium merchants grew increasingly wealthy. Meanwhile, Egyptian poppy growers were profiting from the rising demand for opiate medicines in Europe (see chapter 5). But the Portuguese involvement in the opium trade was fairly light; they preferred to concentrate their efforts on their New World colonies and on the booming slave trade. It was left to another European power to capitalize on Asia's demand for poppies.

The Dutch East India Company

When the Vereenigde Oost-Indische Compagnie (Dutch East India Company) entered the Asian markets at the beginning of the seventeenth century, it was at a distinct disadvantage. The Asian markets had little interest in European goods, demanding cash for their products. And while Portugal and Spain could rely on the mines of their New World colonies for gold and silver, the Dutch Republic was faced with a Spanish silver embargo after winning its independence from Spain.

To make the most of their limited resources, Dutch merchants concentrated on the inter-Asia market. By 1603 they had established a profitable opium trade in the Indonesian archipelago, and by 1613 had expanded their markets to China, Burma, the Moluccan Islands, and Siam (Thailand). In 1640 they began purchasing Indian opium to supply opium users in Java and other Dutch colonies and trade markets.

This first multinational corporation returned excellent dividends to its shareholders, thanks in no small part to the poppy trade. In 1664 François Valentijn, a Dutch clergyman living in Java, claimed that the company's 1,000 crates of opium were matched by another 3,200 crates of smuggled opium and that opium was "the most important kind of profitable business."[2] In 1688 the company purchased approximately 11.5% of Bengal's total opium output, and between 1659 and 1771 they exported 67,831 chests from Bengal to their markets in Jakarta.[3] The expanding European commerce stimulated both supply and demand. Like the Islamic traders before them, European merchants favored opium as a low-weight, high-value commodity. When sold in Jakarta, Bengali opium could fetch merchants a gross profit of 125%.[4]

Like many other goods of the colonial era, what had been a luxury available only to the wealthy soon became an invaluable part of the lives of many common folk. Indeed, a recurring problem for the Dutch was meeting the opium demands of their colonial subjects. The Indian merchants who controlled the Bengal opium trade also sold their wares to British and French merchants. Some years the company could buy only 50% or less of the opium they hoped to sell from Bengal. While this drove up their price, it also encouraged smuggling and corruption among officials.

It was not the Chinese, Arabic, or British merchants who were the main competitors of the Dutch East India Company, but rather its own employees. At the retirement of Governor-General Johan Van Hoorn of the Dutch East Indies in 1709, his possessions were estimated at ten million guilders. The governor of East Java in that same time increased his 2,400 guilders annual income to 100,000 guilders by various extralegal means. A governor of Moluccas was able to increase his income from 160 to more than 4,000 guilders a month.[5] Nor were high-ranking officials the only ones to profit from this extralegal demand. In the 1720s company employees in Jakarta discovered two pilot vessels loaded with more than 30,000 pounds of hidden opium smuggled in by fellow employees.[6] The company's attempts to enforce its monopoly kept running headlong into true (albeit unauthorized) capitalism.

By 1745 the company decided that the best way to beat this problem was to yield to it. The Dutch East India Company set up a new private company, the Soceititjt tot den Handel in den Amphioen (Society for the Trade in Opium), and proposed to sell all opium purchased in Bengal to that new company at a fixed price. The Society for the Trade in Opium would then have a monopoly on all opium trade in Java. Because it would be in their interest to eradicate competition from smugglers, the Dutch East India Company expected the black market would be weakened. Its three hundred shares were fully subscribed within six weeks. But while it was profitable for a few years, the Society for the Trade in Opium found itself facing a new competitor and colonial power—Great Britain.

Opium and the British Empire

*The wicked Suraj-ud-Dowlah came with a vast army,
destroyed almost 40 innocent English gentlemen in one
night in the Black Hole. Calcutta was overset by him. For
my share, I have lost 16,000 rupees.*

ARMENIAN MERCHANT TO HIS SON, 1756[7]

On June 21, 1756, Bengali ruler Suraj-ud-Dowlah attacked a British East India Company garrison and imprisoned the captives in a poorly ventilated 18 x 15 foot room. According to the reports that reached Europe, 146 prisoners were shoved into the cell; only twenty-three escaped alive.* Outrage over this "Black Hole of Calcutta" led to an immediate response. Major Robert Clive, one of Britain's most capable commanders in India, retook the garrison and the city of Calcutta, then overthrew Suraj-ud-Dowlah and replaced him with a pro-British ruler. By 1765 Clive was the governor of Bengal, and Britain formally ruled over India's wealthiest opium-growing region.

Until that time Britain's primary import from India was textiles, especially the lightweight "flimsy muslins" and printed cottons. These had become wildly popular with the British people. In 1684 more than a million cotton pieces were imported into England. Spurred by lobbyists from the local wool and linen industries, England banned most East Indian fabrics in 1721. But the craze continued unabated, as English textile manufacturers used Indian dye and mordant technology—as well as imported Indian plain cotton fabrics, threads, and fiber—to duplicate the now-illegal imports.

With the Indian fabric industry now facing competition from home industries, the British East India Company turned its attention to Bengal's opium fields. As early as 1729, Emperor Yung Cheng issued an edict banning the smoking of opium. But imperial proclamations

---

*Today scholars believe that no more than sixty-five to seventy adults were in the "Black Hole" and that the death toll was considerably lower than the first accounts.

were of little avail against China's demand for opium. To make up for the trade deficit incurred by the British demand for tea, the East India Company began taking steps to meet that need. Because the company relied on the Chinese government for its legal trade in tea, it did not ship opium into China. Rather, it sold its production at annual auctions in Calcutta to licensed private firms. These "country traders" shipped the drug in specially built and heavily armed opium clippers to fortified receiving ships off the coast of southern China. From there, multi-oared "fast crabs" and "scrambling dragons," crewed by Chinese pirates, took the opium to coastal and riverine depots. With the aid of bribed officials, the opium was then distributed through extensive smuggling networks.

> *This item, opium, spreads deadly poison. Rascals and bandits indulge in it and cannot do without it even for a second. They do not save their own earnings for food and clothes, but instead exchange their money for the pleasure of this narcotic. Not only do they willingly bring ruin upon their own lives, but they also persuade friends to follow their example. There is no doubt that opium will harm the morality of our people.*
>
> JIAQUING EMPEROR, 1811[8]

Within China, selling opium for smoking purposes was an offense in the same category as robbery or murder, and violators could face banishment or execution. While Chinese officials meted out harsh punishments to local dealers and drug addicts, the Calcutta opium markets grew ever larger and Britain's ties to smuggling grew increasingly blatant. By the 1830s, 10% of revenues collected by the British government in India came from taxes on the opium trade.[9]

While British liberals and humanitarians were beginning to recognize the horrors of addiction, closing the opium markets was unthinkable; they were far too profitable and the competition from other colonial powers was too intense. In 1773 India Governor-General William Hastings stated that opium was a pernicious article of luxury that ought not to be permitted and "which the Government should carefully restrain from internal consumption."[10] Yet when faced with a shortage of Spanish silver, the only currency acceptable to Chinese tea traders, Hastings turned to smuggling. (Alas, his investment in two ships full of opium proved unsuccessful. One was captured by French privateers; the other did not attract any interested buyers, and the cargo was finally sold at a loss in Malaysia.)[11]

Fifty years later an American trader, Warren Delano, said he could not pretend to justify the opium trade on moral grounds, "but as a merchant I insist it has been ... fair, honorable and legitimate," and no more objectionable than the importation of wines and spirits to the United States.[12] Delano grew wealthy from his role in the trade. His grandson, Franklin Delano Roosevelt, would go on to become the thirty-second American president.

The Opium Wars

Chinese officials continued to make public statements about their growing opium problem. The East India Company agreed to follow all applicable laws, then bribed customs officials to overlook their smuggled shipments. Finally in 1834 a Peking official proposed legalizing the trade. He argued that since the trade could not be stopped, it was better to admit the drug, tax it, and stop the outflow of silver bullion by making opium saleable only by barter. The emperor sacked the official expressing these views, deciding instead to follow the counsel of officials who advocated suppression of the opium trade.

In 1838 Canton's viceroy, seized a few cases of opium and expelled two notorious English traders, including William Jardine of Jardine Matheson & Co. English trade superintendent Captain Charles Elliot assured the Chinese government there would be no intervention on behalf of the smugglers and cleared the Canton River of opium ships.

Smugglers and crooked customs agents on both sides assumed it would be business as usual once the fanfare died down. They had not counted on the new imperial commissioner, Lin Tse-hsü.

> *Even though the barbarians may not necessarily intend to do us harm, yet in coveting profit to an extreme, they have no regard for injuring others. Let us ask, where is your conscience? I have heard that the smoking of opium is very strictly forbidden by your country; that is because the harm caused by opium is clearly understood. Since it is not permitted to do harm to your own country, then even less should you let it be passed on to the harm of other countries.*
>
> LIN TSE-HSÜ, IN A LETTER TO
> QUEEN VICTORIA, 1839[13]

A brilliant scholar and rising star within Chinese imperial bureaucracy, Lin was determined to rid China of the "foreign mud" shipped in from British India. In March 1839 he sent out orders to the English that all opium in foreign hands was to be turned over for destruction. When the British did not comply, Lin surrounded their compound with Chinese soldiers and held them hostage until 20,283 chests of opium were surrendered to him. After this was destroyed, Lin sent trade superintendent Elliot a letter demanding that Her Majesty's government not only withdraw from the opium trade but stop making opium, and promising that any vessel carrying opium in Chinese waters would be confiscated.

Communications between British forces in Asia and the home front took months. But when the message finally got through, Britain's response was swift. If British bribes could not shake Lin's resolve, British gunboats would be brought in to play. An expeditionary force of four thousand troops, sixteen warships, and twenty-eight transports occupied positions around Canton. The Chinese were technologically and tactically outmatched. After enduring continual military defeats from 1839 to 1842, they were forced to sign a humiliating peace treaty and cede the island of Hong Kong to Great Britain. From there opium could reach the Chinese mainland unmolested. Lin Tse-hsü was removed from his office in disgrace and transferred to a remote northwestern outpost.

The Chinese government would make a few more efforts to staunch the flow of opium. In 1856 Chinese officials boarded the *Arrow,* a Hong Kong registered ship, and detained twelve Chinese nationals for piracy and smuggling. The British used this as an excuse to launch the Second Opium War in 1857. At its end in 1860, China was forced to legalize the opium trade, cede part of Kowloon to Britain, open Tianjin as a trade port, allow missionary activity, and pay reparations to Britain and France. (Though not as belligerent, Russia also took advantage of China's weakness to claim approximately four hundred thousand square miles of Chinese territory.)

Flush with these triumphs, Britain began exporting larger quantities of Indian opium not only to their Chinese customers but also to the European mainland. There a new generation of doctors and pharmacists were taking advantage of the poppy's healing powers. But as British merchants transformed opium from a rare, mysterious, and costly drug into an affordable commodity, they would soon find their countrymen facing the same plague that had troubled China.

7

THE WAR ON DRUGS

Even as they prepared for the First Opium War, the British government expressed concerns about the drug trade. Trade Superintendent Elliot said, "As a public officer I have steadily discountenanced it by all the lawful means in my power, and at the total sacrifice of my private comfort in the society in which I have lived for years."[1] The foreign secretary soothingly reassured him that "Her Majesty's government by no means disputes the right of the government of China to prohibit the importation of opium into China."[2]

Despite these pious assertions, many British politicians remained skeptical. Future prime minister William Gladstone delivered an eloquent, angry speech against the "infamous and atrocious traffic."[3] Gladstone knew opium's dangers all too well; his sister Helen was an addict. After her family refused to sanction her marriage to her first love, the always-sensitive Helen retreated to the seductive comforts of laudanum and Roman Catholicism. Her brother made repeated attempts at saving her from both, proclaiming, "She is poisoned much in body and, more, in mind, by the use of that horrible drug" and declaring the needle punctures on her arm "self murder . . . a kind of Cain's mark."[4]

(Helen remained unwavering in her commitment to Papism and opium, despite her family's best efforts at convincing her otherwise. At one point she took volumes of Protestant theology into her bathroom, where she placed them near her toilet with pages ripped out "under circumstances which admit of no doubt as to the shameful use to which they were put."[5] Yet when the family grudgingly relented and allowed her to live as a Roman Catholic, Helen was able to give up laudanum and morphine for long periods. Like many modern twelve-steppers, she overcame her addiction through a personal relationship with her Higher Power. Feminist therapists might argue that she escaped laudanum once she was allowed to establish a self-identity that set her apart from her domineering family.)

Parliament ultimately supported the First Opium War in a close vote of 271 to 262, swayed by arguments that Britain was fighting not for opium smuggling but for free (and profitable) trade. But the writing was on the wall; a considerable number of people sympathized both with China's right to defend its territory and with its antidrug laws. After seeing opium's impact on Chinese society, liberals, humanitarians, and evangelists began to question its effect on their own culture and turned their zeal against their country's native drug trade.

> *A CAUTION TO MOTHERS. At a critical season like the present, where children are teething, the utmost attention ought to be paid them, particularly as the measles and chill-cough are so prevalent; if the irritation of the gums comes with any other disorder, very few infants recover; mothers ought never to be without the AMERICAN SOOTHING SYRUP in the nursery.*
>
> ADVERTISEMENT FOR OPIATED MEDICATION, 1810[6]

In 1840, the year the First Opium War began, Britain imported some two hundred thousand pounds of opium from India. While the English were not so fond of smoking, they consumed a great deal in the form of various syrups, powders, and pharmaceutical concoctions. At the time, pharmacists and quacks alike used opium for ills ranging from diarrhea to insomnia and diabetes. Few other medications were available, and laudanum could cure many ailments, alleviate pain, and lift the spirits of almost everyone sick in body or soul. And this wonder drug was not only effective but cheap. At a penny an ounce, laudanum could be had for about the price of a pint of beer. One druggist sold half a gallon of an opiated cordial and between five and six gallons of a less potent "quietness" every week; by one source, five out of every six working-class families in Manchester were habituated to opium.[7] In England's swampy Fen country, many laborers took their pint with a piece of opium: the local "sleepy beer," brewed with poppies, took many an unwitting traveler by surprise.

In 1844 Friedrich Engels wrote *The Condition of the Working Class in England,* noting:

> Many women give the children [opiates] while they are newborn infants, and go on dosing them without realising the harmful consequences of this method of "strengthening the heart" until the children die. When the child's system develops a greater resistance to the effects of opium, the dose is gradually increased. . . . The effects on the children dosed in this way can easily be imagined. They grow pale, stunted and weak, generally dying before they are two years old. The use of this medicine is widespread in all the great cities and industrial towns of this country.[8]

And while opiates were the opiate of the masses, they were also favored by the gentry. Gladstone, who condemned his sister's habit, was not averse to calming his nerves with laudanum before important speeches. As early as 1682 John Dryden, one of the greatest writers of seventeenth-century Britain, satirized Thomas Shadwell's laudanum habit (along with his weight, intelligence, poetic ability, and other qualities) in the poem "MacFlecknoe." After declaring the hapless Shadwell "confirmed in full stupidity," Dryden gave him a fitting crown:

> *His temples, last, with poppies were o'erspread,*
> *That nodding seemed to consecrate his head.*

Meanwhile, a growing number of artists and rebels were spending their trust funds on opium (and other substances like cocaine and hashish); a few even took to smoking opium in an Orientalist nod to decadent China. Thomas De Quincey's (chapter 16) *Confessions of an English Opium-Eater* may have introduced the public to a new illness, but by and large morphinism was seen as a flaw that needn't trouble people with the right sort of breeding and character.

To regulate usage among those who weren't to be trusted with drugs, the Pharmacy Act of 1868 introduced a list of drugs, including opium, that could be sold only by "pharmaceutical chemists." But these restrictions faced stiff lobbying pressure from the pharmaceutical establishment. While they were happy to see the sale of poisons restricted to qualified dealers, they did not wish new restrictions on opium to interfere with their trade. As a result, "preparations of opium" were distinguished from "preparations containing opium." Only the former, defined as containing 1% of opium or more, were regulated under the act. Most opiated patent medicines could still be sold over the counter.

Despite this, the act caused an immediate decline in the number of infant and child fatalities—from 20.5 per million population between 1863 and 1867, to 12.7 per million in 1871. It remained at that level until the 1880s, when a further decline to between 6 and 7 per million took place.[9] Apart from these restrictions, there were no further legislative efforts to control opiate drugs in the UK until the Dangerous Drugs Act of 1920 (prohibiting the unlicensed import or export of morphine) and the Dangerous Drugs Regulations of 1921 (regulating the production, supply, prescription, and possession of opiates). Even with those, Great Britain generally treated addiction and drug abuse as a social rather than a criminal problem—an approach that continues to this day. The stance taken across the water was a bit more severe.

The American War on Drugs

Opium and morphine never became as popular among America's lower classes as they had in Britain. In the nineteenth century, most of

America's opiate addicts were middle class or wealthy women. Opium and morphine preparations were regularly used for menstrual cramps. They were also frequently prescribed for depression, anxiety, and other "feminine complaints," much as barbiturates and diazepam (Valium) would be used in the mid-twentieth century. And because women were not welcome in the men-only confines of the saloon, many turned to laudanum in place of alcohol.

In the later part of the nineteenth century, patent medicines containing opium, morphine, or cocaine became widely available. An 1883–1885 survey of Iowa, which then had a population of less than two million, found three thousand stores in the state where opiates were on sale—and this did not include the physicians who dispensed opiates directly. Users unable or unwilling to patronize a nearby store could order laudanum and morphine by mail.[10] Those worried about becoming habituated could order medication that promised all of opium's benefits without its addictive potential. When already ensnared they could purchase syrups and pills to cure their habit—medications that typically contained opium, morphine, or heroin.

In 1906 the Pure Food and Drug Act prohibited false or misleading label statements and required the makers of patent medicine to state the presence and quantity of alcohol and certain narcotic drugs, including opium, morphine, and the recently discovered heroin. This helped to stem the tide of opiated patent medicines, especially when combined with muckraking journalism that exposed the dangers posed by cocaine, alcohol, and opium. A backlash was growing against the poppy and its juice, one based on its supposed "Oriental" origins.

Opium and the Yellow Peril

English and American Protestant missionaries had long been critical of Britain's role in the opium trade. The Society for the Suppression of the Opium Trade, a Quaker reform group, pressured Parliament to stop opium traffic to China. They attracted the patronage of the Archbishop of Canterbury and other influential spiritual and political leaders. The Reverend Silvester Whitehead of Canton's Wesleyan Missionary Society said, "The missionaries of China are absolutely one on this important position. . . . The whole six hundred of them with one accordant voice proclaim the opium a curse, and they tell you that the trade in the past was a monstrous wrong, and thus it is still a gigantic evil."[11]

In Britain these reformers had a limited impact on the official church and on government policy. In America, evangelical Christianity (not to mention a burgeoning "temperance movement") was more popular. American missionaries returning from China preached to large congregations about the evils of opium abuse and its potential to lead an individual into moral degradation. These advocates of temperance and clean living spoke out against the horrors of drunkenness and addiction. To them, abuse and habituation were not medical issues or social problems, but sins. Their message found a receptive audience, albeit one whose perceptions were colored by the xenophobic fears of the time.

During the California Gold Rush thousands of Chinese laborers came to America to seek their fortune. They laid railroad tracks, worked in fisheries, picked crops, and did other menial jobs. But an economic downturn in the 1870s increased already high tensions against the "rice-eaters." Chinese laborers became increasingly subjected to mob violence and racist legislation. And a favorite target of politicians and journalists alike was the Chinese penchant for smoking opium. Newspapers regaled their readers with lurid tales of white women fraternizing with Chinese men in opium dens, and laws were passed against these locations. The first American law regulating opiates was an 1875 ordinance by the city of San Francisco prohibiting the smoking of opium in smoking-houses or dens. By 1914, the year Congress passed the Harrison Act, twenty-seven cities had similar ordinances.[12] These would provide a template for actions that were to follow.

On its face, the Harrison Act merely required licensing for manufacturers, importers, pharmacists, and physicians prescribing narcotics. Physicians were expected to keep a record of narcotic drugs dispensed or prescribed and were allowed to provide narcotics "in the course of their professional practice only."[13] But providing opiates to an addict was held to be outside the scope of that practice, since addiction was not a disease. Following the lead of the antiopium missionary societies and the temperance movement, law enforcement officials instead treated drug abuse as a moral failing and a crime, an affront against decent society, and a threat to the American way of life. With the same zeal they showed toward the new Prohibition laws, federal agents began arresting doctors who prescribed opiates to addicts.

Between 1914 and 1926, at least twenty-five thousand physicians were arrested on narcotics-selling charges, with three thousand serving time in jail as a result and thousands more losing their medical licenses.[14] Clinics that helped addicts to taper by providing gradually smaller doses were shut down, because giving *any* opiate to a junkie was a crime. The Supreme Court ruled that physicians could prescribe to addicts under certain circumstances in *U.S. v. Linder* (1925), but the Treasury Department continued its attacks on doctors. Rather than risk their careers or their freedom, most medical professionals refrained from working with addicts altogether, and the pharmacist was replaced by the "dope peddler."

Meanwhile, the gangsters who traded in bootleg whiskey frequently had a brisk side business in illicit drugs. After Prohibition ended, their booze earnings dried up, but the continuing demand for opiates provided them with a lucrative new market. But these users also felt the government's wrath. The Jones-Miller Act of 1922 provided for a fine of up to $5,000 or incarceration for not more than ten years for anyone who imported, concealed, bought, sold, or assisted in the sale of illegal narcotics. Simple possession was now held as evidence of intent. Antidrug crusaders created lurid stories of "pushers" leading dewy innocents into corruption, vice, and race mixing. Grandmother's arthritis medication was now a scarlet letter of shame, and we were in a new "Great War" against the scourge of addiction—a war that would soon be helmed by an uncommonly dedicated general.

Harry J. Anslinger and His Aftermath

In 1930 Harry J. Anslinger was reassigned from the alcohol division to the newly created Federal Bureau of Narcotics (FBN). For the next thirty years Anslinger would lead a tireless crusade against recreational drugs. Anslinger felt that Prohibition would have worked if the penalties for alcohol possession and sale had been more severe. While some respectable citizens might disagree with him on that, few were ready to speak up in favor of opium, heroin, or other "foreign" poisons that they now associated with Negroes, the Chinese, foreigners, and tenement hoodlums.

Anslinger happily provided soundbites that fed into respectable American issues with race and class. In 1957 he told a reporter that adolescent heroin addiction occurred almost entirely "among Negro people in police precincts with the lowest social and economic standards,"[15] and in 1951 he held up before Congress a bag of "Lions Globe" heroin that the Chinese Communists were allegedly shipping to American troops in Korea. (Lions Globe heroin was actually manufactured by forces under the control of our anti-Communist allies.)[16] Through stories planted in popular magazines, press releases, and leaks of official documents to sympathetic columnists, the FBN tied heroin and other drugs to the worst sort of organized crime and espionage.

> *A sixteen-year-old kills his entire family of five in Florida, a man in Minnesota puts a bullet through the head of a stranger on the road; in Colorado husband tries to shoot his wife, kills her grandmother instead and then kills himself. Every one of these crimes had been preceeded by the smoking of one or more marijuana "reefers."*
>
> HARRY ANSLINGER, 1961[17]

We may laugh at some of Anslinger's wilder claims, but we still live under policies he inspired. Today many physicians are reluctant to provide opiates even to patients suffering from severe pain. In 2005 thirty state attorney generals complained that the federal drug policy was interfering with legitimate medical practice. High-profile arrests and prosecutions of physicians (up to two hundred per year, by one estimate) have caused many doctors to underprescribe or refuse to see new patients.[18]

The war against drugs has had some triumphs. By 1943 opiate use in New York was so rare that voluntary commitments for heroin detoxificaton were almost unheard of, and the federal government considered closing its narcotics hospital in Lexington, Kentucky.[19] But our victories have invariably been short-lived. The Corsican Mafia, Vietnamese gangs, Mexican drug cartels—all these and other criminal organizations have profited from our efforts as demand for an illegal substance provides incentive for criminals to become suppliers. To stem this violence we have responded with ever harsher antidrug state and federal initiatives.

In 1956 the federal Narcotic Control Act outlawed the sale of heroin to a minor on penalty of death. The first person tried under the law, Gilbert Zaragoza, was a twenty-one-year-old Mexican American with an IQ in the low 70s. Zaragoza sold a small quantity of heroin to a seventeen-year-old fellow addict. At first, Zaragoza refused to sell to him, but the young man pleaded with him, stating he was about to get dope sick. Zaragoza finally relented and sold the young informer two caps, whereupon police broke in and arrested him. The jury balked at handing down the death penalty, and the judge sentenced Zaragoza to life without the possibility of parole, saying, "Society should use your life to set an example for others."[20] In 1962 President Kennedy commuted his sentence to a twenty-year term; in 1970 Zaragoza was paroled after serving thirteen years.

In 1973 New York's Rockefeller drug laws made heroin dealing a felony equal to first- and second-degree murder. To avoid stringent mandatory minimum sentences, juveniles (who could not be tried in adult court) took over street-level sales, a trend that encouraged the rise of gang culture in many inner cities. New York's prison population swelled from 12,500 in 1972 to 73,000 in 2002, with approximately 19,000 people in jail under the Rockefeller laws. Meanwhile, researchers estimate that 250,000 heroin addicts live in New York, a number that has remained fairly constant for decades.[21]

Once we honored Poppy as a sacramental plant. Today we protect her with numerous taboos. Those who lack a prescription are forbidden to sample her wares on penalty of civil punishment. Those who would abuse her sacred rites for mere pleasure are incarcerated, even killed. And yet as one country eradicates its poppy trade, another region steps up to meet demand. Poppies have now spread to the Western Hemisphere in earnest, as South America coca lords have expanded their offerings to include home-brewed "black tar heroin" (see chapter 10). Poppy is happy to fulfill our needs so long as we propagate her species. To her, our "war" is like locust invasions and droughts—an annoyance but hardly something that will endanger the continued existence of her children.

PART TWO

ALCHEMY

Today we have isolated *Papaver somniferum*'s active chemicals. We have also used them as precursors and inspiration for our own new painkillers. Many of our experiments tried to take the addictive sting out of opium. To date we've had little luck with that; despite the efforts of our best chemical minds, Poppy still demands her bargain. The substances we have brewed with her and in her honor have as many uses and dangers as the mother alkaloids that first attracted humanity's attention. We have found no real substitute for the painkilling properties of morphine or other poppy-derived alkaloids, no chemical that gives us the poppy's benefits without extracting its price of addiction. Even as we go to war with Poppy, we are forced to do business with her.

8

MORPHINE

As the nineteenth century dawned, chemistry was a booming industry. The last third of the 1700s had seen a "chemical revolution," with numerous refinements in techniques of analysis and experimentation. In the 1790s King Friedrich Wilhelm II of Prussia gave chemist Franz Carl Achard a salary and estate in exchange for his work on manufacturing sugar, and many French chemists held leading positions as inspectors.[1] An ambitious young man with a sharp mind and meticulous eye for detail could go places. Friedrich Wilhelm Adam Sertürner, a twenty-two-year-old pharmacist working in Hanover, Germany, was such a man. Though he had no scientific training or university education (merely a five-year apprenticeship to a local apothecary), Sertürner had a keen interest in the medicinal and therapeutic properties of opium. While most of his contemporaries were focused on inorganic substances (mineral acids, alkalis, metals, and salts) that could be purified to a comparatively high degree with the available laboratory techniques, Sertürner concentrated on organic substances, with a particular focus on opium.

In an 1805 experiment, Sertürner dissolved opium in a mix of alcohol and water, then placed it in a separatory funnel, a large glass cone with stoppered openings on the top and bottom. After closing the funnel, Sertürner shook it vigorously and inverted it. As the alcohol and water layers separated, Sertürner was able to open the tap and separate the two layers. Because most substances have different solubilities in alcohol and water, the composition of each layer was different. Sertürner tested the alcohol extract of opium on four dogs and a mouse that he found wandering in his laboratory. On a dose of 12 grains (approximately 780 milligrams), the dogs vomited, had convulsions, and appeared sedated but did not fall asleep; one "gentle little dog" died.[2] Although it appears now that his extract was quite impure, he published his results in a paper titled "Representation of the pure poppy acid (opium acid) together with a chemical investigation of opium with excellent regard to a material discovered therein and the remarks due there."

Then, in 1814, two French pharmacists announced the results of their own work with opium. Parisian pharmacist Jean-Francois Derosne added potassium carbonate to an extract of opium, then isolated the crystals, which he called "sel de Derosne." In 1814 the French academy published a paper that had been written in 1804 by another chemist, Armand Seguin, titled "Sur l'Opium." The race to find opium's "basic principle" was on, and in 1817 Sertürner responded with a series of dangerous experiments on himself and three young friends.

For this experiment Sertürner used a different technique for the extraction of opium, adding ammonia to the water mixture and separating the colorless crystals that precipitated therefrom. He wrote of the experiments:

In order to test my earlier experiments strictly, I encouraged three persons, none older than seventeen years, to take morphine with me simultaneously. Warned by the previous effects, however, I merely administered half a grain [approximately 32 milligrams] dissolved in half a drachma of alcohol and diluted with several ounces of distilled water. This produced a generalized redness of cheeks and eyes [perhaps due to the alcohol] and the vital functions appeared generally enhanced. After half an hour, another half-grain was taken; the condition was aggravated markedly, while a transient tendency to vomiting and a dull pain in the head with narcosis was felt.

After another 15 minutes, we swallowed another half-grain of morphium, undissolved, as a coarse powder, with 10 drops of alcohol and a half-ounce of water. The outcome with the three young men was decidedly rapid and extreme. It presented as pain in the region of the stomach, exhaustion, and severe narcosis that came close to fainting. I also was subject to the same fate. Being in the supine position, I fell into a dream-like state and sensed in the extremities, particularly the arms, a slight twitching which accompanied the pulse beats. These distinct symptoms of true intoxication, particularly the frail condition of the three young men, caused me so much concern that I, half unconscious, drank more than a quarter of a bottle (6 to 8 ounces) of strong vinegar and also had the others do the same. This led to such severe vomiting that, several hours later, one who was of a particularly delicate constitution and whose stomach had already been emptied completely, found himself in a continuous state of a most painful and highly alarming retching. In this condition, I gave him carbonated magnesia, upon which the vomiting subsided instantly.

The night passed under deep sleep. Although the vomiting recurred in the morning, it immediately subsided after a strong dose of magnesia. Lack of opening of the body, loss of appetite, narcosis, and pain in the head and body disappeared only after several days. Judging from these highly unpleasant experiences, I deduce that morphine, even in small quantities, acts as a strong poison. . . . As none of the other components of opium possesses effects such as those described here, the important medicinal properties of opium probably result from pure morphium, which I have to leave to the physicians to test.[3]

Sertürner named his crystalline material "morphium," derived from Morpheus, the Roman god of dreams and son of Somnus, the god of sleep. It was another French chemist, Joseph Louis Gay-Lussac, who introduced Sertürner's substance, under the name "morphine," to the world. Gay-Lussac, a professor at the prestigious École Polytechnique, had the academic and social credentials Sertürner lacked. With Gay-Lussac's support, morphine was available throughout Europe by 1822. This success allowed Sertürner to purchase the main apothecary in Hamelin, where he worked until his death in 1841.

Physicians working with opium had to contend with natural variations in potency; depending on the batch, a particular dose might have little effect or be lethally strong. With morphine it was easy to standardize dosages, and because morphine was considerably stronger than raw opium, far less was required. But critics noted that morphine was used in a distressing number of suicides and murders. In Balzac's 1830 *Comédie du diable,* the Devil credits morphine with a sudden population increase in Hell. Even Sertürner weighed in, stating, "I consider it my duty to attract attention to the terrible effects of this new substance in order that calamity may be averted."[4]

Morphine is a potent *analgesic*—it alleviates or abolishes pain without inducing the loss of consciousness. (This is contrasted with an *anesthetic* like ether, which alleviates pain by rendering the patient insensible.) To this day morphine remains the gold standard for analgesics; it is inexpensive, easy to produce, and approximately fifty times more potent than aspirin for relieving pain.

Unfortunately morphine also has several nasty side effects. At higher doses it can depress respiration and induce unconsciousness. (Hence Sertürner's name for his discovery.) Morphine (along with other opiates) suppresses coughs but often triggers nausea and vomiting. It causes the sphincter to contract and reduces peristalsis (movements of the bowel muscle that propel its contents forward), and opiate use is frequently accompanied by constipation. While some consider morphine-induced euphoria an advantage, most trying to live with chronic pain would prefer a clear head. Continuous usage can rapidly produce tolerance, requiring ever-greater dosages to deliver the same effect.

And although doctors originally hoped that morphine could provide opium's beneficial effects without causing dependence and addiction, they soon discovered that Sertürner's discovery was not only more potent but also more addictive than raw opium. An ounce of laudanum contains about 60 milligrams of morphine, and a heavy user might consume two or three ounces a day. By contrast, there were accounts of habituated morphine users whose daily dosage was as high as 2,500 milligrams, or over a quart of laudanum!

Despite that pesky dependence problem, most considered morphine to be yet another scientific breakthrough. Then (as now) addiction was seen largely as a problem of the lower classes. People of good breeding, it was thought, could use opiates with impunity, becoming the type of user "who fulfils his duties to his government, to his family, and his fellow citizens in an irreproachable manner."[5] It remained, however, less popular than opium—a cheaper and already proven remedy—until the syringe became widely available (see chapter 31). Subcutaneous shots of morphine were much more effective and less likely to cause hives and allergic reactions than opium injections.

Morphine in the Third World

Today morphine remains one of the cheapest and most effective analgesics. A hospice in Uganda mixes its own liquid morphine, and a three-week supply costs less than a loaf of bread. Yet despite this, very little morphine finds its way to the Third World. In 2005 the poor and middle-income countries where 80% of the world's people live consumed only about 6% of the world's morphine. Six countries—the United States, Canada, France, Germany, the United Kingdom, and Australia—consumed 79%.[6] Another study found that the two million people who died of HIV/AIDS and cancer in sub-Saharan Africa in 2005 consumed less than 1% of the quantity of morphine that was required (76.5 metric tons): only 2% of the pain needs of dying HIV/AIDS and cancer patients in Asia were met.[7]

The problem is not so much morphine's cost as its legal status and its potential for abuse. Some governments have banned the importation of morphine entirely, while in other countries it is available only to wealthy and well-connected citizens. Many larger governments have concerns about the potential diversion of large quantities of scheduled pharmaceuticals. They press for regulations that allow only doctors to prescribe morphine, forgetting that doctors are few and far between in many of these countries. They also forget that local prejudices against painkillers may be even higher than our own. Surgeons at one Papua New Guinea hospice complained that prescribed analgesics are frequently not given, even when the patient is crying in pain. Nurses are concerned that "morphine is addictive" and "I saw a patient who had morphine and she died."[8]

Even in countries where morphine is readily available, health care providers may run in to some unexpected barriers. Because morphine is given widely (and comparatively liberally) in many hospices, some patients believe morphine is only for dying patients and are hesitant to take it because they aren't dying.[9] And those who are dying are all too often undermedicated by doctors who fail to take their increasing tolerance into account, or who worry that overmedicating pain may kill already fragile patients. But a study of more than 1,300 hospice patients, conducted by Dr. Russel K. Portenoy of New York's Beth Israel Medical Center and his colleagues at thirteen different centers, suggests those concerns are exaggerated. Portenoy's study compared the survival of patients on relatively low morphine doses with patients whose doses had been pushed up, often to very high levels, to keep them as comfortable as possible at the end of life. The data showed that high doses of morphine create only a tiny risk, if any at all, of premature death for a patient whose body has become accustomed to the medication.[10]

Unfortunately, morphine is also considered desirable by recreational users and addicts. When heroin is unavailable, abusers may use morphine as a substitute. Eugene O'Neill's mother (chapter 18) and Nelson Algren's Frankie Machine, the Man with the Golden Arm (chapter 19), were both morphine addicts. Morphine pills are available in instant-release and extended-release formulations. While recreational users are generally disappointed with oral morphine's euphoria, it is still extremely effective for pain relief and other uses. (Those looking for a more pleasurable formulation of oral morphine may find poppy tea more to their liking. See chapter 27.) Many IV users report that morphine gives a prickly "pins and needles" rush that distinguishes it from heroin's smoother onset. Some enjoy this sensation, while others find it unpleasant.

In the past morphine was used as an antidepressant, antipsychotic, and antianxiety agent. A 2001 study suggests morphine may still have uses as a psychiatric medication. When given low doses of oral morphine, patients whose obsessive-compulsive disorder had not responded to standard SSRI (selective serotonin reuptake inhibitor) treatment noted a marked improvement in their symptoms.[11] Other studies have found that nineteenth-century uses of morphine for melancholia and manic psychosis would have had at least some clinical effect. It also had an antidepressant effect on psychotics who even today are resistant to standard antidepressant treatment.[12]

Today a morphine habit is a quick way to land in rehab. In 1889 Dr. J. R. Black published a paper titled "Advantages of Substituting the Morphia Habit for the Incurably Alcoholic" in the *Cincinnati Lancet-Clinic*. Black pointed out that morphine "is less inimical to healthy life than alcohol" and that it "calms in place of exciting the baser passions, and hence is less productive of acts of violence and crime; in short . . . the use of morphine in place of alcohol is but a choice of evils, and by far the lesser."[13] An English physician noted in 1873 that opium users "are not uproarious, and don't swear. There are none of the deeds of brutal violence that are inspired by beer, and none of foul language."[14]

9

CODEINE

Pierre Jean Robiquet found the active ingredient in the notorious aphrodisiac cantharides, or "Spanish Fly," and discovered the substance that makes urine smell funny after people consume asparagus. And when he turned his attention to opium, he had even greater success. While Sertürner had isolated opium's most powerful alkaloid, Robiquet discovered two that were less potent but no less pharmaceutically useful. In 1817 Robiquet isolated narcotine (now known as noscapine). In 1832 he isolated an alkaloid that he named after the Greek for "poppy capsule." This substance, codeine, is today the world's most widely used opiate.

Codeine is less powerful than morphine. To produce the same analgesia as 30 milligrams of morphine, a 200 milligram oral dose of codeine would be required. But higher doses of codeine are impractical. Unlike morphine, codeine has a "ceiling" of 300 to 450 milligrams; any consumed after that will not be metabolized but may contribute to side effects like hives, itching, constipation, and intense lethargy.

But codeine is still very effective in many situations. While its analgesic qualities are not as strong as morphine, it is an equally effective antitussive (cough suppressant) and antidiarrheal medication. It is also less sedating and less likely to induce nausea and vomiting. And while it might not be as powerful a pain reliever as morphine, it is more than adequate for many cases that are too much for aspirin or other NSAIDs (nonsteroidal anti-inflammatory drugs) but not bad enough to warrant the risk of more powerful substances. In 1911 physician and pharmacist W. Hale White wrote of codeine:

> In man its physiological action is in all respects much less than that of morphine. It often relieves the hacking cough of phthisis [tuberculosis]. It is also used for ovarian pain and to diminish the glycosuria [excretion of glucose in urine] in diabetes which it does more effectually than opium itself and as an analgesic. It is an excellent substitute for morphine as an ingredient of cough mixture.[1]

While we now treat diabetes with insulin rather than opiates, the rest of Dr. White's advice still holds true. Codeine (generally mixed with aspirin, acetaminophen, or other substances) is available over the counter in many countries and is widely prescribed in most others. But an average opium sample comprises between 8% and 17% morphine by weight: by contrast, only 0.7% to 5% is codeine.[2] Because of the great demand for codeine and codeine products, as much as 90% of the licit morphine produced is transformed by methylization into codeine.

Once it gets in our bodies most of us will transform at least some of it back. Codeine is a *prodrug:* it is largely inactive until it is processed by the body. Typically, about 10% of a dose of codeine is converted in the body by the enzyme CYP2D6 to morphine; the rest is metabolized by other agents to inactive compounds. But some people have a genetic variant that produces limited CYP2D6 activity and slow metabolism of CYP2D6 substrates. In them, conversion of codeine to morphine is reduced, as is codeine's analgesic efficacy.[3] Another gene variant produces extra CYP2D6, thereby increasing codeine's potency. Mothers who carry this and who use codeine—a drug frequently prescribed for postpartum pain—can give their newborn a dangerously high dose if they breastfeed.[4]

Although codeine is also physically addictive, its lower potency makes it less dangerous than more powerful opiates. It is also useless to intravenous opiate users. IV codeine can induce a powerful and painful histaminic reaction that may result in pulmonary edema (fluid in the lungs) and other potentially lethal complications. But codeine can indeed be used for entertainment. As a result, pure codeine, or formulations containing larger quantities of codeine, are generally available only by prescription and may require special safeguards and record-keeping. They are also increasingly difficult to find; most cases requiring higher doses of codeine will be treated instead with hydrocodone or oxycodone (see chapter 12). However, tablets containing smaller amounts of codeine are widely available. This has often led to enthusiastic young folks consuming multiple pills to get the right dosage—an approach that, depending on the other ingredients, can have terrible consequences.

Cold-Water Extraction

When the liver gets overwhelmed with acetaminophen (a dose that can range from 2 grams to 12 grams, depending on a number of factors), it begins to metabolize it into a toxic substance called NAPQI (short for N-acetyl-p-benzo-quinone imine). As NAPQI builds up in the liver, it causes horrible damage. The patient may be unaware of this for a few hours or even days until their skin yellows and their upper abdomen grows increasingly tender. One study found almost half of the 622 patients treated at twenty-two transplant centers were poisoned by acetaminophen and that it was the leading cause of acute liver failure.[5]

Many of these poisonings came from people who were taking acetaminophen in combination with an opiate. Codeine is commonly combined with acetaminophen in cold remedies and tablets. Taken in small doses, the two analgesics potentiate each other, increasing the pain relief. But small doses can quickly add up, especially when you are chasing a high and not just trying to alleviate a cough and achy joints. Taking ten Tylenol 2 tablets will give 150 milligrams of codeine, a large but still safe dose—but it will be combined with 3 grams of acetaminophen!

A few inspired opiate devotees created a process by which users could maximize their codeine experience while avoiding cirrhosis. Codeine is very soluble in water at any temperature. Acetaminophen, by contrast, is moderately soluble in warm water and almost insoluble in cold. By taking advantage of this, it is possible to separate most of the acetaminophen from codeine tablets using a process of cold-water extraction, commonly called CWE.

The pills are first crushed, and a small amount of water is then added. Too little and a gloppy paste results; too much will leach out more unwanted substances. This is stirred until it is a cloudy liquid, then placed in the freezer until it becomes very cold but not quite frozen. When the liquid is cold, it is filtered through a piece of closely woven cotton, like the back of a dress shirt, or through a coffee filter that is first wet down with ice water. This process is repeated until the water is relatively clear, drawing out most (although not all) of the acetaminophen. The white grit filtered out (which contains acetaminophen and nonsoluble binders) is discarded. The water, which contains most (although not all) of the opiates, is consumed.

This helps protect against liver damage from acetaminophen. It can also be used to extract hydrocodone and oxycodone from Vicodin and Percocet and has been used by both pain patients and recreational users worried about their acetaminophen intake. In 2006, 63% of unintentional acetaminophen overdoses involved prescription medications.[6] Chronic pain sufferers who increased their dosage over time, or who had taken over-the-counter medications for other complaints, were at risk for acute major cardiovascular events, liver damage, stroke, and serious upper gastrointestinal problems[7]—not from the opiates, but from the nonprescription additive.

It should be stressed that cold-water extraction is no cure-all. CWE changes the nature of the medication prescribed. It may hit you faster in a liquid solution than it would as a pill. And because you are taking away the acetaminophen, you may be making the remaining codeine less effective for its intended purpose; you are also losing a greater or lesser amount of the drug than if you were taking it intact. Instead of resorting to kitchen chemistry to get your medicine safely, you might do better to cut out over-the-counter remedies containing acetaminophen until such time as you no longer need your prescription meds.

"Homebake Heroin"

For many years heroin was rarely seen in New Zealand. Then, in the late 1970s, high-quality Southeast Asian heroin became available for the first time. But its time in the spotlight was brief. Subsequent operations by New Zealand, Australian, and British police led in 1980 to the collapse of the responsible group, the so-called Mr. Asia drug syndicate. After a few more busts the amount of heroin available declined dramatically. By the early 1980s seizures of imported heroin were once again a rarity.

Then, in January 1983, Auckland police seized a drug laboratory that was converting widely available codeine tablets to heroin. In the three subsequent years, Auckland police seized more than fifty such laboratories, either fully functional or as disassembled "kits," and moe than ninety were seized in New Zealand as a whole.[8] Laboratories have been encountered in kitchens and bathrooms in most parts of the country. The homemade product of these do-it-yourself drug operations has become known as "homebake."

The equipment required is very simple, and homebake is normally made in small batches for the addict's own use. Homebake chemists mix crushed packets of codeine tablets with water then filter to remove the binders—starches, talc, and other items that can be lethal if injected. The filtered liquid is then placed in a separating funnel; lye is added to make the solution strongly alkaline. Chloroform is added, drained off, and evaporated using gentle heat (typically a very low flame on a stove). The water layer is discarded. After the chloroform evaporates, white crystals of codeine base remain.

These codeine crystals are combined with pyridine hydrochloride and heated; the mixture is then added to a separation funnel along with water and a lye solution. Another chloroform extraction is performed; this time the water layer (which contains morphine) is retained. After filtering, this is stirred with a "seeding stick" (often a wooden clothes peg) while hydrochloric acid is added until powder precipitates. This morphine powder is then recovered through yet another filtration and placed in a spoon. A small amount of acetic anhydride is added and the mixture ignited. The result is a brown or black tarlike residue containing diacetylmorphine (heroin) and monacetylmorphines (metabolites of heroin and powerfully psychoactive in their own right).[9]

This mixture can be smoked or injected, and the quality can vary widely depending on the amateur chemist's skill. The mixture may contain excess codeine. Intravenous codeine can cause a massive histamine release (otherwise known as an allergic reaction) and fatal pulmonary edema (fluid in the lungs). Pyridine is a known carcinogen, and acetic anhydride is corrosive. A sloppy batch may send an unacceptable amount into your circulatory system or lungs, and missed shots frequently lead to abscesses.

Codeine tablets are still widely available in New Zealand, but less often abused than in the past. With a new proliferation of morphine sulfate tablets on New Zealand's legal and illegal pharmaceutical markets, homebakers often use morphine instead when brewing their wares. Yet the number of homebake users (and opiate users in general) remains relatively low. One survey found the number of Kiwis who had ever used an opiate rose from 3% in 1990 to 4% in 1998; current users rose from 0.5% to 0.6%, most using legally prescribed medication. Still, it is estimated that New Zealand has nearly 10,000 addicts.[10]

Fours and Doors: Codeine and Glutethimide

In 1984 the infamous recreational drug methaqualone (sold as Quaalude or Sopor) was pulled from U.S. markets. Seeing an open market, the pharmaceutical company William H. Rorer began marketing another sedative-hypnotic, glutethimide (Doriden). Glutethimide was presented as a safer alternative to barbiturates and Quaaludes. This had more to do with its legal status than its actual safety in a pharmaceutical setting. An American investigation of drugs used in suicide attempts found an overall mortality of 13.9% from glutethimide versus 0.7% from barbiturates; a similar study in Copenhagen reported corresponding values of 14.1% and 1.8%.[11] But Doriden was listed as Schedule III, allowing multiple refills and requiring less paperwork than the more restrictive Schedule II classification of most barbiturates.

As glutethimide was rediscovered by doctors it became increasingly popular among a certain discerning set of opiate users. They found that Doriden combined with codeine produced a powerful, euphoric high. With glutethimide, Tylenol 4—an easily acquired painkiller used for outpatient surgery and minor injuries—could make for a great day on "fours and doors." Codeine cough medicine combined with Doriden was nicknamed "pancakes and syrup." Glutethimide is a CYP2D6 enzyme inducer, and this causes more of the codeine to be converted into morphine. And because glutethimide is also a strong sedative, it increases the opiate nod. A typical dose of two Doriden (1,000 milligrams glutethimide) and four Tylenol 4 (240 milligrams codeine) was said by many addicts to be comparable to a heroin shot—and because it could be taken orally, there was no risk of track marks or abscesses.

The combination was known as early as the 1970s. In 1982 a number of glutethimide/codeine deaths were reported in Newark, but it soon spread to a wider audience. Between 1987 and 1991 reports of abuse came from Washington, Baltimore, Philadelphia, and New York City, then spread throughout the country. Unfortunately, the combination was not only entertaining but dangerous. Glutethimide is slowly and erratically absorbed from the gastrointestinal tract and has a half-life longer than morphine or codeine (the half-life is the amount of time it takes a user to process 50% of the drug). As a result, users might take another "load," then fall into a coma as the excess Doriden combines with the codeine to suppress respiratory function.

From January to July 1987 the Philadelphia county coroner's office received more than nineteen fatalities from "fours and doors." Chronic users were taking up to twenty "loads" per day, with heavy abusers ingesting up to 12 grams of glutethimide and more than 2.5 grams of codeine (often in combination with acetaminophen or aspirin) on a daily basis. When forced to stop their habit, they faced withdrawal from both opiates and Doriden.[12]

Faced with the increased abuse, the DEA rescheduled Doriden to Schedule II. Rorer quickly lost interest in Doriden and withdrew it from the American market by the spring of 1993. Today, glutethimide is no longer available in most of the world. (It is still sold in Eastern Europe. Konstantin Bojanov's 2005 DVD *Invisible* chronicles Bulgarian addicts who use glutethimide and codeine, along with other substances, in their quest for oblivion.) However, a slightly less potent CYP2D6 inducer and sedative, promethazine, is combined with codeine in cough syrup used to make Houston's famous "purple drank" (see chapter 25).

Noscapine

Robiquet's earliest discovery was soon overshadowed by its flashier sibling. Noscapine caused little sedation and no euphoria, although it did show some use as a cough suppressant. Today we are slowly discovering noscapine may be a valuable weapon in our long fight against cancer. In February 2007 a study reported that noscapine administered orally to animals had a tumor inhibition rate of 60% and reduced metastasis by just over 65%, with no reported toxicity.[13] Noscapine has also been studied as a treatment for breast, ovarian, colon, lung, and brain cancer and for various lymphomas, chronic lymphocytic leukemia, and melanoma. A 1998 study on noscapine at Emory University (Atlanta) involved animals that had been transplanted with human breast cancer tumors. By using noscapine, they were able to reduce tumor volume by 80% within three weeks, without any visible toxicity to the animals' vital organs or obvious weight loss.[14]

Noscapine appears to work by disturbing the assembly of microtubules, structures involved in cell division. In normal cell growth, microtubules are formed when a cell starts to divide. Once the cell stops dividing, the microtubules are either broken down or destroyed. Noscapine stops the microtubules in cancer cells from breaking down, causing them to become so clogged with microtubules that they cannot further grow and divide. This is the same mechanism of affect used by popular, and very expensive, chemotherapy drugs like paclitaxel (Taxol)—only noscapine can be delivered orally and does not produce the nausea, mouth sores, hair loss, and other side effects commonly associated with Taxol.

This is not so exciting a scientific breakthrough as it may seem. In 1958 cell culture studies performed for the United States National Cancer Institute found noscapine to possess significant cytotoxic (cancer-killing) properties. This was similar to findings that had also been reported in 1954. But, perhaps because noscapine was no longer patentable, no further studies were carried out to determine its effect on treating cancer. While Emory University was able to patent noscapine as a cancer drug, its other and more common uses are not covered. Hence, any company investing heavily in clinical trials of noscapine would not have sole rights to the drug. Although Emory University researchers remain cautiously optimistic about striking a partnership with a company or foundation, they also realize that they are unlikely to find commercial sponsorship to further develop noscapine.[15]

10

HEROIN

Like many other chemists in 1874, Charles Romley Alder Wright was looking for a nonaddictive alternative to morphine. After combining morphine with various acids, Wright set about boiling it for several hours in a solution of acetic anhydride. He then provided the resulting compound to F. M. Pierce, a lecturer and scientist at Owens College (Manchester), who reported,

> Doses . . . were subcutaneously injected into young dogs and rabbits . . . with the following general results . . . great prostration, fear, and sleepiness speedily following the administration, the eyes being sensitive, and pupils dilated, considerable salivation being produced in dogs and slight tendency to vomiting. . . . Respiration was at first quickened, but subsequently reduced, and the heart's action was diminished, and rendered irregular.[1]

Unimpressed with the results, Wright did no further work with his new compound. Then, in 1897, researchers with the German chemical company Bayer repeated Wright's experiment. Bayer chemists had recently combined acetic anhydride with salicylic acid, a popular febrifuge (fever reducer), an anti-inflammatory agent, and a mild pain reliever that was notoriously rough on patients' stomachs. Examining Wright's work with what he called "tetra-ethyl morphine," Bayer chemist Heinrich

Dresser realized that it was the same approach Bayer had used to create acetylsalicylic acid.

Repeating the process, Dresser's team once again synthesized diacetylmorphine in 1897. Within a few months workers and chemists were experimenting on frogs and rabbits, then on themselves. The reports were glowing, with repeated claims the drug made its users feel "heroisch." Thus inspired, Bayer's marketing people—who had recently introduced acetylsalicylic acid as aspirin—brought out its newest wonder drug, heroin.

Believing (incorrectly) that heroin produced less respiratory depression than codeine, Bayer presented heroin as a safer children's cough suppressant. It was also touted as a cure for morphine addiction and a panacea against, among other things, depression, bronchitis, asthma, tuberculosis, and stomach cancer. Doctors were provided with leaflets, information, and samples. A 1900 catalog for Dow's Anti-Trust Drug Store of Cincinnati, Ohio, described heroin in glowing terms as "the safe substitute for the opiates," claiming it "acts as a general analgesic without narcotic influence. Devoid to a great extent of the unpleasant after-effects of morphine, such as constipation, lassitude, headache, etc."[2] By 1899 Bayer was producing about a ton of heroin a year and exporting the drug to twenty-three countries. Heroin was available as pastilles, cough lozenges, tablets, water-soluble salts, and an elixir within a glycerin solution.

Alas, it quickly became apparent that heroin use was every bit as addictive as morphine. By 1902 French and American researchers were reporting cases of "heroinism." When the American Medical Association approved heroin for medical use in 1906, it was with the caveat that heroin was strongly habit-forming. This had little effect on its use in patent medicines. Although Bayer held the patent on the name *heroin,* the process of making diacetylmorphine was simple, and any ambitious local pharmacists could easily make some for their own miracle cures. (This was especially true after 1919, when Bayer lost its trademarks on heroin and aspirin under the Treaty of Versailles.)

In 1905 American journalist Samuel Hopkins Adams penned a blistering exposé of the patent medicine industry. In response, Congress passed the Pure Food and Drug Act of 1906, which required pharmaceutical companies to list the ingredients of their medicines. When that failed to sufficiently discourage opium consumption among users of recreational drugs like morphine and cocaine, the Harrison Act of 1914 made the nonmedical use of narcotics a crime.

But even this could not staunch the demand for heroin. While it was no longer available at the local pharmacist, there were still many underground sources. In New York a new culture of street hoodlums grew up around heroin. When they weren't committing robbery, prostitution, or other crimes to feed their habits, they scoured the streets for scrap metal. Alarmed by these "junkies," heroin was made illegal in 1924; by 1928 one-third of America's jail inmates were violators of the Harrison Act.[3]

The Pharmacology of Heroin

Like codeine, heroin's effect comes when it breaks down after absorption. Once heroin is ingested the acetyl groups (free ions formed from acetic acid) are stripped away by metabolic processes; the remaining morphine and 6-MAM (another metabolite, which is considerably more potent than morphine) then attach to opioid receptors to produce pharmacological and psychological effects.

But those acetyl groups give morphine (and many other organic molecules, including aspirin and acetaminophen) an improved ability to penetrate the blood-brain barrier (see chapter 30). When ingested as heroin, more morphine gets through to the central nervous system— enough to make it twice as powerful per milligram.

This effect is not particularly pronounced when heroin is swallowed. While it will have a slightly faster onset than morphine, stomach acids will remove the acetyl groups before most of it ever hits the bloodstream. But when heroin is sniffed or smoked—and especially when it is injected—it can make an enormous difference. As the diacetylmorphine goes through the user's system and pours into the central nervous system, it produces an intense rush of euphoria and a physical sensation that has been likened to having an orgasm throughout your body.

For almost a century this instant orgasm has been manufactured in clandestine laboratories around the world. Raw opium is added to oil drums filled with boiling water and stirred; insoluble twigs, soil, leaves, and other materials are removed, leaving the opium in solution. Slaked lime (often in the form of chemical fertilizer) is then added to the mixture, converting the morphine into soluble calcium morphenate. The other alkaloids and unwanted substances precipitate out of the solution, becoming sediment at the bottom of the barrel. The water (which now contains the morphine in solution) is then strained through burlap rice sacks or other filters into large cooking pots. There it is reheated. Ammonium chloride is added, and the solution is then allowed to cool. As it does, the morphine base settles on the bottom of the pot. It is then filtered out and dried to a coffee-colored powder in the sun. This may be further purified by dissolving it in hydrochloric acid, then adding activated charcoal, heating, and filtering it. This may be repeated several times.

The purified morphine hydrochloride is then formed into small brick-size blocks in a press. These are wrapped in paper or cloth and transported to heroin processing laboratories, where the bricks are pulverized and placed in pots with acetic anhydride. These pots are then tightly covered and heated for about two hours over low heat, maintaining a constant temperature of approximately 185°F (85°C) as the chemist tilts and swirls them to make sure all the morphine dissolves. When the pots are opened and cooled, the morphine and acetic anhydride have bonded to become heroin. Water is now added along with activated charcoal; the mixture is then filtered. Sodium carbonate (baking soda) is added to the solution, causing the crude heroin base to precipitate out.

This base can be prepared in different ways. To create the smokable form favored in much of Europe, the base is adulterated with caffeine (which lowers the melting point and allows the heroin to be vaporized before burning away) and other flavorings like strychnine or quinine (a holdover from the days when legal smokable heroin was made by Chinese labs in Hong Kong). Because this "heroin no. 3" is insoluble, users must mix it with a mild acid (typically lemon juice or vitamin C) to prepare it for injection; this makes snorting it a rather painful proposition. It will, however, produce a quick and powerful high for smokers who "chase the dragon" (chapter 29), and it can be used for other purposes with a little bit of work.

The most sophisticated labs prepare a product that is ready for snorting or injection. The heroin base mixture is dissolved in water, and chloroform is added, precipitating off colorful impurities and a red, greasy liquid. The aqueous solution is then poured in a clean pot. Activated charcoal is added, and the mix is filtered to remove still more impurities. This is repeated until the light-yellow water solution is colorless. Then sodium carbonate is added. Unlike the coffee-colored product of the first production, this batch is white.

This is then filtered yet again, in a dangerous process involving highly flammable chemicals. The base is dissolved in boiling ethyl alcohol, then recrystallized. A precisely measured amount of acid is added, converting the purified base into soluble (and injectable) heroin hydrochloride. Alcohol and ether are then added, until the heroin hydrochloride recrystallizes into pure, sparkling white crystals with a bitter taste and a powerful kick. This is adulterated with various substances to increase its volume and distributed to addicts around the world.

Heroin on the Black Market

Heroin is cheap and easy to produce. Opium poppies can be grown around the world, and the required chemicals are not difficult to procure. The market generates enormous sums of untraceable cash. As a result, there has been no shortage of suppliers—and no shortage of government officials willing to look the other way or actively assist in the trade. Powerful leaders around the world have declaimed against heroin in the strongest terms while offering aid and assistance to smugglers and producers. The War on Drugs has often taken a backseat to national security.

At first the Sicilian Mafia resisted involvement in drugs. They concentrated on bootleg liquor and left the dope to Jewish mobsters like Dutch Schultz and Meyer Lansky. But as Prohibition ended, enterprising mobsters like Charles "Lucky" Luciano moved into selling bootleg heroin. Much of their supply came from heroin laboratories in and around Marseille, France, and run by the Unione Corse (Corsican mob). At the beginning of World War II these criminal organizations were at a low point, as war made smuggling more difficult than usual and Mussolini declared war on organized crime.

But during Operation Husky, the Allied invasion of Sicily in 1943, the mob provided Allied forces with invaluable support. The army recruited Sicilians who had been deported from America for racketeering and other offenses as translators and go-betweens. Later, they appointed many to official positions in Sicily's postwar reconstruction. Corsican mobsters helped break communist-led strikes in Marseille, thereby gaining control of the docks.

With these powerful crime families now restored to power, a sophisticated heroin network arose. Raw opium from Turkey's Anatolian plateau was smuggled into Lebanon, where it was distilled into morphine base. This was then shipped to factories in Sicily and Marseille, where it was turned in to heroin then packaged for export. Transported in shipments of candy, fruit, or vegetables, they were then resold on the American market. In 1945 an estimated 20,000 addicts lived in the United States. By 1952 America had 60,000 addicts, a number that would grow to 150,000 by 1965.[4]

In the 1960s Turkey's role in the opium trade came under scrutiny. Faced with an ever-increasing number of American junkies, President Richard Nixon decided to take action. Ever the tactician, Nixon sought to stem the tide of heroin at its source, stating in a memo to Attorney General John Mitchell,

> If we do not disrupt the heroin traffic now, it is likely shortly to drift into the hands of middle-class Americans, and may become unstoppable. . . . What is needed is a major diplomatic initiative, accompanied by economic inducements, and if need be, sanctions designed to get Turkey . . . out of the business.[5]

By 1972 Turkey, under increasing American pressure, banned the cultivation of opium. This, combined with the famous "French Connection" busts of 1972, led to a U.S. drought in heroin. Heroin became expensive, hard to find, and heavily adulterated; a typical street bag in 1973 contained as little as 2% heroin, sometimes less.[6] Many addicts cleaned up or signed up for the new methadone programs (chapter 13). But the victory was short-lived as competing markets stepped in to fill the void.

Mexico and Vietnam

To bolster their position in Vietnam, Americans made alliances with just about anybody who hated the North Vietnamese communists. Many of these new bosom buddies had longtime connections to the local opium trade. In exchange for their support and information, U.S. officials looked the other way when they shipped heroin out of the "Golden Triangle" region where Laos, Burma (Myanmar), and Thailand meet. When U.S. Congressman Robert H. Steele claimed in July 1971 that high-ranking Vietnamese general and U.S. ally Ngo Dzu was one of Asia's largest heroin traffickers, the U.S. mission declared publicly (and incorrectly), "There is no information available to me that in any shape, manner or fashion would substantiate the charges Congressman Steele has made."[7]

In Harlem, a hustler named Frank Lucas used his connections with a black army sergeant stationed in Vietnam to acquire large quantities of Southeast Asian heroin. Through "the Country Boys," a network of relatives and acquaintances from his rural North Carolina hometown, Lucas distributed his stamped "Blue Magic" heroin to an appreciative clientele. As Lucas explains,

> with Blue Magic, you could get 10 percent purity. Any other, if you got 5 percent, you were doing good. We put it out there at four in the afternoon, when the cops changed shifts. That gave you a couple of hours before those lazy bastards got down there. My buyers, though, you could set your watch by them. By four o'clock, we had enough niggers in the street to make a Tarzan movie. They had to reroute the bus on Eighth Avenue. Call the Transit Department if it's not so. By nine o'clock, I ain't got a fucking gram. Everything is gone. Sold . . . and I got myself a million dollars.[8]

In 1975 an arrested Lucas turned state's evidence. His testimony led to fifty-two of the seventy officers who had worked in New York's notoriously corrupt Special Investigations Unit being arrested or indicted. Later Denzel Washington portrayed Lucas in the 2007 film *American Gangster*. And while the end of the Vietnam War, and Lucas's incarceration, meant that there was less Southeast Asian heroin on America's streets, a new supply was coming in from south of the border.

Mexican poppy growers had long produced a cheap, lower-potency, brown heroin that was popular among Mexican American addicts but rarely available outside Spanish-speaking circles. As the illicit drug industry became larger, more lucrative, and more sophisticated, the quality of Mexican heroin improved significantly—and so did the quantity. The western United States found itself awash in cheap, potent "black tar heroin," which could be smoked or injected. Meanwhile, other gangs were shipping in South American heroin.

As the supply grew, the cost decreased and the purity increased. From purity levels of 5% to 10% in the 1970s, the national average purity for retail heroin from all sources in 2000 was 36.8%.[9] This new heroin was strong enough that users could get high from snorting or smoking it. As a result, many who would never use a needle began dabbling in heroin through other modes of ingestion. Those who had become addicted to other painkillers often found black market heroin to be a more cost-effective way of handling their habit. Nixon's prophecy was realized, as a growing number of middle-class youths began using heroin as a recreational drug.

Today only Great Britain uses diacetylmorphine in medical settings. Many British doctors find its added potency useful when prescribing drips or subcutaneous injections to cancer patients or others suffering from intractable chronic pain. In most other places heroin is relegated to the recreational marketplace, while other, equally addictive opioids are used in its place.

11

KOMPOT

Drug addiction is not a serious social and health problem in the USSR. This is due to general social and economic conditions as well as to the specific steps taken by the Soviet Government. There is no unemployment in the Soviet Union; the people's standard of living is constantly rising, economically and culturally, and such social phenomena as prostitution, begging and vagrancy have been eliminated. All this militates against the spread of drug addiction.

E. A. BALININ, REPRESENTATIVE
OF THE USSR IN THE UNITED NATIONS
COMMISSION ON NARCOTIC DRUGS, 1971[1]

During the Cold War era, communist officials claimed that drug abuse and addiction were products of capitalism, not a problem that occurred in proletarian societies. Meanwhile, chronic shortages of necessities and luxuries led to a thriving trade on black markets, which also did not officially exist. Those who had money could get whatever they wanted; those who didn't learned to make do. Authority was something to be avoided if possible and bribed if necessary, and dreams of a better life were as hollow as the slogans about a proletarian paradise. Many sought to numb their pain by any means available. Much as they had learned to improvise for other necessities, they discovered the numbness they sought in dead flowers and sulfuric acid.

Kompot: The Rise of Polish Heroin

"Life in Poland these days for young people is so awful,"
says Witold, a Polish heroin addict. "I don't want to be an
ordinary man with an ordinary life." When asked about
AIDS, Witold simply shrugs. "By the time it reaches us,"
he says, "I will probably already be dead from kompot."

JENNIFER HULL, 2001[2]

Since the Middle Ages poppy seeds have been an important part of Central and Eastern European cuisine. Whether it be called *makivek* (Ukraine), *mohnkuchen* (Germany), *makowiec* (Poland), *cozonac* (Romania), or *beigli* (Hungary), poppy seed cake is a regional Christmas tradition. Lithuanians greet the holiday with *aguonų pienas,* a sweet poppy seed beverage, while Ashkenazic Jews throughout the region celebrate Purim with *hamant-aschen* (poppy seed cookies). Poppy fields decorate the landscape throughout the area, providing seeds for cooking and bedding for the cattle. But these fields also provide the fixings for a potent homemade heroin. Called *kompot* in Poland, *chornyi* in Ukraine, and *hanka* or *chernaya* in Russia, this injectable cocktail is the drug of choice for millions of addicts in the former Warsaw Pact and Soviet states.

According to legend, the classic kompot recipe was created in the early 1970s by an anonymous chemistry student at Poland's Gdansk university. It is produced by simmering large quantities of poppy straw (dried poppies) for several hours, until most of the morphine and other water-soluble chemicals have been extracted. *Kationit,* a nonsoluble solid that contains large quantities of sulfuric acid, is then placed into the brew. The morphine alkaloids react with the sulfuric acid and become salts within the kationit block. The blocks are then removed from the pot and the remaining brew is discarded. They are then washed again, producing a solution of morphine sulfate. Ammonia water is then added to the solution until it becomes alkaline. This causes the morphine to precipitate out and, upon evaporation, crystallize into a "plaster" of morphine freebase. After dissolving this freebase in ether or acetone, it is distilled for several hours at 185°F (85°C). When the solvents have almost evaporated, acetic anhydride is added. The end result is a brownish liquid containing a mix of morphine, heroin, and other trace opiates.

From Poland, this recipe quickly spread among disaffected youth throughout the Warsaw Pact and Soviet countries. The recipe was simple and its ingredients widely available. Because the party said there was no drug abuse in communist countries, there was no reason for police to harass nonexistent addicts, nor was there any incentive for politicians to admit their country had been infected by capitalist decadence.

The collapse of the Warsaw Pact and the fall of the Soviet Union brought "freedom" but not prosperity. The transition to free markets produced massive layoffs and a rapid rise in unemployment. The social safety nets of communism, such as they were, were ripped away. Gangsters and black market strongmen became wealthy, and the average citizen went from poor to poorer. Marxist-Leninism may have created a culture without hope; its downfall produced a society that dared to hope only to be bitterly disappointed. As drug abuse became more widespread, the new regimes were forced to acknowledge their growing population of addicts—especially as kompot's destructive potential became increasingly clear.

Kompot is frequently provided in preloaded syringes, but in some cases it is sold in a communal pot in which users dip their syringes and draw up the amount they pay for. This is extremely unsanitary, and regular users often report abscesses and infections. More serious is the risk of anaphylactic shock should the kompot contain any stray plant proteins or particles. The user's antibodies react to this foreign material by attacking it; as it circulates through the body the immune system goes haywire. The blood pressure drops, and fluid begins to accumulate in the lungs; hives may appear all over the body, including on the tongue and eyelids. The windpipe and throat may swell, causing difficulties in breathing. If left untreated, death may follow.

Anecdotal evidence suggests that some producers of kompot also drop fresh blood into the solution. This supposedly neutralizes the acid and causes contaminates and plant proteins to precipitate out. There is also a belief among some brewers that human blood makes the end result more potent. If that blood comes from a person infected with HIV or hepatitis, anyone using that batch has a high likelihood of becoming infected even if they use sterile needles. In addition, many larger producers use "slaves" as testers. They draw from the batch and report on its quality, and as payment, they are allowed to take another draw, typically using the same unsterilized needle.[3]

The number of addicts and opiate users in Eastern Europe and the former Soviet Republics may be as high as three million—a figure that would represent 20% of the world's opiate users and about 1% of the region's population over the age of fifteen.[4] A good number of these users support their habits, and themselves, through prostitution, and their usage of condoms is often as sporadic as their usage of clean needles. This has encouraged the spread of AIDS from a few high-risk groups to the general population—and has served to further demonize addicts among law enforcement and to isolate them from their countrymen.

A Free Eastern Europe Fights Kompot

People don't become drug addicts just because there are drugs. It has causes in society. And in Poland, those causes go deep—the hopelessness of life, the sense of discrepancy between declared values and what young people actually see going on around them, the lies, bribery and corruption.
        JERZY ZURAWSKI, A WARSAW SOCIOLOGIST, 1987[5]

During the Warsaw Pact years, Poland had its fill of repressive rules and arbitrary enforcement. As the Communist Party's grip on power began to loosen, Polish legislators sought a more rational and humane approach. Its 1985 Law on the Prevention of Drug Abuse penalized only those acts or behaviors that contribute to creating the supply of drugs—cultivation, production, processing, import, export, transit, trade, making drugs available, and similar activities. Consumption, purchasing, and possession of drugs were not treated as a criminal offense. At worst, those drugs could be confiscated. Instead of imprisoning addicts, efforts were made to control the distribution of poppy straw.

To that end, the government required poppy farmers to register with the state. During the latter part of the 1980s, up to 70% of Poland's drug arrests consisted of farmers cultivating poppies without the appropriate permits. Most were not involved in the kompot trade; they were just growing their crops as they always had, unaware that the laws had changed or unconcerned with yet another illogical directive from some faceless bureaucrat. But whether or not these laws were fair or justly applied, they served their intended purpose as poppy straw became more difficult for kompot addicts to acquire.

Although well-intentioned, these efforts had unexpected consequences. During the seventies and eighties, the Polish drug culture was largely self-sufficient. Addicts produced kompot for themselves and their friends, and there were few "pushers" selling to an addicted clientele. The only cost involved the cheap (often free) poppy straw and the inexpensive chemicals used in producing kompot. But as poppy straw became harder to come by, various criminal groups moved in and began taking control of the production and distribution of kompot. In time they would expand their reach into new markets. Today between 10% and 25% of all amphetamines in Europe are produced in clandestine Polish labs, and Poland is a major transit hub for heroin imported into Western Europe from Turkey and Afghanistan.[6]

Ultimately the attempts to control poppy growing proved futile, and so Poland created a system for tracking the twenty-two precursor chemicals outlined in the 1988 UN drug convention. The pharmaceutical department of the Ministry of Health issued licenses for domestic production and the use of precursor chemicals. Of the chemicals used in making kompot, only acetic anhydride was licensed. But this did little to slow the making of kompot as scientifically minded addicts and crime syndicates made their own by reverse-engineering easily obtained acetylsalicylic acid (more commonly known as aspirin). Less knowledgeable users skipped the process of acetylizing their kompot. The final product of their labors had morphine rather than heroin as its active ingredient but could still provide a powerful euphoric rush and stave off withdrawal symptoms.

Other countries in Eastern Europe have had no better luck controlling the poppy trade. In Lithuania poppy cultivation is a criminal offense, and Lithuanian police destroy acres of illicit poppy fields every year. But despite their efforts Lithuanian smugglers regularly export poppy straw and kompot to neighboring Latvia and the Kaliningrad region of Russia.[7] In Hungary, where in 1927 chemist János Karday patented the first process for brewing morphine from poppy straw, many poppy fields are guarded by armed security personnel. Despite this, kompot and other drugs are sold openly in the underground pedestrian walkways of Budapest's Moscow Square. Police are reluctant to patrol these areas due to the massive numbers of discarded needles all over the place.

Kompot: Treatment and Punishment

She stares at the range and admits that not a day goes by that she doesn't wish she could have some kompot again. "Not just because it made me feel good, but because life is so unutterably bleak, so awful."

Marek nods. "This country really doesn't offer people anything at all anymore. There's no chance for apartments, for jobs, there's nothing to buy. Young people have no diversion, no place to go for release. The great joy in life here is being able to buy some kielbasa or toilet paper."

ZOFIA SMARDZ, 1987[8]

Efforts toward HIV education and harm reduction have been hampered by poverty and a scarcity of resources. In the Czech Republic addicts frequently scavenge syringes from hospital dumps. In Slovenia 58% of users share needles, while 60% to 80% of users in three Ukrainian cities report sharing syringes, with only 15% to 20% using a new syringe with each injection.[9] As a result AIDS and hepatitis C have become increasingly common among intravenous drug users throughout the region. As many as 1.8 million people may be living with HIV or full-blown AIDS. The Russian Federation, Ukraine, Latvia, and Estonia are experiencing some of the world's fastest-growing HIV epidemics.[10]

Poland's MONAR (the Polish acronym for Youth Movement Against Drug Abuse) takes its cues from American recovery programs like Phoenix House and Synanon. New members wear gray, prisonlike uniforms, have their heads shaved, and perform menial duties. At regular "group therapy" sessions they are subjected to criticism and abuse in an effort to, in founder Marek Kotanski's words, "break down their characters first to reveal the flaws and weaknesses that make them vulnerable to drug addiction."[11] In Yekaterinburg, Russia, a syndicate of socially conscious gangsters has given back to their local community with a tough antidrug program. Patients spend their first week handcuffed to a radiator, with breaks only to eat and use the toilet, with brief walks allowed on their second week. Those who are uncooperative or who attempt to escape face violent beatings from the staff, most of whom are former addicts themselves. This all in keeping with the center's policy that "a drug addict is a wild beast, an animal, who cannot be treated with pity."[12]

While some treatment programs and needle exchanges have been set up in urban Eastern Europe, for the most part ex-communist governments rely on a punitive approach. In Russia doctors who lobby for methadone programs (see chapter 13) can face criminal sanctions for engaging in "drug propaganda":[13] Human Rights Watch has found that the treatment offered at state drug treatment clinics in Russia was so poor as to constitute a violation of the right to health. Rehabilitation treatment, which helps patients prevent relapses by developing control over urges to use drugs, is available at state clinics in only about one-third of Russia's regions, and more than 90 percent of addicts return to using illicit drugs within a year of entering treatment.[14] In Ukraine, drug users can be arrested and convicted for possession of minuscule amounts of heroin; arrested users are often pressured or tortured to extract information on suppliers, particularly when they are suffering from withdrawal.[15]

But stiff prison sentences have not worked to stem the use of drugs or the spread of AIDS. Treating addicts as criminals has only discouraged them from seeking what little help is available. Drugs are relatively available in many Eastern European prisons, thanks to corrupt guards and long-established prison markets. Needles, by contrast, are scarce. As a result, prison addicts are even more likely to share syringes. Combined with the inevitable incidents of homosexual rape, this has only increased the prevalence of HIV infection among opiate users in and out of custody.

Today, kompot's popularity has declined. This is not due to law enforcement efforts but to the growing availability of inexpensive Afghani and Pakistani heroin. During the 1980s many Soviet soldiers came back from their tours of duty in Afghanistan with heroin habits. Many former Soviet states in Central Asia have become part of the "silk road" leading from Afghanistan and Pakistan to Turkey and the Balkans, while the Baltic republics have become an integral part of the heroin routes into Scandinavia and Germany. Among the ethnic crime syndicates that have been linked to heroin trafficking are the Albanian mob, Kurdish militants, and Bulgarian Roma (gypsies); Ukrainian and Russian criminal organizations are also deeply involved in the trade. In Latvia a dose of heroin costs less than a Big Mac at a local McDonald's, and heroin and other drugs are readily available at nightclubs and bars. In eastern Russia a gram of heroin (more than twenty doses) can be had for $30 to $40. Seventeen thousand residents of Irkutsk, a gritty Siberian city of six hundred thousand, are

HIV-positive, thanks largely to needle-sharing among local addicts. Perhaps sixty thousand more are infected but have not registered with the authorities.[16]

The black market channels that functioned during the Communist era are still in place and have now been repurposed to meet the ever-growing demand for drugs. While the demand for heroin in Western Europe has been stabilized for some time, the market in the East is booming. Smuggling represents one of the region's few growth industries. And because poppies are still widely grown throughout the area, it is unclear how effective any attempt to stop heroin smuggling will be. In 2001 Estonia witnessed a rise in kompot usage as a Taliban crackdown on poppy growing caused Afghani heroin to become more expensive and less pure.[17]

12

OXYCODONE

In 1834 a French chemist named Pierre-Joseph Pelletier isolated yet another opium alkaloid. Pelletier, who had earlier discovered caffeine and chlorophyll, named this new drug paramorphine because he believed its structure was similar to morphine. He was more or less right, but his new substance (now known as thebaine after the famous opium industry of Thebes) behaved nothing at all like codeine or morphine. Thebaine has no analgesic properties; in fact, its clinical activity is similar to strychnine. The symptoms of thebaine poisoning include life-threatening convulsions; sensitivity to light, sound, and touch; frantic pacing; and muscle tremors caused by involuntary muscle contractions.[1]

Traces of thebaine will frequently be found in specimens from people who consume poppy products; none should appear as a result of heroin or morphine use. As a result, many drug tests now check for thebaine to distinguish between heroin-abusing workers and employees who like poppy seed bagels.[2] This has led to more accurate testing, but it has also led to a rumor among junkies that you can beat a drug test by eating poppy seed bagels beforehand.

While pure thebaine in itself has little pharmaceutical value, under the right conditions it can be extremely useful. It is the starting ingredient for a variety of semisynthetic opioids and pharmaceuticals, including popular drugs like hydromorphone (Dilaudid), oxymorphone (Opana), hydrocodone (Vicodin), and the powerful narcotic antagonist naloxone (Narcan).

Tasmanian growers have invested a great deal of time and resources into the development of poppies that produce elevated levels of thebaine. Through selective breeding and the use of mutagenic chemicals, they created a strain called "top1" or "Norman" (for "no morphine"). While *P. somniferum* normally synthesizes thebaine into morphine, researchers shut down the genes responsible for that synthesis. This produces a poppy that looks identical to a normal morphine-producer save for its latex, which is red or pink instead of the more typical white.

Tasmania's climate is ideal for growing poppies, and its island location provides some protection against thieves who would steal these valuable plants. And while longstanding treaties require American pharmaceutical companies to purchase 80% of their opium from India and Turkey, they are under no such constraint when buying thebaine. As a result, Tasmania supplies nearly 40% of the world's legal *P. somniferum* and is the unquestioned leader in top1/Norman poppies, producing 66% of the world's thebaine. The economy in this Australian state has boomed, especially with the rise of a powerful, and controversial, painkiller.

Oxycodone

Oxycodone was first synthesized in Germany in 1916, some years after Bayer had stopped producing heroin. Scientists hoped that a thebaine-derived drug would retain the analgesic effects of morphine and heroin with less of the euphoric effect that leads to addiction and overuse. To some extent this was achieved, as oxycodone's effects are not as long-lasting as heroin or morphine. But oxycodone has other advantages over natural opiates. Unlike morphine or heroin, it has a high oral *bioavailability*. Oral oxycodone has an absorption of 60% to 87%, more than twice as high as morphine's 25% or so. While intramuscular or IV doses of morphine and oxycodone are roughly equal, oxycodone is twice as strong as morphine when given orally.

Oxycodone may be slightly less likely than morphine to produce nausea and cause delirium in high therapeutic doses. It also produces somewhat less of a histaminic release and attendant opiate itches. And because of its high oral bioavailability, instant release formulations of oxycodone are often prescribed along with another, longer-lasting pain relief solution. In cases of "breakthrough pain"—sudden intense flare-ups of pain that are not suppressed by the long-lasting opiate—the patient can take a small amount of oxycodone for quick relief. Then, in 1996, Purdue Pharma introduced a new, longer-lasting formulation, OxyContin.

The Contin System

In 1984 Purdue Pharma begin selling Uniphyl, a once-a-day asthma medication. Uniphyl contains the popular asthma drug theophylline in a homogenous matrix of cellulose and other binders. As the tablet dissolves, its active ingredient was gradually and evenly released. In 1985 Purdue brought out a morphine tablet, MS Contin. These were and still are particularly popular with oncologists, because they gave sustained relief to the chronic pain endured by many cancer patients. In 1995 MS Contin commanded an 80% share of the cancer pain market, bringing in $110 million in sales and 25% of Purdue Pharma's net profit.[3]

In the late 1980s many states began passing guidelines or laws recognizing the therapeutic value of narcotics in treating severe intractable pain. Physician organizations and patient rights groups also began lobbying against DEA interference with doctors and pharmacists. In many cases these groups were funded by pharmaceutical companies, whose salespeople saw a large untapped market for pain relief. Purdue Pharma was one of those investors, donating large sums to medical organizations like the Pain and Policies Support Group, the American Pain Society, and the American Academy of Pain Medicine.[4]

In 1997 OxyContin will be launched into the non-malignant market. . . . The most common diagnoses for non-malignant pain are back pain, osteoarthritis, injury and trauma pain. The major competitors for these diagnoses will be hydrocodone and oxycodone combination products, as well as Ultram. OxyContin will be positioned as providing the equivalent efficacy and safety of combination opioids, with the benefit of twice daily dosing.

PURDUE PHARMA MEMO, 1996[5]

OxyContin provided a sustained gradual release of oxycodone over a twelve-hour period. Its payload was suspended in an acrylic matrix that would release a steady supply of the drug as the tablet passed through the stomach and intestines. While earlier formulations of oxycodone like Percodan and Percocet typically contained 2.5 to 10 milligrams of oxycodone and were to be taken every six hours, these twelve-hour tablets could contain as much as 80 milligrams (and later 160 milligrams) of oxycodone.

Purdue Pharma claimed that the Contin time-release function limited the addiction risk. Because an OxyContin tablet provided a steady flow of oxycodone over an extended period, it did not give the euphoric high associated with intravenous narcotics. Purdue felt OxyContin could be prescribed not only by oncologists and pain specialists but general practitioners as well. They supported OxyContin's release with an extensive media campaign aimed at general practitioners instead of pain specialists. This was supported by paid three-day seminars on pain management and its undertreatment. Held at resort locations in California, Arizona, and Florida, these seminars introduced two thousand to three thousand doctors to OxyContin and recruited hundreds for its "Speakers Bureau" as pain management educators.[6]

While FDA regulations forbade direct-to-consumer advertising, Purdue established Partners Against Pain (PAP), a campaign aimed at patients suffering from long-term pain. While Partners Against Pain material did not specifically mention OxyContin, it encouraged doctors and patients to take a more aggressive stance against chronic pain, including opioid treatment when necessary.[7] PAP-created pamphlets and videotapes appeared in physician waiting rooms, urging patients to talk with their doctors about pain and its possible treatment.

All this footwork paid off: by 2000, 6.5 million OxyContin prescriptions were written, making OxyContin the eighteenth bestselling drug in America and the most popular opioid painkiller.[8]

OxyContin Comes to Rural America

No one knew what was going on. These are a bunch of pot smokers, drinkers, just mellow people. This drug just took us by storm. A whole community, at least a hundred people I know around here. They're all into the addiction. These are guys I used to smoke pot with and drink beer with in the woods. I grew up with them all, having parties and that. And now there's not one of them—not one of them— that don't use pills.

CURT, 26, RECOVERING
OXYCONTIN ADDICT, 2001[9]

OxyContin found a ready market in small, blue-collar towns throughout rural America. Laborers and farmers were frequently injured on the job; back strains and joint aches were a part of their everyday life. For them OxyContin offered a chance to continue in their jobs until they made their twenty-year pension, to hold on to the family farm until the children were ready to take over responsibility. The time-release mechanism meant they could take their pills in the morning and evening rather than every four to six hours—a much easier schedule for hard-working people.

Recreational users soon learned that they could defeat the time release by crushing the tablet, thereby getting twelve-hours worth of oxycodone in one dose. Many OxyContin users shunned the needle and its attendant stigma, preferring to snort or swallow their drugs. They did not realize that oxycodone's high oral bioavailability meant they were getting nearly as much of the drug into their system as IV users. Other users began injecting the pills, seeing them as a safer pharmaceutical alternative to "street drugs." (In fact, street heroin is far less likely to contain talc, silicates, wax, starches, insoluble binders, and other fillers that can lead to talcosis, pulmonary obstructions, and horribly infected abscesses.) Like the opium-eating peasants of England's fen country, small-town America was caught up in an epidemic of "hillbilly heroin."

But where opium and pod tea were cheap and readily available in the fens, black market OxyContin was selling for $1 a milligram or more. Because a habituated abuser could require a daily 500-milligram or more dose to stay well, "oxy" was an expensive addiction. Many OxyContin addicts turned to other opiates. A $500 per day OxyContin habit could be appeased with less than a gram of heroin, which goes for $60 to $100 in most American markets. While some OxyContin users claim oxycodone is more stimulating and euphoric than heroin, each will stave off withdrawals from the other.

Still other users turned to crime. In October 2000, 5.5% of Kentucky's drugstores and 4% of Maine's drugstores were robbed. A six-week period ending July 2001 saw fourteen pharmacies in Boston and its suburbs terrorized by gun-toting bandits who ignored the cash register and demanded the stores' OxyContin instead. Similar incidents were reported from New England to the Appalachians to as far south as Florida and as far west as California and Washington State. In response two of New England's largest supermarket chains announced they would no longer carry OxyContin in their pharmacies; another small Boston pharmacy placed a sign in its window saying, "For everyone's safety, we no longer stock the painkiller OxyContin."[10] Similar signs can still be seen in pharmacies across America. Explaining why he

would no longer sell products containing oxycodone, pharmacist Ken
Ritter said,

> The addiction is so strong. The desperation is so strong. We have to
> take a stand and do something, so I'm taking my stand. . . . You can't
> imagine what it's like to have someone walk up to you and put a gun
> in your face. . . . The desperation to get the drug is out of control.[11]

Medical professionals who avoided OxyContin-related crime also
had to watch out for DEA raids. As the crisis grew, law enforcement
began to concentrate on doctors who wrote an "excessive" number of
scripts and pharmacies that filled an "excessive" number of prescriptions
for OxyContin. Yet there was no official description of what consti-
tuted "excessive." One doctor, Frank Fisher, was arrested on charges that
included the death of a patient taking opioids—who died as a passenger
in a car accident. A Florida doctor, James Graves, is serving sixty-three
years for charges including manslaughter after four patients overdosed
on OxyContin he prescribed—all either crushed and injected their
OxyContin or mixed it with alcohol or other drugs. A FAQ offering
guidelines on how doctors could stay within the law was erased from
the DEA website in October 2004 after one of the authors used it to
testify on behalf of a pain doctor charged in a DEA bust.[12]

Once derided as "hillbilly heroin," OxyContin soon began showing
up in higher social strata as well. In October of 2003 conservative talk
show host Rush Limbaugh announced he was addicted to painkillers.
That same month Courtney Love was taken to the hospital after an
OxyContin overdose. In May 2007 Lindsay Lohan's estranged father
announced she was abusing oxycodone, and in January of 2008 Heath
Ledger died after ingesting a cocktail of oxycodone, hydrocodone, and
several antianxiety drugs. Some younger users began smoking their
OxyContin, receiving a quick, intense rush and lasting lung damage
from burning wax and acrylic. Others got into trouble when raiding
their parents' medicine cabinets. A single OxyContin 80 can easily kill

a youth with no opiate tolerance, especially if combined with alcohol or other drugs.

The growing abuse of OxyContin led to numerous lawsuits and increasing government scrutiny. On May 15, 2007, Purdue Pharma and three of the company's current and former executives pleaded guilty to misleading the public about the safety of its painkiller OxyContin. Under the terms of the settlement, Purdue pleaded guilty to one felony count of fraudulently misbranding a drug. In a settlement brokered by former New York mayor and presidential candidate Rudy Giuliani, the company paid $600 million in fines, including $160 million to state and federal health care programs and $130 million to resolve pending private lawsuits. Purdue CEO Michael Friedman, general counsel Howard Udell, and former Chief Scientific Officer Paul Goldenheim each were hit with fines ranging from $7.5 million to $19 million, but none were given any jail time. The total amount of the penalties represented approximately 90% of the profit that Purdue had earned from OxyContin to date. OxyContin remains on the market and is still widely available.

13

METHADONE

As World War II began, trade routes between Europe and Persia, India, and Turkey grew increasingly blocked. To limit dependence on the imported opium required to produce morphine, German scientists worked overtime to develop synthetic substitutes. (Among their greatest successes was the painkiller pethidine, which remains in usage today under the names meperidine and Demerol.)

In 1939 chemists at I. G. Farbenkonzern's pharmaceutical laboratories synthesized a compound they labeled Va 10820. Because they had developed many other compounds that year, it was not until 1942 that they were able to explore its potential as a painkiller. But while several experimental trials were performed on Va 10820 (also known as Amidon), the results were not particularly impressive. The researchers underestimated its strength, and the initial doses were too high, resulting in intolerable opioid side effects. Consequently, the compound was never brought into widespread usage in the Third Reich.

After the war's end, the records on I. G. Farbenkonzern's research were confiscated by U.S. forces and brought to the United States. The original patent rights were no longer protected, and so any pharmaceutical company interested in the formulas could purchase the rights for production for $1.[1] In 1947 the AMA's Council on Pharmacy and Chemistry gave Va 10820 the generic name methadone. Pharmaceutical company Eli Lilly sold their methadone formulation under the trade

111

name Dolophine (from the Latin *dolor* for "pain" plus *finis,* "end").

Like natural opiates, methadone attaches itself to opioid receptors within the body. These receptors are proteins found within the membranes of some cells, particularly the central nervous system and the gastrointestinal tract. Opioids bind to these receptors, as do a number of endogenous chemicals called endorphins (the substances that produce the famous "endorphin rush" and "runner's high"). Most of the non-endogenous opioids are directly or indirectly derived from poppy alkaloids. Methadone, by contrast, is entirely synthetic.

While morphine's half-life (the amount of time it takes a user to process 50% of the drug) is approximately two hours, methadone has a half-life of twenty-four to thirty-six hours. If treated like morphine— regular doses every four to six hours—a patient will soon develop dangerously high blood levels of methadone. When methadone was first introduced, doctors using it for pain relief often increased their patients' dosage until they reached concentrations that caused sedation, respiratory depression, and overdose.[2] As a result, methadone gained a reputation as a dangerous, potentially toxic drug that was little used when safer alternatives like morphine were available.

Doctors at the U.S. Public Health Service Center in Lexington, Kentucky, recognizing methadone's extended effect, began using it to treat patients who were detoxing from opiates. An addict would be given a small dose of methadone, which was progressively reduced to zero over a period of approximately ten days—a process that took longer than going "cold turkey" but involved considerably less suffering. But this usage was limited by the Harrison Act of 1914.

As interpreted by law enforcement, doctors were forbidden to prescribe opiates to an addict to maintain his habit. Under the Harrison Act narcotics could be dispensed or prescribed only by a physician. Addiction was now seen by the government as a crime rather than a disease. Accordingly, opiates provided by a physician to an addict were not being supplied in what the Harrison Act defined as "the course of his professional practice." In *Webb v. U.S.* (1919) the Supreme Court held that it was not legal for a physician to prescribe narcotic drugs to an addict-patient for the purpose of maintaining his or her use and comfort. In 1922 they further declared, in *U.S. v. Behrman,* that a narcotic prescription for an addict was unlawful, even if the drugs were prescribed as part of a "cure program."

While they later reversed themselves, in *Linder v. U.S.* (1925), and held that addicts were entitled to medical care like other patients, the damage had already been done. Many doctors had been imprisoned for providing narcotics to addicted patients and many others had seen their careers ruined. Most physicians were now unwilling to treat addicts under any circumstances, and only a very few would provide any kind of drug treatment to wean a dope fiend off the habit. Those who were unwilling to check into the Lexington "narcotics farm"—a grim place where most of the patients were convicts sent by court order—would have to undergo withdrawal without medical aid.

All these laws and regulations did little to stop opiate sales as an underground drug market quickly sprang up to keep addicts satiated. By the early 1960s heroin was the leading cause of death among people age fifteen to thirty-five. Hepatitis was spreading rapidly through the use of contaminated needles, while jails were overcrowded with addicts arrested for drug-related offenses and property crimes undertaken to support their habits.[3] Faced with this crisis, two brave doctors in New York proposed a radical solution.

The Beginnings of Methadone Maintenance

Vincent Dole came to his work on addiction by a circuitous path. After receiving a degree in mathematics from Stanford, he crammed seven semesters of biology into one summer to qualify for admittance to medical school. During World War II he helped develop the copper sulfate method of measuring blood density in shock victims. (The blood is dropped into a copper sulfate solution of known specific gravity. Blood that contains sufficient hemoglobin sinks rapidly due to its density, whereas blood that does not floats or sinks slowly. This test is still used to determine whether potential donors have enough hemoglobin to give blood.)

Later Dole turned his attention to obesity. His studies found that many obese people metabolize food differently from others. He also noted that their cravings for food were similar to a cigarette smoker's craving for tobacco or an addict's craving for narcotics. Like smokers and junkies, obese people tended to relapse after dieting even after periods of abstinence. When most other doctors were claiming that obesity was a character flaw caused by gluttony, Dr. Dole's research suggested that these relapses had a metabolic and biochemical origin. Following his work on obesity to its logical conclusion, Dole theorized that opiate addiction, like obesity, might be a biochemical imbalance rather than a weakness of will.

Dole joined forces with Dr. Marie Nyswander, a psychiatrist who specialized in addiction. The author of *The Drug Addict as a Patient* (1956), Nyswander had more than twenty years' experience working with narcotic users. She knew that conventional psychotherapy, detoxification, and incarceration were of little use in keeping addicts from relapse. Rather than blaming the addict for a lack of motivation, she believed that the problem lay in a lack of effective treatment options. To keep addicts from relapse, medicine would first have to address the insatiable craving that gnawed at them even after the physical dependence had been conquered.

To test their theory, Dole and Nyswander admitted six long-time heroin users to their program at the Rockefeller Institute (now Rockefeller University). Each had more than five years' history of addiction and two or more failed treatment attempts; all had criminal records related to their heroin abuse. With this singularly unpromising test group, they hoped to find an answer to the problem of addiction.

Their patients were started on small doses of morphine, 15 milligrams four times a day. As with Dole's earlier obesity project (which began with patients being given as much food as desired), they were allowed to increase their doses as they pleased. Within three weeks they were requesting and getting eight shots totaling 600 milligrams (10 grains) a day. "Much of the time they sat passively, in bathrobes, in front of a television set," Dr. Nyswander later recalled. "They didn't respond to any of the other activities offered them. They just sat there, waiting for the next shot."[4] While Dole and Nyswander continued to study the metabolic factors and mechanisms of these short-acting opiates, it was clear that these addicts were as resistant to this form of treatment as to anything else they had tried so far.

In accordance with FBI regulations, Dole and Nyswander were expected to help the patients with detox then discharge them after the metabolic tests on morphine were completed. To do this they followed the then-standard protocols for detoxification. But instead of beginning an immediate methadone taper, Dole and Nyswander kept them on high doses for a longer period so they could run metabolic tests comparing the metabolism of morphine and methadone.

As their addicted patients continued taking methadone, Dole and Nyswander noted startling behavioral changes. Instead of sitting passively and waiting for their next shot, they sought stimulus from other outside activities. One began painting; another started taking classes for his high school equivalency diploma. The methadone did not produce the highs and lows of repeated morphine doses, and there was little incentive to up the methadone dose, because it did not provide the "rush" of intravenous drugs. While on methadone the subjects were apparently free of both physical and psychological cravings. Should they be tempted, the methadone produced a cross-tolerance, or "blockade." This ensured users would feel no euphoria from a normal dose of morphine, heroin, or other opiate. In a 1965 report Dole and Nyswander concluded that "with [methadone] and a sufficient program of rehabilitation, patients have shown marked improvement; they have returned to school, obtained jobs and become reconciled with their families."[5]

From the original six patients the program expanded exponentially. By October 31, 1969, 1,866 New York heroin addicts were on methadone; by October 31, 1970, there were 3,485 patients with forty-two methadone distribution centers in New York City and four in Westchester County. Eighty percent of patients remained on methadone for at least five years. Their rates of arrest and conviction dropped from 52 convictions per 100 man-years of addiction to 5.8 convictions, and 88% of patients maintained arrest-free records while on methadone.[6]

Methadone Meets Resistance

While doctors hailed methadone as a major breakthrough in the treatment of addiction, law enforcement was more skeptical. The Federal Bureau of Narcotics (FBN) believed that methadone was just another narcotic and that giving it to an addict was no different from providing any other opiate. Bureau agents informed Dole that he was breaking the law and could go to prison. Armed with the legal backing of the Rockefeller trust, Dole calmly suggested they arrest him so they could go to court and get a binding determination on the issue.

Their bluff called, the bureau backed away from their threat, but their hostility to methadone treatment continued. Agents infiltrated the clinics where the research was being conducted. Records were stolen and Nyswander was followed. Her activities including vacation plans were reported to the bureau by an unknown surveillant. Many years later under the Freedom of Information Act, Nyswander obtained a censored record of these activities. The file was the size of the Manhattan telephone book.[7] Bureau agent Malachi Harney lectured President Nixon, stating that in the FBN's view, methadone "legitimizes opiate addiction in our society, tends to make it acceptable and respectable. It maintains a large nucleus of drug addicts from which addiction will proliferate."[8]

Methadone clinics also faced opposition from neighborhood residents who were afraid they would draw crime—after all, they catered to criminals. This opposition still continues; those who try to open methadone clinics regularly face zoning challenges and hostility from local governments. Because of this, many methadone patients face long drives to get to their nearest clinic and receive their morning dose before going to work. Thanks to this community pressure methadone clinics are often situated in the worst parts of town, thereby propagating the idea that methadone leads to crime and discouraging addicts from entering the program.

Richard Nixon praised methadone as a crime reducer. This led many black activists to believe that methadone clinics were a plot to sterilize the black population. According to one urban legend, methadone was intended by the Third Reich to sterilize Jews and was given the name Dolophine in honor of Adolf Hitler. (As stated above, the name Dolophine was first used in 1947 and had nothing to do with Der Führer. Furthermore, methadone users frequently regain their libidos when their dosage is stabilized, while hard-core heroin users generally exhibit little interest in sex.) Given that in 1972 the infamous "Tuskegee Syphilis Experiment" on 399 black sharecroppers was brought to light, it is not difficult to understand the black community's mistrust of government doctors in their community.

Offenders enrolled in methadone maintenance programs are rarely allowed to continue treatment behind bars. Very few jails provide continuous treatment for inmates on methadone, except for pregnant inmates. One study found that for detoxification purposes only 2% of jails used methadone or other opiates, while 30% used only ibuprofen or acetaminophen and 20% reported providing no symptomatic treatment.[9] Because methadone's half-life is longer than the half-life for heroin or morphine, the withdrawal period is correspondingly longer. Patients who abruptly cease taking methadone by choice or coercion may endure weeks, not days, of horrible suffering. Most doctors recommend a gradual and medically supervised taper for those seeking to wean themselves from methadone.

Methadone appeases cravings for opiates and limits their euphoric potential. It does not block the effect of cocaine, alcohol, or other drugs, and it is not uncommon for heroin addicts to be dependent on other substances. But methadone patients seeking inpatient treatment for other addictions are generally expected to get off the methadone first. Methadone patients are not allowed to speak at Narcotics Anonymous meetings or to lead groups. The official position of Narcotics Anonymous is that "our program approaches recovery from addiction through abstinence, cautioning against the substitution of one drug for another."[10] Much as law enforcement officials benefit by promoting the idea of addiction as crime, many drug addiction counselors (particularly those who cannot prescribe medication themselves) have a vested interest in promoting "drug-free living" as the only real form of recovery.

However, the dangers associated with methadone are very real. Methadone users who also abuse tranquilizers are at increased risk of overdose. Some addicts on MMT (methadone maintenance therapy) will try increasing their previous dose of heroin to get the old "rush." This can result in either euphoria or death. If the methadone dose is small enough, a patient can maintain a dual heroin and methadone habit. And despite efforts to control the distribution of methadone through licensed clinics, methadone occasionally is diverted into the black market. Inexperienced users who try methadone frequently get themselves in trouble. Unaware of methadone's long half-life, they redose within a few minutes in search of a high—then discover too late that they have taken more than they should.

Nobody suggests that diabetics should abstain from insulin or transplant patients should kick the habit of immunosuppressant drugs. Yet because of methadone's connection to the "character weakness" of addiction, its usage garners continuing controversy. This means that many addicts (not to mention pain patients who could benefit from methadone's extended half-life) are unable to take advantage of what is to date their best hope of a normal existence.

14

FENTANYL

In 1960 Paul Janssen, a Belgian biochemist and founder of Janssen Pharmaceutica, first synthesized fentanyl. He expected the compound to show analgesic properties similar to other synthetic opioids like meperidine or methadone. He got something far more potent. Animal tests conducted by the Janssen Pharmaceutica research group showed that the analgesic potency of fentanyl was 470 times that of morphine.[1]

Fentanyl quickly became a favorite among anesthesiologists. It is far less likely to cause histamine reactions in patients and can cause a deep, complete sedation with a comparatively small dose. Then, in 1990, Janssen introduced a new delivery system—the Duragesic patch. The Duragesic patch allows for a controlled dose of fentanyl. The fentanyl is mixed in a gel/hydrocellulose matrix, then delivered at a consistent rate through the skin through a sophisticated membrane.

The patch could provide relief for patients unable to swallow pills and could be scaled up to meet the demands of even the most severely ill cancer patients. Marketed through Janssen's primary shareholder and American partner, Johnson & Johnson, Duragesic patches became a billion-dollar business, used not only for cancer but also for arthritis, neuropathy, and other chronic pain conditions. Fentanyl lollipops and lozenges provided quick relief for breakthrough pain; while fentanyl is largely broken down in the stomach, it is quickly and efficiently absorbed through the cheek and gum membranes.

But Duragesic patches also found a ready audience among the users of street drugs. Today recreational users cut open the patches and smoke the gel or apply multiple patches; a few enthusiastic if self-destructive souls have even tried to extract the fentanyl and inject it. On December 15, 2005, forty-four-year-old Jacqueline Young died in bed at the Greenwood, Indiana, hotel where she was living. She was wearing two pain patches and had applied heating pads to accelerate the delivery of fentanyl. On March 21, 2006, police officers arrived at the home of Anna Layton of Shelbyville, Tennessee, to tell her about her son's death only to find her dead. Both mother and son had eaten and injected fentanyl from patches. Toxicology reports showed that Anna Layton had nearly fifteen times the lethal dose of fentanyl in her system, and her son had nearly three times the lethal dose. In 2004 fentanyl patch abuse was found to be responsible for 115 deaths in Florida alone.[2]

Fentanyl is intended only for users who are already opiate tolerant, typically patients who have been on pain medication for long periods of time. Those with less tolerance can easily experience fatal respiratory depression. Even those who are used to painkillers need to approach fentanyl with care. If the membrane is damaged an excessive quantity of the drug could leak onto the skin, and combining fentanyl with other depressants like alcohol or benzodiazepines can be deadly.

Fentanyl has long been popular among junkies as "China White," heroin of legendary, sometimes lethal, potency. Many street chemists have attempted to brew their own fentanyl. While relatively complicated, the synthesis is not beyond most bright graduate students—and because one gram of fentanyl can be cut into approximately seven thousand doses, this can be a lucrative undertaking. By mixing a bit of fentanyl with low-quality heroin, or even with inert cut, a dealer can make a killing (figuratively and literally) with batches of "magic" or "China white." But this potency also makes fentanyl extremely dangerous. Between April 5, 2005, and March 28, 2007, American researchers identified 1,013 deaths caused by injections of fentanyl-laced heroin—a number that was likely underreported.[3] And if the chemist is careless, the compound that is created may be one of fentanyl's more powerful analogs—or something else altogether.

MPTP and the "Junkie Statues"

In 1976 Barry Kidston, a young graduate student in Bethesda, Maryland, was hospitalized with symptoms of severe Parkinson's disease. When treated with levodopa, the standard treatment for Parkinson's, he regained some of his mobility. It was then revealed that Kidston, a chemist, had been brewing and injecting the synthetic opiate 1-methyl-4-phenyl-4-propionoxy-piperidine (MPPP) for several months. Two years later, Kidston's psychopharmacology career ended as he died of a cocaine overdose. An autopsy revealed a substantial loss of dopamine-producing cells in the substantia nigra part of his brain, a hallmark of Parkinson's disease.

Then, in July of 1982, a forty-two-year-old named George Carillo arrived at the Santa Clara Valley Medical Center in San Jose, California. Carillo was literally frozen like a statue in a bent, twisted position. Neurologists suspected catatonic schizophrenia, but psychologists were certain it was a neurological disorder. Then a neurologist in Watsonville, some thirty miles away, reported a case of two brothers in their twenties, both addicts, who showed advanced symptoms of Parkinson's. Alerts were issued warning of a new batch of bad heroin on the streets. Ultimately seven addicts would come down with these alarming symptoms. William Langston, M.D., described his experiences with one of these unfortunates.

> After a day or two, we learned two things about this patient. One is that he was totally mentally normal inside, which was a shocker. A medical student actually put a pencil in his hand and asked him to write, held a legal tablet up to his hand. Because he couldn't talk, we didn't know whether he was normal in there or not. And he wrote: "I'm not sure what is happening to me. I only know I can't move; it

just won't come out right." And that was the first time that we knew he was mentally normal—and [also] an exquisite definition, I think, of the feeling a Parkinson's patient must have.

The second thing was, in taking [his] history, we asked him if he was on any medications. And to our shock, he wrote the word "heroin"—not a traditional medication, but that was our first clue that he was using heroin. And that ultimately led to other heroin addicts and the discovery that the heroin was actually the cause.[4]

A sample of this tainted heroin was analyzed. One of the toxicologists who examined it recalled reading about an unusual case of Parkinson's in *Psychiatry Research*. William Langston, the neurologist who first treated Carillo, looked up the paper, which dealt with the Kidston case. He found that Kidston had prepared his synthesis based on a 1947 paper by Albert Ziering, a researcher at the Hoffmann–La Roche pharmaceutical company.

But when he went to the Stanford University library to check *The Journal of Organic Chemistry* in which it had appeared, he discovered that Ziering's paper had been cut out. It was clear now that some enterprising college chemist was cooking up MPPP and selling it as heroin. It was equally clear that he, like Kidston, had made a mistake in his recipe. Further study of MPPP revealed that if Ziering's original synthesis was not followed exactly, a contaminant called MPTP was produced—and when injected into monkeys, MPTP triggered symptoms of Parkinson's disease.[5]

Upon entering the bloodstream, MPTP is converted into another molecule, MPP+. This molecule attacks the dopamine-producing cells of the substantia nigra, producing damage identical to that seen in Parkinson's patients. This meant that researchers could now reproduce Parkinson's disease—and study its treatments—in the laboratory with animal subjects. This allowed for research into stem cell treatments and experimental medications deemed too risky for patients—and has provided several promising breakthroughs in experimental technologies and treatments for Parkinson's. Other researchers suspect that MPP+, metabolized from industrial chemicals or other contaminants, is responsible for many cases of Parkinson's disease. Studies found increased Parkinson's associated with pesticide use; consumption of well water; exposure to herbicides; and proximity to industrial plants, printing facilities, and quarries.[6]

But the addicts who injected the tainted heroin paid a heavy price for these advances. While L-Dopa relieved some of their symptoms in the short term, it had many side effects, including hallucinations and psychotic states. Later, tolerance to L-Dopa developed and the tremors and catatonia returned. A few received some measure of relief from fetal cell implants. Another, William Govea, was helped by a deep brain electronic stimulator developed thanks to research begun in the post-MPTP era. It has helped relieve many of his symptoms. Unfortunately, due to crimes he committed while suffering from L-Dopa-fueled psychosis, he is currently incarcerated in the Atascadero State Hospital until at least 2026.

The *Nord-Ost* Siege of 2002

We will start killing them, the people who are here. One by one we will kill them—all of them. . . . We didn't come here to go home again, we came here to die. We are all suicide fighters.

ABUSAID, REPRESENTATIVE
OF CHECHEN REBELS[7]

Tensions between Russia and Chechen separatists have existed for centuries. On the night of October 23, 2002, they broke out into open warfare. During the second act of the popular Russian musical *Nord-Ost*, a group of forty-one Chechen separatists took more than eight hundred Moscow theatergoers hostage. The Chechens were armed with small arms and machine guns; they also carried a large amount of explosives strapped to their bodies and promised to detonate them should Russian authorities attempt to storm the theater by force.

Hours dragged on. Captives and captors alike waited in the auditorium without food or water. The orchestra pit became a makeshift lavatory. Pictures of the female soldiers among the guerillas—burqa-wearing "Black Widows" with explosive belts around their waists—became symbols of Islamic terrorism's new face, as all Russia reeled from what its papers were calling "our own September 11."

In April, President Vladimir Putin had declared the war in Chechnya over. These rebels were proving him wrong and taking the war to the heart of the Russian empire. His rise to power had been based in no small part on his "tough on terrorism" persona and his uncompromising stance against Chechen and other separatists. The hostage keepers repeatedly referred to themselves as *smertnik*—those condemned to death, or martyrs—and as the "Islamic Suicide Squad." There was little hope that this would resolve itself in any way but a bloodbath.

At about 5 a.m. on October 26, some fifty-seven hours after the siege began, rebels and hostages noticed what they thought was smoke. It soon became apparent that something else was going on. The gas "caused a sleepiness—a quiet slipping into sleep," hostage Lyudmila Fedyantseva said. "I asked my mom, a medical worker, if it was ether. She said, 'No, this is something different.'"[8]

> *When the shooting began, they (the rebels) told us to lean forward in the theatre seats and cover our heads behind the seats. But then everyone fell asleep. And they (the rebels) were sitting there with their heads thrown back and their mouths wide open.*
>
> GEORGY VASILYEV, THEATER DIRECTOR[9]

Thirty minutes later a force of two hundred Spetsnaz (Russian special forces) began their full-scale assault. Those rebels who had not succumbed to the effects of the gas put up a fierce fight but were ultimately overwhelmed; unconscious rebels were executed with shots to the temple. Less than two hours after the battle began, at 7:20 a.m., Russian forces declared the building secured. "We killed all the terrorists and didn't shoot a single hostage, and not one of our fighters was hurt," said one soldier to Russia's popular *Ivzestiya* newspaper.[10]

But the operation had taken a tremendous toll on the captives. Almost all required hospitalization for gas poisoning. Some died from respiratory depression, while others choked on their own vomit. One hostage had been shot by the Chechen rebels and another wounded during a tense moment near the end of the crisis. The rest of the 130 hostages killed during the siege died as a result of the Spetsnaz gas.

Speculation arose about its nature, including discussion about whether it was permissible under the chemical warfare provisions of the Geneva Convention. Other experts noted that the rescue forces who entered the building after the gas was used were supplied with the powerful narcotic antagonist naloxone and suggested the Russians had used some kind of weaponized narcotic. Finally, on October 30, Health Minister Yuri Shevchenko confirmed that the gas was aerosolized fentanyl. While he acknowledged the deaths, Shevchenko stressed that the fentanyl gas, widely used in medical practice, "cannot in itself be called lethal" and attributed the hostage deaths to stress, dehydration, and hunger caused by the captivity.[11]

The Analogs

While fentanyl is an extremely strong opiate, some of its analogs (similar molecules with minor differences in composition) are even more powerful or have valuable pharmaceutical properties of their own.

Although remifentanil (Ultiva) is no more powerful than fentanyl, it is metabolized much more quickly. Within four minutes after an Ultiva IV drip is stopped, the patient will return to a baseline state. A relatively large dose can be administered; then, after the procedure is done, the patient can quickly be awakened. This is particularly useful in outpatient surgeries, allowing for rapid room turnover and quick recovery from anesthesia.

Sufentanil (Sufenta) is five to ten times more potent than fentanyl. Unlike most other opiates, it does not cause histamine release and the consequent itching. At present Sufenta is indicated for use only by anesthesiologists and trained professionals. However, pharmaceutical company Durect is presently working on a sufentanil patch using its Transdur transdermal system. These patches are smaller than comparable fentanyl patches and longer lasting, providing up to seven days of relief whereas a fentanyl patch must be changed after three.

And when you're talking about powerful painkillers, they don't come much stronger than carfentanil, which is approximately one hundred times more potent than fentanyl and ten thousand times stronger than morphine! One 10 milligram dose of carfentanil was enough to sedate a 5,000-kilogram (11,000 pounds) Asian elephant through an operation on his foot abscess.[12] Carfentanil citrate is the drug of choice for chemical capture of large North American hoof stock such as free-ranging moose, elk, bighorn sheep, and bison. Zookeepers and naturalists using carfentanil are cautioned to avoid holding used darts in their mouths, to wash thoroughly should any carfentanil come in contact with their skin, and to have first-aid kits containing resuscitation aids and opiate antagonists on hand at all times.[13]

PART THREE

ACOLYTES

Unlike many of the plants that act as spirit allies, *P. somniferum* actively seeks out followers. Artists, writers, musicians, and other creative types seem particularly drawn to her glamour. Many have cursed the toll she has exacted from them. Some have lost their families, their careers, and even their lives to her enchantment. And yet Poppy's allure remains undimmed.

If we are going to understand Poppy as an ally, we must know not only her history but also her art. To that end here are some of those she has touched, for better and for worse.

15

SAMUEL TAYLOR COLERIDGE

In Xanadu did Kubla Khan
A stately pleasure-dome decree:
Where Alph, the sacred river, ran
Through caverns measureless to man
Down to a sunless sea.
So twice five miles of fertile ground
With walls and towers were girdled round:
And there were gardens bright with sinuous rills,
Where blossomed many an incense-bearing tree;
And here were forests ancient as the hills,
Enfolding sunny spots of greenery.

In a note published with "Kubla Khan," Samuel Taylor Coleridge explained that in 1797 he had retired to a lonely farmhouse due to ill health. After a slight indisposition "an anyodyne had been prescribed"[1] that had caused him to fall asleep while reading Samuel Purchas's *Pilgrimage.* In a series of vivid dreams he composed "from two to three hundred lines, if indeed that can be called composition in which all the images rose up before him as things, with a parallel production of the correspondent expressions, without any sensation or consciousness of effort."[2]

Rousing himself from his reverie, Coleridge took up his pen and wrote down the fifty-four lines that have come down to us. But then he was called upon by a businessman from the neighboring village of Porlock, who detained him for more than an hour. Returning to his writing table, Coleridge found that his vision had faded but for a few scattered lines and images.

A private note Coleridge wrote on a manuscript copy went into more detail about this anodyne and the circumstances under which "Kubla Khan" was composed.

> This fragment with a good deal more, not recoverable, composed, in
> a sort of Reverie brought on by two grains of Opium taken to check
> a dysentery, at a Farm House between Porlock & Linton, a quarter
> of a mile from Culbone Church, in the fall of the year, 1797.[3]

For many scholars, the story of "Kubla Khan" is a fitting metaphor for Coleridge's career. By the time he was thirty, Coleridge had written the poetry for which he is remembered today. His later prose work was notoriously inconsistent. While his Shakespeare criticism (particularly his treatment of *Hamlet*) is still consulted, many of his writings were turgid and unfocused, and many of his projects went unfinished. His lifelong addiction to opium is presented both as the cause of his poetic brilliance and his ultimate failure.

The Early Life of Coleridge

Speaking of his childhood, Coleridge told a friend:

> I was driven from life in motion, to life in thought and sensation. I
> never played except by myself, and then only acting over what I had
> been reading or fancying, or half one, half the other, with a stick
> cutting down weeds and nettles, as one of the seven champions of
> Christendom. Alas! I had all the simplicity, all the docility of the

little child, but none of the child's habits. I never thought as a child, never had the language of a child.[4]

A sensitive and sickly lad, nine year-old Coleridge's life was thrown into upheaval upon the death of his beloved father in 1781. Sent as a charity student to the Christ's Hospital boarding school, Coleridge was, in his own words, a "depressed, moping, friendless, poor orphan, half starved."[5] Despite his sufferings, he excelled academically thanks to his excellent memory and keen, searching intellect. (He had begun reading at three and impressed fellow students and teachers alike by reciting Homer in the original Greek.)

Graduating at the top of his class, he won a scholarship to Cambridge, where, in 1791, he began his studies. In 1792 he won the Browne Gold Medal for his abolitionist "Ode on the Slave Trade." Coleridge became a passionate supporter of the French Revolution and Unitarianism—a great disappointment to his family, who had hoped he would follow in his father's footsteps and become an Anglican minister.

Coleridge's college career soon ran into other difficulties. The small allowance given him by his brother George was insufficient to support his growing fondness for alcohol and opium. Burdened with a £150 debt and distraught over an unrequited love affair, Coleridge decided he was through with academic life. Gambling the last of his savings on a losing lottery ticket, he contemplated suicide before deciding instead to join the military.

In December 1793 he ran away from Cambridge and enlisted in the Fifteenth Light Dragoons, a cavalry unit, under the name Silas Tomkyn Comberbache. Alas, he soon found that he was not cut out for the military life either. Unable to ride a horse and useless in the cavalry, Coleridge occupied himself with odd jobs like mucking the stables and nursing the sick. When the Coleridge brothers finally found their prodigal sibling in April 1794, they had little trouble convincing his superiors to release him from his enlistment under the "Insanity" clause.

Now back at school, Coleridge soon fell in with another poet, the free-thinker and intellectual Robert Southey. Together they came up with a plan to establish a utopian colony on the banks of Pennsylvania's Susquehanna River. To that end Southey married Edith Fricker, and Coleridge married her sister Sarah in October of 1795. But their plans for an American free love commune were scuttled by lack of funds and farming experience. Southey went off to Portugal with his new wife, Edith, and Coleridge was trapped in a loveless and unhappy marriage.

In 1797 Samuel and Sarah moved in to a drafty, poorly heated cottage in Nether Stowey, the last house before the town's poorhouse. There they lived in squalid, impoverished conditions that only served to exacerbate Coleridge's ill health, particularly his neuralgia and tooth-aches. To deal with the pain, Coleridge turned once again to opium. Often he would take his laudanum before sitting down to write, then produce haunting, dreamlike images. But the inspirations that flashed through his writing were transient and ethereal; Coleridge had great difficulty capturing them on paper. He frequently started large-scale visionary literary and poetic projects that never came to fruition—a recurring theme throughout his life. Still, Coleridge's poetry and literary criticism (mostly reviews of then-popular Gothic potboilers) began to attract the attention of a wider audience. Among them was the poet William Wordsworth.

> *And when—O Friend! my comforter and guide!*
> *Strong in thyself, and powerful to give strength!—*
> *Thy long sustainèd Song finally closed,*
> *And thy deep voice had ceased—yet thou thyself*
> *Wert still before my eyes, and round us both*
> *That happy vision of belovèd faces—*
> *Scarce conscious, and yet conscious of its close*
> *I sate, my being blended in one thought*

(Thought was it? or aspiration? or resolve?)
Absorbed, yet hanging still upon the sound—
And when I rose, I found myself in prayer.
COLERIDGE, FROM "LINES TO
WILLIAM WORDSWORTH," 1807

Together Wordsworth and Coleridge published *Lyrical Ballads* in 1798. It included some of their greatest poems, opening with Coleridge's "The Rime of the Ancyent Marinere" and concluding with Wordsworth's "Lines Written above Tintern Abbey." While it received mixed reviews among critics, *Lyrical Ballads* was surprisingly popular with readers, providing much-needed income to the impoverished Wordsworth and Coleridge households.

That year Coleridge also received the patronage of the Wedgwood brothers, heirs to the Wedgwood pottery fortune. They promised him £150 a year to write poetry. Since before this event he had been eking out a living on a patron's £40 a year, this represented a sizeable increase. To celebrate, Coleridge and Wordsworth, along with Wordsworth's sister, Dorothy, went on a tour of Germany. Ever gifted with languages, Coleridge taught himself German and studied the works of Kant and the German idealists; later, he would translate Romantic poet Frederich Schiller into English.

But then tragedy struck as Coleridge's baby son Berkeley died of smallpox. For months Sarah hid the death from her high-strung husband, dealing with the grief on her own. When she finally told her husband, he went on a long walk—but stayed in Germany with Wordsworth and Dorothy. This caused an increasing rift between the couple, which only grew worse when Coleridge fell in love with Sara Hutchinson in 1799. Burdened with debt, they argued frequently over Sarah's hot temper and Coleridge's "indolence" (a contemporary term for opium addiction). Coleridge rarely saw his wife after 1804 and in 1806 obtained a legal separation.

Coleridge the Addict

Southey saw to the support of the Coleridge family on his tiny income, but he was greatly displeased with his old friend's dereliction of duty. Southey had been a college radical, but his politics drifted to the right with time, and in 1807 he was granted an annual allowance by the conservative Tory government. While Southey remained in contact with Coleridge, relations between the two were severely strained. In 1809 he forbade Coleridge to enter his property after he sought reconciliation with Sarah. Wordsworth stated, "His habits are so murderous of all domestic comfort that I am only surprised Mrs. C. is not rejoiced at being rid of him."[6]

In 1810 Coleridge and Wordsworth quarreled, spawning a breach that never fully healed and troubled Coleridge for the rest of his life. As Dorothy Wordsworth sadly wrote in a letter:

> I know that [Coleridge] has not written a single line. . . . We have no hope of him. . . . His whole time and thoughts . . . are employed in deceiving himself and seeking to deceive others. . . . This Habit pervades all his words and actions. . . . It has been misery, God knows, to me to see the truths which I now see.[7]

Meanwhile, others noticed Coleridge's increasing unreliability. His lectures had long been famous as entertaining off-the-cuff rambles that often bore little resemblance to the original topic. (One speech on Shakespeare's *Romeo and Juliet* became, before its conclusion, a defense of flogging in school. But where once he arrived unprepared, now he often would not arrive at all.)

By 1812 a disgusted Josiah Wedgwood had cut off his half of Coleridge's annuity. Coleridge was unable to earn the difference as he sank deeper into his opium habit. By now he consumed as much as two quarts of laudanum a week. Supported by the kindness of friends and admirers, believing that all his earlier poetic genius had departed,

Coleridge fell into an abyss of poverty and despair. Repeated efforts to free himself of his opium habit failed. Finally, in 1816, Coleridge sought the aid of James Gillman, a Highgate physician who later became his first biographer. He lived with the Gillman family for the remainder of his life, and under Dr. Gillman's watch he was able to gain some measure of control over his dependence on opium.

The Final Years

> *In those two Miles be broached a thousand things—let me see if I can give you a list—Nightingales, Poetry—on Poetical sensation—Metaphysics—Different genera and species of Dreams—Nightmare—a dream accompanied by a sense of touch—single and double touch—A dream related—First and second consciousness—the difference explained between will and Volition—so many metaphysicians from a want of smoking the second consciousness—Monsters—the Kraken—Mermaids.*
>
> JOHN KEATS ON COLERIDGE, APRIL 1819[8]

With Gillman's encouragement, Coleridge published some fragments of poems that he had started at the beginning of his career but never completed. The fragments "Kubla Khan" and "Christabel" appeared in print and influenced a whole new generation of Romantic poets. They saw *Lyrical Ballads* as a seminal work of their own movement, viewed Coleridge as an elder statesman, and acclaimed his newly published works as equal to his earlier work.

Coleridge also continued to write on philosophy and especially political topics, and like his old friend Southey, he grew more conservative in his old age. He also began seeing visitors and admirers, among them author James Fenimore Cooper, poet John Keats, and American Transcendentalist philosopher Ralph Waldo Emerson. An annuity gained after becoming a Fellow of the Royal Society of Literature in

1824 helped ease many of his financial worries, allowing him a comfortable if not luxurious standard of living.

In 1827 Coleridge finally achieved reconciliation with Wordsworth when they toured the Rhineland together. While he was glad to make amends with his old friend, he was not so impressed with Cologne, stating in an 1828 poem,

> *In Köhln, a town of monks and bones,*
> *And pavements fang'd with murderous stones*
> *And rags, and hags, and hideous wenches;*
> *I counted two and seventy stenches*[9]

Then, in 1830, the ailing Coleridge met his long-suffering ex-wife Sarah. They were reconciled, and an absent father became a doting grandfather. With Gillman controlling his opium dosage, Coleridge was less tempted (and less able) to sink into his old "indolence." Coleridge and Sarah would have many more cordial meetings over the next three years until his death in 1833. In the end he would say, "In fact, barring living in the same house with her there are few women that I have a greater respect and ratherish liking for, than Mrs. C."[10]

16

THOMAS DE QUINCEY

*The druggist—unconscious minister of celestial pleasures!
—as if in sympathy with the rainy Sunday, looked dull
and stupid, just as any mortal druggist might be expected
to look on a Sunday; and when I asked for the tincture
of opium, he gave it to me as any other man might do,
and furthermore, out of my shilling returned me what
seemed to be real copper halfpence, taken out of a real
wooden drawer. Nevertheless, in spite of such indications
of humanity, he has ever since existed in my mind as the
beatific vision of an immortal druggist, sent down to earth
on a special mission to myself.*

THOMAS DE QUINCEY, 1821[1]

At thirteen Thomas de Quincey wrote Greek with ease. By fifteen he composed Greek verse in lyric meters and was able to converse in Greek fluently, thanks to daily extempore reading from the newspapers into the best Greek he could furnish. "That boy," said one of his headmasters, "could harangue an Athenian mob better than you and I could address an English one."[2] Heir to a wealthy Manchester linen merchant's fortune, the brilliant young man had a bright future ahead of him in academia, law, or any other career to which he might aspire.

And yet at seventeen de Quincey rebelled against the constraints of the school and his family's evangelical prejudices. Running away from his school with a copy of Wordsworth and Coleridge's *Lyrical Ballads* and a collection of Greek plays, he spent several months living on the streets of London. There, for survival, he relied on charity, scavenging, and the kindness of a young prostitute named Anne of Oxford Street. In extremity he availed himself of moneylenders, one of the habits that would plague him throughout his life. Finally de Quincy was reconciled with his family. They called in a few favors, and in 1804 the prodigal genius began his career at Worcester College, Oxford.

But the long months of exposure and hardship had taken its toll on de Quincey's body; he was now given to stomach upset and susceptible to tic douloureux. Tic douloureux (trigeminal neuralgia) manifests as sudden, severe shocks of pain on one side of the face. An attack can be triggered by talking, eating, brushing the teeth, or even a gust of cool air on the face. The agony is among the most severe known and has caused many unfortunates to take their own lives, thereby earning it the name "suicide disease." After suffering this anguish for twenty days, de Quincey paid a visit to his local chemist. There he acquired another lifelong habit.

> That my pains had vanished was now a trifle in my eyes: this negative effect was swallowed up in the immensity of those positive effects which had opened before me—in the abyss of divine enjoyment thus suddenly revealed. Here was a panacea, a φαρμακον [*pharmakos,* or medicine] for all human woes; here was the secret of happiness, about which philosophers had disputed for so many ages, at once discovered: happiness might now be bought for a penny, and carried in the waistcoat pocket; portable ecstacies might be had corked up in a pint bottle, and peace of mind could be sent down in gallons by the mail-coach.[3]

At Oxford de Quincey abandoned poetry to concentrate on philosophy. Yet once again he left school on the brink of his degree, failing to appear for his final oral examination after turning in several brilliant papers. While still only seventeen de Quincey had written Wordsworth a glowing letter and the poet, in turn, invited him to visit. Instead of taking his degree, de Quincey decided to take Wordsworth up on his offer. Traveling in a coach with Samuel Taylor Coleridge and his family, he arrived at Dove Cottage, Wordsworth's home in the remote Lake Country.

Once he arrived de Quincey discovered the Wordsworths were in the process of moving; he also discovered that his inheritance had nearly run out. Undaunted, he moved into their old home as a tenant. There he would stay for several years as caretaker, friend, critical reader, and benefactor of Wordsworth's charity. De Quincey brought some thirty chests of books and gave evidence of having read them all. Coleridge's friend Robert Southey said de Quincey was the "most well-informed man of his age" that he had ever met—no mean praise, given Southey's many friends in the English intelligentsia.[4]

He also brought quantities of opium, which he continued to use for its stimulating and euphoric effects. But in 1813 the stomach troubles that plagued him during his vagabond days in London returned in earnest. The death of Wordsworth's three-year-old daughter, Kate, brought back memories of de Quincy's beloved sister Elizabeth, who had died when he was five. The recovered trauma left him in physical and emotional agony, and he found that only his old friend could relieve his sufferings. Before long he was consuming over a pint of laudanum a day. The opium left him deeply depressed, shuffling about through a twilight world between consciousness and sleeping. When he tried to cut his dosage, he was beset by lucid nightmares and visions as he withdrew from both opium and its alcohol base.

But through his struggles he still found time to marry Margaret Simpson, a local farmer's daughter, in 1817. Their first son, William, had arrived in 1816. They would go on to have seven more children before Margaret's death in 1837. This marriage led to tension between him and the Wordsworths, who thought her beneath their station, and after watching Coleridge sink into dependency, they were also uncomfortable with de Quincey's habit. As Wordsworth's sister-in-law, Sara Hutchinson, put it, "He does himself with opium and drinks like a fish."[5] (It didn't help that he had cut down her beloved wild plants at Dove Cottage to get more light in at the windows.)

His inheritance long gone, de Quincy racked up mounting debts as his family grew. Desperate for ways to earn a living, the indigent intellectual turned his hand to writing for newspapers and periodicals. The editor at *The London Magazine* gave the new writer helpful advice: write about what you know. To that end, de Quincey gave him a long essay that would shock and titillate readers for generations to come.

Confessions of an English Opium-Eater

Opium consumption had long been common among Britain's poor and wealthy alike. Doctors and scholars had written at length about the habit and its deleterious consequences. *Confessions of an English Opium-Eater* was the first volume written by a devotee. De Quincey openly admitted to using opium for recreational as well as medical reasons. Not only did laudanum take away his pain, it turned a trip to the opera into an ecstasy of sensation where

> the choruses were divine to hear, and when Grassini appeared in some interlude, as she often did, and poured forth her passionate soul as Andromache at the tomb of Hector, &c., I question whether any Turk, of all that ever entered the Paradise of Opium-eaters, can have had half the pleasure I had.[6]

In his colorful style, de Quincey gave an insider's guide to the pleasures of laudanum, with livid descriptions of his Orientalist dream-visions and mystical raptures. And if he was lavish in singing opium's praises, de

Quincy was equally clear about its pitfalls, providing florid accounts of withdrawal and the nightmarish hallucinations it engendered.

> I was stared at, hooted at, grinned at, chattered at, by monkeys, by parroquets, by cockatoos. I ran into pagodas, and was fixed for centuries at the summit or in secret rooms: I was the idol; I was the priest; I was worshipped; I was sacrificed. I fled from the wrath of Brama through all the forests of Asia: Vishnu hated me: Seeva laid wait for me. I came suddenly upon Isis and Osiris: I had done a deed, they said, which the ibis and the crocodile trembled at. I was buried for a thousand years in stone coffins, with mummies and sphynxes, in narrow chambers at the heart of eternal pyramids. I was kissed, with cancerous kisses, by crocodiles; and laid, confounded with all unutterable slimy things, amongst reeds and Nilotic mud.[7]

Creating a structure that would become the standard for addiction narratives, de Quincey provided readers with the vicarious enjoyment of his drug usage, along with an appropriate amount of suffering and ruination. The rogue may enjoy his sins, so long as he repents and pays the appropriate price for his evil entertainment. *Confessions* would find a ready audience among English readers. Published in two parts in *The London Magazine* in 1821, *Confessions* was soon released in book form.

While English readers were thrilling to the scandal of de Quincey's drug addiction, the literati on the Continent were more impressed by his intimate knowledge of altered states of consciousness. French composer Hector Berlioz loosely based his 1830 *Symphonie fantastique,* a musical setting of an opium dream, on de Quincey's *Confessions;* later on, poet and addict Charles Baudelaire included a French translation of *Confessions* with his own essay on hashish in his 1860 book *Les Paradis artificiels* (Artificial Paradises).

It seemed that the stage was set for de Quincey to take his place as a major English writer and thinker. But, in keeping with his previous history, he managed to avoid success at every turn. His literary triumph led not to fame but to decades of grinding poverty and financial pressure as he tried to support himself, his family, and his habit.

Journalism, Habituation, and Debt

Self-discipline had never been a strong point with de Quincey, particularly when faced with routine tasks. Editors who hired him soon became accustomed to lengthy excuses for missed deadlines. But they also became accustomed to excellent work when it finally arrived. Throughout his youth de Quincey had been an avid reader and collector of books. His knowledge touched upon Greek and Roman literature and history, German literature and philosophy, politics, and economics. Any or all of those might be referenced in his essays, which also featured a sardonic wit and fascination with crime that seemed at odds with his gentle, soft-spoken manner.

Not all publications were impressed with this wild talent. De Quincey's 1819 editorial stint at the *Westmoreland Gazette* lasted only four months, during which time he regaled readers with grisly murder trials alongside essays on philology, politics, and German philosophy. The quality of his writing and the breadth of his interests ensured that he would always find a publisher, while his natural tendencies toward procrastination and idleness, along with his addiction to laudanum, often left him in search of new markets. One of his most notable essays was "On the Knocking at the Gate in *Macbeth*" (1823), an incisive study of *Macbeth*'s famous "drunken porter" scene that is considered an early example of psychological criticism and the psychoanalytic approach. It is still read today. Another darkly comic essay, "On Murder Considered as One of the Fine Arts," appeared in *Blackwood's* in 1827 and became a seminal work in the burgeoning fields of crime and detective fiction.

But if de Quincey's editors were used to delays, so too were his creditors. Mounting bills forced him to leave London and set up housekeeping in Edinburgh. In 1831 de Quincey was prosecuted and briefly imprisoned for debt; in 1833 he was twice prosecuted for debt and forced to flee to the debtor's sanctuary at Holyroode; 1834 saw him in debtors' court three times; while in 1837 he was prosecuted twice and in 1840 prosecuted yet again.[8]

While he was able to write lengthy, eloquent articles about economic theory and the wealth of nations, de Quincey was incapable of managing his household expenses. During his binges, bills and requests for material piled up unread. Yet when he ceased to use laudanum he was "subject to affections which are tremendous for the weight of wretchedness attached to them" and unable to work even at the "wretched business of hack-author, with all its horrible degradations."[9] As a result, his periods without opium were as unproductive as his debauches. Added to this was his kindly nature and irresponsible generosity; de Quincey frequently gave large sums of money to friends and even acquaintances who were unable or unwilling to pay him back.

Finally, in 1840, his daughters took charge of his financial affairs. Renting a cottage at Lasswade, seven miles from Edinburgh's center, the now-widowed de Quincey set about the remainder of his life and writing career. In 1845 de Quincey capitalized on his past success with *Suspiria de Profundis* (Sighs from the Depths), a sequel to *Confessions*. A compilation of opium visions and essays, *Suspiria* was an example of what de Quincey called "impassioned prose"—ornate dream-narratives that straddled the line between poem and essay. These were enormously popular, in the original and in Baudelaire's translation, with the French Symbolist painters and with the Decadents of the late nineteenth century. A century later they inspired Italian director Dario Argento in his films *Suspiria, Inferno,* and *Mother of Tears: The Third Mother.*

De Quincey added other narratives to *Suspiria,* but, like "Kubla Khan," it remained an unfinished work upon the author's 1859 death. While prolific in his writings, de Quincey was given to losing or misfiling manuscripts. His opium-inspired tendency toward somnolence led him, on regular occasions, to set his work (or his hair!) on fire while writing by candlelight.

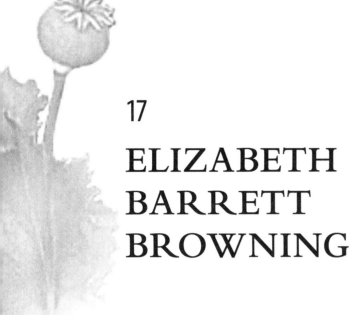

17

ELIZABETH BARRETT BROWNING

Can I be as good for you as morphine is for me, I wonder,
even at the cost of being as bad also?—Can't you leave me
off without risking your life,—nor go on with me without
running all the hazards of poison?

ELIZABETH BARRETT BROWNING
TO ROBERT BROWNING, 1846[1]

By the standards of the early nineteenth century, Elizabeth Barrett received a remarkable education. Born in 1806, she was tutored alongside her brothers throughout her childhood and availed herself of the family's extensive library. Before Elizabeth was ten she had read a number of Shakespeare's plays; during her teen years she read Homer's *Odyssey,* Ovid's *Metamorphoses,* and Dante's *Inferno* in their original languages and wrote plays for family performance in both English and French.

Barrett's father supported her in all these intellectual endeavors. The son of wealthy Jamaican sugar planters, Edward Barrett Moulton Barrett encouraged all his twelve children in musical and artistic pursuits. Elizabeth's life on Hope End, a beautiful 500-acre estate in the

Malvern Hills of England's West Midlands, seemed on the surface an idyllic one. And the children were certainly devoted to the loving pater-familias. In her 1826 poem "To My Father on His Birthday," twenty-year-old Elizabeth wrote,

> *No name can e'er on tablet shine,*
> *My father! more beloved than thine!*
> *'Tis sweet, adown the shady past,*
> *A lingering look of love to cast—*

But the pastoral bliss of Hope End had a dark side. Moulton Barrett exercised complete emotional and financial control over his issue. Above all else, he forbade his children, sons and daughters alike, to marry. Biographers have long speculated about his reasons for this odd pro-hibition, and various Freudian and other motives have been attributed to the Barrett patriarch's behavior. Julia Markus, author of *Dared and Done: The Marriage of Elizabeth Barrett and Robert Browning,* has sug-gested he lived in shame and terror that the family's secret might be revealed. The Moulton Barretts had acquired a fortune in Jamaica—but they had also picked up some Creole ancestors along the way. Edward feared the African heritage would be revealed in dark-skinned, kinky-haired grandchildren. To keep the honor of his lineage, Moulton Barrett resolved that it would be severed with this generation.

Moulton Barrett had other reasons to worry about his oldest daugh-ter. From her teen years Elizabeth had been physically and emotionally fragile. At fifteen she was stricken with an unexplained illness whose symptoms resembled what is today called chronic fatigue syndrome and fibromyalgia: headache, fever, lassitude, body aches, and muscle spasms. From that point forward she remained frail, with little appetite and a propensity for fainting. Unable to determine a specific cause, doc-tors treated her symptoms with the standard medicines of the day—laudanum and morphine.

In 1832, after her mother died and reduced circumstances forced

Moulton Barrett to sell Hope End and move to London, Elizabeth developed asthma. Their move to London in 1837 exacerbated her condition; the sooty, smoggy air and damp climate soon had her spitting up blood. For rest her doctors once again prescribed laudanum, along with leeches and bleeding for her feverish spells. When these proved ineffective, they urged that Elizabeth be transferred to a warmer environment. Dr. Chambers, her London physician, recommended the Mediterranean. Unwilling to send his daughter so far away, Moulton Barrett finally allowed her to move to Torquay, a coastal town in southern England with healthier air and a milder clime.

But even in Torquay Elizabeth's health continued to decline. Much of her day was spent on the couch wrapped in blankets; her nights were sleepless without laudanum's aid. In 1840 Elizabeth's beloved younger brother Edward drowned in a sudden squall. He had traveled to Torquay to be by her side. Wracked with guilt, Elizabeth returned to their house on Wimpole Street, London. There she retreated to her third-story room, insulating herself from London's noise and pollution with two thick doors, sealed windows, and liberal doses of opiated medicines.

Robert Browning

> *My family had been so accustomed to the thought of me living on and on in that room, that while my heart was eating itself, their love for me was consoled, and at last the evil grew scarcely perceptible. It was no want of love in them, and quite natural in itself: we all get used to the thought of a tomb.*
>
> ELIZABETH BARRETT BROWNING, 1846[2]

Shut in her room, she continued to take advantage of the Barrett library. When she was well, family members carried her down to her sofa. During her frequent weak spells, she read in bed, voraciously consuming French, German, Greek, Latin, Hebrew, and Italian texts. She also dedicated herself to poetry and correspondence. Since the early days of her illness, she had maintained epistolary relationships with like-minded souls. These were typically older men, like eighty-year-old Greek teacher Uvedale Price, or safely married, like the blind classical scholar Hugh Stuart Boyd. Other friends critiqued her poems and even printed them in magazines like the *New Monthly* or other publications. She wrote to them on the topics of the day and on the questions of the ages, maintaining lively intellectual conversations despite her shut-in condition and reliance on poppies.

Elizabeth's existence was narrow and constrained on all sides, but it was a safe one. Her father's morbid preoccupation with her chastity freed Elizabeth from the domestic duties of entertaining suitors and maintaining a conjugal home, allowing her to concentrate on intellectual pursuits. Her writing began acquiring a small circle of discerning fans. In a letter, American author Edgar Allen Poe declared her "the noblest of her sex." Then in early 1845, thirty-eight-year-old Barrett received a letter from someone she had long admired, poet Robert Browning.

In 1844 Barrett had praised Browning's *Bells and Pomegranates* in her "Lady Geraldine's Courtship," saying that it showed "a heart within blood-tinctured, of a veined humanity." Browning wrote to thank her. As they corresponded, they found that Robert shared Elizabeth's passionate abolitionist sentiments. He had refused to take over the Browning family's Jamaican plantations because of their slave holdings, even though it meant forfeiting his share in the family fortune. Like the Barretts, the Brownings had skeletons in their ancestral closet; some claimed they had Jewish heritage, while others whispered that his grandmother in the West Indies had "a strain of Negro blood, a dash of the tar brush."[3]

Courtship

The two began a passionate yet chaste relationship. She poured out her hopes and fears to her ardent beau, lamenting, "I would give ten towns in Norfolk (if I had them) to own some purer lineage than that of the blood of the slave! Cursed we are from generation to generation."[4] Browning reassured her, calling her "my little Portuguese" and sending her flowers repeatedly. And where the critics had treated the monologue poems of Browning's 1842 *Dramatic Lyrics* unkindly, Elizabeth encouraged him as a writer and poet. Over the next eighteen months they exchanged 573 letters and met in Elizabeth's room 91 times.

The topic of Elizabeth's habit arose on several occasions. At first she expressed surprise that Robert should care so much about her usage and declared that she needed poppies to function, referring to morphine as "my elixir . . . the tranquillizing power has been so wonderful."[5] She assured him that her use of poppies was purely clinical, and that she never used more than her prescribed dose. Still, touched by his worry, she promised to "get to do with less . . . at least."[6]

At first Elizabeth refused Robert's ardent offers of marriage. She feared burdening him with an invalid wife, but she was also terrified of her father's wrath. In addition, money was a concern; Browning's annual income at the time was around £100, and Elizabeth was spending more than £80 a year on her medicine. But despite her hesitation Elizabeth was also falling in love with the erudite and charming poet. Her feelings were reflected in the work she composed at that time, poems that she called, in reference to Robert's pet name, *Sonnets from the Portuguese*.

> *How do I love thee? Let me count the ways*
> *I love thee to the depth and breadth and height*
> *My soul can reach, when feeling out of sight*
> *For the ends of Being and ideal Grace.*
> *I love thee to the level of every day's*
> *Most quiet need, by sun and candlelight.*
>
> FROM SONNET XLIII,
> *SONNETS FROM THE PORTUGUESE*

Ultimately the attraction between the two proved stronger than illness or parental disapproval. On September 12, 1846, Elizabeth sneaked out of the family home and met Robert at St. Marylebone Parish Church. There they were united in holy matrimony. Elizabeth returned to the family home for a week, then left for Europe with her husband. Upon learning of her marriage, Moulton Barrett immediately disinherited her. He never again spoke to his beloved daughter, returning her letters unread and later refusing to see his infant grandson.

Marriage

While Elizabeth and Robert were passionately in love, she was devastated by her father's rejection. Two years after her marriage, while she was recovering from her second miscarriage, Elizabeth wrote to a friend, "I should choose the smile of my own father to that of my own child . . . oh yes I should & would."[7] While she maintained warm relations with her siblings, her father would never come around, not even after two other Barretts eloped and were disinherited.

Friends worried the duo would starve, but they had little to fear. Throughout her life Elizabeth had relied on a small allowance from her father, spending a goodly share of it on her medicine and the rest on her books. Her new husband shared her thrift. With income earned from shares Elizabeth had received from an uncle and money earned from their writings, they were able to live comfortably. Settling in Italy, the couple set up housekeeping in Florence, where the weather was warm and the cost of living low. There, save for brief journeys, Elizabeth spent the remainder of her life.

Over the next two years Robert wrote very little as he became acclimated to his new home. Elizabeth, by contrast, became a more focused and politically involved poet. She was active in the Florentine independence movement and also published (with Robert's encouragement) *Sonnets from the Portuguese* and the long poem "The Runaway Slave at Pilgrim's Point," a lurid antislavery narrative of rape, miscegenation, murder, and suicide. She also made efforts to limit her morphine consumption after two miscarriages, efforts that bore fruit in 1849 when she gave birth to the couple's only child, Robert "Pen" Weideman Barrett Browning.

Then, in July of 1850, she had a third miscarriage. According to her attending physician, she lost "above a hundred ounces of blood" in twenty-four hours.[8] While she survived the ordeal, her already frail health was weakened further and her dependence on opiates became even greater than before. Still this did not stop her from working. In 1853 she released another edition of her poems and in 1856 published *Aurora Leigh,* an autobiographical poem/novel in blank verse that focused on the difficulties its narrator faced in being taken seriously as a woman and a poet.

In 1857 Edward Moulton Barrett died, still unreconciled with his disobedient daughter. A heartbroken Elizabeth turned once more to the consolation of laudanum. An old rival, American abolitionist Julia Ward Howe (author of "Battle Hymn of the Republic"), took the opportunity to get some digs in with her poem "One Word More with E.B.B."

> *There are those who thread unmeasured heights*
> *With spirits for their bodyguard*
> *Who vex, with ill-directed flight*
> *And sentence, mystical and hard.*
> *I shrink before the nameless draught*
> *That helps to such unearthly things,*
> *And if a drug could lift so high,*
> *I would not trust its treacherous wings;*
> *Lest, lapsing from them, I should fall*
> *A weight more dead than stock or stone,—*
> *The warning fate of those who fly*
> *With pinions other than their own.*[9]

Robert was outraged by this public attack on his beloved bride. Elizabeth was unruffled, stating that the poem was "perfectly true, so far, that life is necessary to writing, & that I should not be alive without the help of my morphine."[10] Until her death in 1861, Elizabeth insisted that her usage of opiates was for medical purposes; she treated the idea that she might be an addict as beneath contempt and unworthy of her consideration. Alas for her—and the generations of opiate users that followed—society was beginning to see her beloved medicine as a dangerous and shameful poison. While laudanum and morphine remained popular, the lines between patient and addict, user and abuser, were becoming simultaneously more clearly drawn and more indistinct.

18

EUGENE O'NEILL

Gene talks to me for hours, about a play in his mind of his mother, his father, his brother and himself in his early 20s in New London! Autobiography. A hot, close, sleepless night—An ache in our hearts for things we can't escape!

CARLOTTA MONTEREY O'NEILL, 1939[1]

In June of 1939 Eugene O'Neill was even sicker and more despairing than usual. After five years' work on an extensive cycle of plays, he felt he had reached a creative impasse. An increasingly troubling hand tremor—a symptom of the neurodegenerative disease that would ultimately end his career—made the very act of writing painful. Feeling his mortality and haunted by the growing war in Europe, O'Neill turned instead to a more intimate and autobiographical art.

One of the stories he wanted to tell concerned his father, a famous actor; his alcoholic, self-destructive brother; and his convent-educated mother. The play forced O'Neill to face the scars of his childhood and his sad, damaged family. He spared neither their failings nor his own. He replayed all their painful dramas and the tragic flaws that doomed them. Trying to make sense of the wreckage of his own personal life, he turned back to his past in an attempt to understand them and himself. When he finished the play in March 1941, he wrote in his diary,

"Like this play better than any I have ever written—does most with the least—a quiet play!—And a great one, I believe."[2]

Indeed, it was so personal and unsparing that he could not bear to see it released. The manuscript was sealed with wax and placed in a vault with instructions that it was not to be published until twenty-five years after his death. But in 1953, after cortical cerebellar atrophy (CCA) finally claimed O'Neill, his wife Carlotta decided not to wait. In 1956 *Long Day's Journey into Night* was released and quickly became recognized as O'Neill's masterpiece. Particular attention was paid to one of O'Neill's most haunted and haunting female characters—Mary Tyrone, standing in for Eugene O'Neill's mother, Ella.

Notoriously secretive and reclusive, O'Neill rarely provided any public insight into his family history. His closest companions heard tales of his father's miserly streak or the great loneliness and sorrow he perceived around him. Only the very closest knew that his mother had been treated for a drug habit related to his difficult birth and the quack physician who attended on them. *Long Day's Journey* went into grim, excruciating detail about Mary Ellen (Ella) Quinlan O'Neill (1857–1922) and her decades-long addiction to morphine.

Long Day's Journey into Night

I don't blame you. How could you believe me—when I can't believe myself? I've become such a liar. I never lied about anything once upon a time. Now I have to lie, especially to myself. But how can you understand, when I don't myself. I've never understood anything about it, except that one day long ago I found I could no longer call my soul my own.

MARY TYRONE, *LONG DAY'S JOURNEY INTO NIGHT*[3]

Ella was a thirteen-year-old convent-educated schoolgirl when she first met the famous actor James O'Neill at her family's home. Four years later, she saw O'Neill once again in New York. Still grieving her father's untimely death that year, she was swept off her feet by the handsome, well-spoken matinee idol. For James the wealthy, innocent, young Ella represented an escape from the grind of his profession and the drab slum existence of his childhood. In 1877 they were married, and young Ella prepared for a life of wedded bliss.

Unfortunately, the sensitive young schoolgirl was ill-suited for the life of a traveling actor. Raised in the security of the convent and her wealthy family's home, she found herself living in an endless succession of cheap hotels. Her three sons (one of whom died in infancy) were born and raised on the road. And it was there, recovering from the difficult delivery of young Eugene, that she was first introduced to morphine.

What followed was a thirty-year struggle, with periods of abstinence and sanitarium cures interspersed with longer periods of usage. In 1903 Ella, desperately depressed and out of medicine, threw herself into a river in a suicide attempt. Soon after, Eugene refused to attend Mass with his father. He would never again regain his faith. Wracked with Catholic guilt, Ella grew increasingly embittered and distant from her family. The O'Neills, for their part, alternated between solicitous care for their ill mother and angry recriminations after each relapse.

O'Neill concentrated those decades of suffering into the form of a classic Greek tragedy, placing their long-running arguments in a single day and location. As *Long Day's Journey* begins, Mary Tyrone has returned from yet another sanitarium; her husband, James, and her sons, Jamie and Edmund, walk about on eggshells trying to avoid doing anything that would trigger another relapse. Edmund has tuberculosis, and his father and his older brother, Jamie, are both ill with alcoholism and self-loathing. As the day progresses, it becomes increasingly clear that their hopes for Mary's cure were hollow; she is once again using morphine. A series of emotional eviscerations follow, as each family member accuses the others of contributing to their mother's illness. Every shortcoming is dredged up, every past failing dragged into the light and used as a weapon.

Jamie blames his mother's addiction for his own; he stumbled upon her with a needle one day when he was young. "Caught her in the act with a hypo. Christ, I'd never dreamed before that any women but whores took dope," he says bitterly.[4] (The earliest records of James Jr.'s misconduct and academic failings began in 1892, when he was fourteen, so this may be around the time he first discovered Ella's morphine habit.) Still mourning the loss of his idealized mother figure, Jamie has spent his entire life trying to degrade himself and everyone around him. Much as Mary uses morphine, he numbs himself with an unrelenting cynicism and liberal consumption of alcohol. His great illusion is that he no longer has any illusions. He idolizes Mary and hopes that her recovery will encourage him to turn his own wasted life around. Yet he is also relieved when she relapses, because he now has an excuse to continue drinking and whoring. Decades before the phrase was coined, O'Neill drew a remarkably accurate picture of codependency.

Edmund alternates between blaming himself and his father for Mary's condition. The doctor who delivered Edmund also got Mary hooked, and Edmund's tuberculosis is arguably the trigger for her latest relapse. But if his ever-stingy father had not hired a quack, perhaps she never would have become an addict; perhaps if he had given her a home instead of taking her touring; perhaps if he had been sober more often . . . This familiar, oft-repeated series of arguments have their own form of comfort. By assigning blame to someone, even themselves, they gain some feeling of agency and control.

Mary is the center around which the Tyrones have made their temporary home. But it is a role she is ill-prepared to fulfill. Unable to shake her conviction that her marriage to James Tyrone was a wrong turn, Mary simultaneously loves her family and sees them as the instruments of her destruction. She looks back fondly on her days in convent school, when she had two dreams—to be a concert pianist or a nun. Mary soothes her present pain by recollecting an idealized past to serve as a reminder of what was and what might have been.

Like the rest of the family, Mary's despair is existential rather than situational. (James suggests, rightly, that she would have been unsuited for life as either a nun or traveling artist.) Her pipe dreams are rooted in something far deeper and more destructive than the morphine. Ignoring reality has become second nature to her. Where Jamie has chosen to affect a world-weary sophistication, Mary has opted for faith in an Edenic past, a world where she never became a wife and mother. On morphine she can live in her idyllic visions, where false happiness helps her to forget her misery.

> MARY: He hasn't the slightest idea— When you're in agony and half-insane, he sits and holds your hand and delivers sermons on will power! . . . He deliberately humiliates you! He makes you beg and plead! He treats you like a criminal! He understands nothing! And yet it was exactly the same kind of cheap quack who first gave you the medicine— and you never knew what it was until too late! *(passionately)* I hate doctors! They'll do anything— anything to keep you coming to them. They'll sell their souls! What's worse, they'll sell yours and you never know it till one day you find yourself in hell!
>
> EDMUND: Mama! For God's sake, stop talking.[5]

Mary Tyrone (and Ella O'Neill) fit the typical pattern of the late nineteenth-century and early twentieth-century addict: older middle-class women who first started taking drugs for medical reasons. An 1878 study of addiction by the Michigan Board of Health reported that of 1,313 addicts, 803 were female.[6] In a Tennessee drug maintenance program that began in 1913, women made up two-thirds of the registered opiate addicts.[7] Like Mary and Ella, most of these addicts got their supply from a local pharmacy or a family doctor. Police saw no need to become involved in what was essentially a family matter between law-abiding citizens.

Because of Victorian attitudes that women were more sensitive to pain than men, female patients were more likely to be prescribed opiates than men. Opiates were the first line of treatment for gynecological problems. They were also regularly used to treat neurasthenia, a condition of chronic physical and mental weakness caused by nervous exhaustion. It would not have been at all uncommon for a physician to prescribe morphine to a patient suffering from postpartum pain or to one suffering from chronic depression. Because women were not supposed to indulge in strong beverages, many used laudanum or morphine tablets for recreation instead. And because it was unseemly to discuss "female conditions" in polite company, addiction was little discussed.

While *Long Day's Journey* gives plenty of attention to Mary's habit, it suggests that morphine is only one of the problems plaguing the Tyrone household; indeed, it has become a mere stand-in for the real and insurmountable issues that plague them. *Long Day's Journey* is not a melodrama about The Evils of Drugs but a tragedy about the suffering that loving families inflict upon each other. In telling the tale of the Tyrones, O'Neill was not only revealing his own family but ours as well. The Tyrones live in a world where the question is not "How do we find happiness?" but rather "How do we learn to live without it?"

Although *Long Day's Journey* contains many autobiographical elements, we should not mistake it for autobiography. Like any playwright, O'Neill condensed, reframed, and exaggerated stories for dramatic effect. Contemporary reports suggest that Ella was far less uncomfortable with life on the road than Mary Tyrone. She had many friends, particularly among younger unmarried actresses. Whatever her habit, she was able to keep her morphine usage under control enough to avoid notice from other actors or contemporary gossip columnists.

Although Ella's addiction apparently caused a great deal of stress within the O'Neill household, she seems to have been for the most part a functioning user, not the disheveled zombie who stumbles through the final act of *Long Day's Journey*. It is interesting to speculate on how much of that tension was based on morphine's changing role in American society. When Ella first became addicted, morphine was readily available at any pharmacy, but as the war on opiates began, what she saw as a useful medicine became a symptom of moral degeneracy. Were the constant arguments caused by Ella's weak will—or by her stubborn refusal to give up a drug that improved her physical and emotional state? Remember that Mary Tyrone comes from Eugene O'Neill's story, not Ella Quinlan O'Neill's.

> *But some day, dear, I will find it again—some day when you're all well, and I see you healthy and happy and successful, and I don't have to feel guilty any more—some day when the Blessed Virgin Mary forgives me and gives me back the faith in Her love and pity I used to have in my convent days, and I can pray to Her again when She sees no one in the world can believe in me even for a moment any more, then She will believe in me, and with Her help it will be so easy. I will hear myself scream with agony, and at the same time I will laugh because I will be so sure of myself.*
>
> MARY TYRONE[8]

Mary Tyrone's claim that she has "lost her faith" suggests she has damaged the opioid receptors that are connected to many of the symptoms of religious ecstasy. According to the play, Mary has been clean for two months. This means she would still be in the midst of intense postwithdrawal syndrome (see chapter 32) and would likely have very little capacity for feeling the reassurance and comfort of religious belief. Psychedelics give us the capacity to experience the divine. Opiates can allow us to experience—or to reexperience—faith.

Long Day's Journey ends with Mary wandering about in a dope-befogged reverie, drifting between the present and a past where she had married James Tyrone and where, she recalls in the play's heartbreaking final words, they were "very happy for a time." Ella O'Neill's story, thankfully, ended on a more upbeat note. In 1914, as the Harrison Act made it increasingly difficult to procure narcotics, she was able to conquer her addiction yet again. Although anecdotal evidence suggests that after a 1917 mastectomy she once again became "used to drugs,"[9] it seems she kept her habit under control until her death.

Perhaps she was helped by her return to the Catholic faith of her youth. After her 1914 cure she began once again attending Mass regularly and taking the Sacraments. Her reclaimed piety helped her through her mastectomy and her husband's agonizing death from stomach cancer in 1920. With her help and encouragement, Eugene's brother, James, was able to get sober for almost two years, until Ella died of a stroke in 1922. The stress of her hospitalization drove him back to drink. James became convinced that Ella died of despair after realizing he had backslid. After her funeral he stated repeatedly that he was now going to drink himself to death; by October of 1922 he succeeded in doing so.

19

NELSON ALGREN

These were people you just went to hear a band with. It was only now and then that it'd come to you—like it might suddenly occur to you that one of your friends was crippled or something—it would come to you that the guy's on stuff. But it didn't stay with you very much.

NELSON ALGREN, 1955[1]

Today Nelson Algren's 1949 novel *The Man with the Golden Arm* is remembered largely for the 1955 film it inspired. Under Otto Preminger's direction, the movie gives us a Caligariesque vision of Chicago's cramped streets and dirty tenements. His back alleys, cheap flophouses, sawdust-floor taverns, and smoke-filled rooms are as grim yet beautifully stylized as Elmer Bernstein's jazz score. Igniting all this darkness is Frank Sinatra in one of his greatest performances, Frankie Machine, a small-time card dealer, aspiring drummer, and morphine addict.

Sinatra's Frankie Machine wants desperately to escape his surroundings and his habit. Yet he is trapped by his paralyzed wife, Zosch—who is actually faking paralysis to continue her desperate hold on her husband. Eleanor Parker plays Zosch with a needy, angry urgency as she descends into scene-chewing murderous madness that would do Joan Crawford proud. Trapped between her, Robert Strauss as Schwiefka, a glad-handling gambling boss, and Darrin McGavin as the predatory morphine dealer Louie, Frankie's every effort to improve his life and become a professional drummer is thwarted.

Frankie's allies in his quest are few. Sparrow (Arnold Stang), a petty thief with Coke-bottle spectacles and a baggy Salvation Army suit, follows him with a fierce if none too bright devotion. His assistance is generally less than helpful; when he steals a suit for Frankie, he winds up getting both of them arrested. Yet Frankie keeps him around with the same amiable if sometimes exasperated loyalty that ties him to his wife.

Zosch's friend Molly is equally devoted and, as portrayed by Kim Novak, far easier on the eyes. Because she's already supporting an alcoholic boyfriend (unaffectionately called "Drunky John" at the local bar), it's not surprising that she falls for the charismatic/pathetic Frankie. Zosch resents the growing attraction between the two and grows ever more clingy and demanding. All this only drives Frankie closer to Louie and deeper into his habit. Finally it reduces him to theft, as he steals enough heroin from Louie to get feeling better before his audition. Alas, his crime is for naught. He is still twitchy at the tryout that was going to be his big break.

When Louie comes around looking for Frankie, he catches Zosch out of her wheelchair. Afraid that Frankie will leave her if he finds out, she pushes Louis out the window. Then, inevitably, the cops come around asking questions. Zosch decides she'd rather see Frankie in prison than in Molly's arms. Letting the cops believe she is still paralyzed, she leads them to believe Frankie was the one responsible for her crime.

But despite all this Molly stands by her man. She allows Frankie to hide out in her apartment so he can go "cold turkey" and face the police clean and sober. There he endures a harrowing withdrawal sequence. Sinatra artfully catches the cramps, anxiety, and jumping-out-of-your-skin discomfort of kicking an opiate habit as he thrashes about in luridly detailed agony. Like the needle-in-arm paper cutouts that Saul Bass created for the film's equally famous title sequence, addiction becomes both a withdrawal and a passion play.

Ultimately a sober Frankie tells Zosch he is leaving her to start a new life with Molly after standing trial. Zosch rises from her chair as the police come in looking for Frankie. Now everyone knows her secret; the cops realize that she, not Frankie, murdered Louie the dealer. Unable to escape, she throws herself from the balcony, dying as Louis died. Now rid of his addiction and cleared of murder charges, Frankie is free to start a new life with the woman he loves.

Today this may seem hopelessly campy. To audiences of 1955 it was a grim and gritty look at the world of dope addicts. What we read today (and what a few critics read then) as stagy melodrama seemed to them to be Realism with a capital R. It was real not because it reflected the actual life of morphine addicts, but because it reflected their expectations and reaffirmed all their beliefs. Frankie cleans up with the love of a good woman and a little bit of willpower. Frankie's sin is without joy, and through his suffering he redeems himself. Because of his virtue, all the problems that might befall him are overcome and he is forgiven. Instead of a junkie and common criminal, he is now the Good Thief and the Good Example, the one all those people could be if they only wanted it badly enough.

Preminger had little choice in the matter. His adaptation was a direct challenge to the restrictive Hays Code. Under the code, motion pictures were forbidden to show the drug trade, to present an adulterous relationship, or to throw the sympathy of the audience "to the side of crime, wrongdoing, evil or sin."[2] In presenting an addict as a hero, Preminger was flying in the face of the code. In 1953 he had shocked the MPAA with his *The Moon Is Blue,* a racy comedy that featured the words "virgin," "seduce," and "mistress." Because that was nominated for three Oscars without an MPAA certificate of approval, United Artists funded *The Man with the Golden Arm* despite knowing it violated the Hays Code.

But Preminger had to take care to shock the censors without overwhelming audiences and studio executives. Molly and Frankie had to wait until his wife was out of the way rather than violate the sanctity of marriage. And Zosch had to be an unredeemable shrew and figure of evil, lest horrified viewers lose sympathy for Frankie as a philanderer who left his wife for another woman. While Frankie could be a junkie, he had to be a good-hearted one. And ultimately the film had to have what could pass for a happy ending. Preminger knew his film could only be as controversial as it was commercial.

In the end, perhaps it did not matter. Sinatra's performance, drawn from junkies he had known and from a visit to a rehabilitation center, was magnetic, realistic, and surprisingly dark. His drive to succeed in music is as infectious as his flubbed tryout is crushing. In the final scene, his body language and the despairing look in his famous blue eyes suggest this new opportunity will be of no more avail than the ones before it. Yet most critics saw it as a story not about degradation but redemption. Now in the midst of the postwar boom, it was impossible for America to envision a social problem that could not be solved. But this was hardly the view of the author of the original book and of an early screenplay that was rejected.

Algren's *Man with the Golden Arm*

INTERVIEWER: How about this movie, *The Man with the Golden Arm?*

ALGREN: Yeah.

INTERVIEWER: Did you have anything to do with the script?

ALGREN: No. No, I didn't last long. I went out there for a thousand a week, and I worked Monday, and I got fired Wednesday. The guy that hired me was out of town Tuesday.[3]

While he was not an addict himself, Nelson Algren met many junkies while working on his novel. He was well acquainted with them and the other has-beens and never-weres who populate his stories. The son of a mechanic, Algren grew up in a Chicago tenement and spent much of his life in poverty. His characters weren't idealized working-class heroes or lovable losers. They were as squalid as the dingy boarding houses and cheap taverns where they lived and moved and had their being. And yet despite all their flaws, Algren also gave them a quiet, somber dignity. His vision was unsparing but never contemptuous; he neither made apologies for his characters nor laughed at them.

In *The Man with the Golden Arm,* considered today his greatest novel, Algren provides an unrelenting panorama of life's losers. Wounded during World War II, Frankie Majcinek is given large doses of morphine to ease the pain of his shrapnel-torn liver. When he comes home he has a "monkey on his back," a phrase Algren heard on the streets and made a common figure of speech. He tries to stay clean, but spends most of the novel (save for his stay in prison) on the stuff. Sparrow is no lovable idiot in Algren's novel; while he's got a history of insanity, he's also a petty thief and hustler who will steal anything small enough to carry away. Frankie is his willing partner in various criminal schemes. We meet the two of them in a holding cell, where burnt-out cop "Record Head" Bednar is checking them in.

Algren suggests that Zosch's paralysis may be hysterical and that she exaggerates it to keep hold of Frankie. But while her injuries may be overstated, her instability is all too real. As Frankie drifts away from her and toward Molly, her grip on reality grows increasingly tenuous. Ultimately she winds up in a mental institution. She is more Blanche DuBois than femme fatale, no more capable of an extended scheme than Frankie or Molly or their friends at the local dive Tug and Maul.

Molly Novotny is a stripper who genuinely loves Frankie but who also seduces him. Frankie may feel guilty about cheating on Zosch, but not guilty enough to quit doing so. It is Frankie, not Zosch, who murders Louie the dealer. Sparrow ultimately betrays Frankie on a plea deal that, unbeknownst to him, will still send him to prison for the rest of his life. And rather than walking off into the sunset, a wounded Frankie hangs himself in a cheap flophouse as the police close in. There is no growing, learning, and hugging at the end of this story, just a police report and a poem in honor of the card dealer whose skill earned him the title "man with the golden arm."

While Algren does not shy away from Frankie's drug addiction, neither does he fetishize it. Frankie's morphine habit is no more destructive than the guilt and lies binding him to Zosch. He and Sparrow may dream of bettering their lot. Their various small-time thefts and schemes break the general mood of despair with glistening shards of pitch-black comedy. But ultimately they know, and the reader knows, that those dreams are empty and their future is as bleak as their present. Morphine is just another way to Frankie's inevitable end, no more hopeless or unpleasant than anything else that might befall him or any of his fellows in the Chicago slums.

The Man with the Golden Arm does not explain away Frankie as a "junkie." It gives him the dignity of his own flaws, of being architect of his own destruction. Frankie is protagonist in his own drama, but it is a tragedy and not a passion play, ending in destruction rather than redemption. Sophocles might have been able to do justice to the fall of Algren's Frankie Machine. Hollywood had to reinvent his end as a new beginning. Morphine became not a brief diversion from a hopeless life but a dragon that the hero had to slay before achieving the American Dream.

INTERVIEWER: Do you try to write a poetic prose?

ALGREN: No. No, I'm not writing it, but so many people say things poetically, they say it for you in a way you never could. Some guy just coming out of jail might say, "I did it from bell to bell," or like the seventeen-year-old junkie, when the judge asked him what he did all day, he said, "Well, I find myself a doorway to lean against, and I take a fix, and then I lean, I just lean and dream." They always say things like that.[4]

Algren's "realistic" writing is as stylized as Preminger's "realistic" direction. Preminger was influenced by European silent films and directors. Algren was influenced by French philosophers (he had a turbulent fling with Simone de Beauvoir and admired Céline and Sartre) and Russian realist writers like Kuprin and Gorky. While his writing was also influenced by American muckrakers and protest novelists, his worldview, which allows salvation neither from God nor Karl Marx, is pure French existentialism. His characters are victims not of capitalism but of the human condition. They seek self-identification in a world that would just as soon ignore them. Being a junkie, a cripple, or a "habitual" is better than being nothing at all.

Algren's Frankie uses morphine to punish himself and hold himself together the same way Zosch uses her wheelchair. He has not chosen his habit any more than Zosch has chosen her paralysis. But, like her, he milks his sickness for everything he has. His addiction becomes both a balm against his failure and an excuse for it. Failing because you are a morphine addict is more comforting than failing because you never had a chance at success. Frankie may have that cold comfort, but Algren never allows it to his readers. They see a world where Zosch can rightly say to herself, "It's just the way things would be if that Nifty Louie was God 'n Blind Pig was Jesus Christ . . . it's just about the way them two'd run things."[5]

The Man with the Golden Arm looked back to better days in an era when progress was king—then suggested that those times weren't all that great, either. If the author's sympathy with the poor and downtrodden wasn't Red, it was downright pink. Yet despite this it garnered a National Book Award in 1950 and became Algren's only bestseller. Something about his unsparing darkness spoke to a generation that had just survived World War II, and his compassion for the underdog resonated in a country that had just recently become a superpower.

Six years later, times had changed, and what was once edgy was now subversive. Algren now had a lengthy FBI file and had, in 1952, been denied a passport for, among other things, contributing a "left-wing article" to the travel magazine *Holiday*.[6] Nelson Algren's story became the basis for a movie promoted as Otto Preminger's *Man with the Golden Arm*. His characters were co-opted by an industry that gave him precious little financial recompense for his contribution, and Algren died broke in 1981. Today he is barely remembered. An author who was compared to Faulkner in his lifetime remains a bit too challenging for the post-postwar world.

20

CHARLIE PARKER

I looked in the mirror, and I saw him stick this needle in his arm. And I screamed, and I got up, and I said "Why?" And he just smiled, and he took the—his tie was his tourniquet. And I was watching, then it came into my mind that on the dresser I'd seen so many of the ties in small ties [knots]. But that was all; he didn't say anything, he just wiped his arm and put his tie 'round his—under his—collar, put his jacket on, and come over and kissed me on the forehead, and he says "See you in the morning."

REBECCA PARKER, CHARLIE'S FIRST WIFE,
DESCRIBING THE EVENTS WHICH LED
TO THEIR 1939 SEPARATION[1]

In 1935 nobody in Kansas City expected much—musically or otherwise—from young Charlie Parker. While his teachers recognized his keen intelligence, they could not ignore his frequent truancy. When he dropped out of school at fifteen, he was still a freshman. And although he was passionate about music, his playing left something to be desired. His debut performance at the High Hat club ended in humiliation. Laughed off the stage by the audience and his fellow musicians, he left in tears and didn't pick up the saxophone again for three months.

But Parker was not to be discouraged. Sneaking into local clubs with the help of sympathetic older musicians, he listened intently to jam sessions featuring great saxmen like Lester Young and Coleman Hawkins. When he got home, he practiced his craft—and practiced, and practiced, and practiced. To the consternation of his neighbors, he spent as much as fifteen hours a day blowing his horn.

Then, in November 1936, Parker was seriously injured in an automobile accident while traveling to a gig in the Ozarks. During his recuperation from broken ribs and a spinal fracture, doctors prescribed morphine for pain. When he recovered, an insurance settlement allowed him to purchase a new alto saxophone, but it was soon pawned to feed his growing heroin habit, a situation that would frequently recur throughout his career.

The next summer, after getting his horn out of hock, Parker returned to the Ozarks. Stuck in a country resort, he used his free time for practice. Listening to 78s of Lester Young with the Count Basie band, Parker mastered Young's solos note for note. When he returned to Kansas City, his fellow jazz musicians noticed the improvement. Better-paying and more prestigious gigs followed. But although his talent was undeniable, so was his growing unreliability. His marriage was crumbling, and one night he attacked a cab driver with a knife and spent twenty-two days in prison.

His life and career in shambles, Parker left Kansas City (and his wife and infant son) in early 1939, heading to Chicago and from there to New York. Making ends meet as a dishwasher at Jimmy's Chicken Shack, a popular Harlem eatery, Parker jammed at nightclubs with New York's finest jazz musicians. There he distinguished himself for his technical wizardry. While lesser saxophonists were content to use a few key signatures and standard riffs, Parker based his melody lines on the higher intervals of a chord. His use of unusual keys and improvisations on the seventh, ninth, or thirteenth of a chord produced dissonant, complex sounds that bore more resemblance to neoclassical composers like Stravinsky than the more popular "swing" sound. Even those players who could keep up with his unusual improvisations were hard-pressed to match his blistering finger speed and his hard-edged, crystal-clear tone.

Along with a few other adventurous musicians, notably trumpeter Dizzy Gillespie and pianist Thelonious Monk, Parker became known for a new style of music and life. A new "hip" subculture was developing among these "beboppers." Sunglasses, goatees, and pork pie hats were its uniform; "cool" slang was its argot; late night "jam sessions" were its religious rituals; heroin was its drug of choice.

The Birth of Bebop

[Heroin] was our badge. It was the thing that made us different from the rest of the world. It was the thing that said, "We know. You don't know." It was the thing that gave us membership in a unique club, and for that we gave up everything else in the world. Every ambition. Every desire. Everything.

TRUMPETER RED RODNEY,
WHO PLAYED WITH PARKER 1948–1951[2]

Unlike the big band/swing sound, bebop was generally played by smaller combos. Fewer players meant more room for improvisation and more time for solos. Dissonances, polyrhythms, new tonal colors, and irregular phrasing were adopted enthusiastically. Instead of just keeping a beat, the bass and drums accented phrases and propelled the melody forward. And while big bands catered to dancers, the soaring melodies and breakneck tempos of bebop were strictly for listening.

Earlier jazz performers acted not just as musicians but also as entertainers. Louis Armstrong was known as much for his showmanship as his virtuoso trumpet playing. To bebop musicians this kind of pandering to the audience was "Tomming"—acting like a black minstrel for the entertainment of white audiences. Parker had no interest in singing, leading a band, or doing anything except playing his saxophone. (Cool bopper and onetime heroin addict Miles Davis took this to the ultimate level. He became famous for playing his trumpet with his back to the audience to show he cared only for the music and not for the reaction it garnered from the fans.) This was not music for the masses but for the rarefied few, played not in enormous dancehalls but in intimate cabarets and private loft parties.

Bebop musicians saw this as a freeing of their art from the demands of an unappreciative and uneducated audience, while old-school jazz musicians saw it as intellectual masturbation and unlistenable noise. Cab Calloway dismissed bebop as "Chinese music," and Louis Armstrong disparagingly referred to it as "slop." Music critics were, at first, equally unkind. In 1948 Weldon Kees wrote in the *Partisan Review,* "I have found this music uniformly thin, at once dilapidated and overblown, and exhibiting a poverty of thematic development and a richness of affectation."[3] But this only served to cement its popularity among aesthetes who wanted something deeper and more challenging than the music favored by "squares" and "moldy figs."

Among the "hipsters" who loved this new music, Charlie Parker was a larger-than-life figure. His technique and feel for melody was the stuff of legend, and so were his Dionysian excesses. Legends circulated of Parker eating buckets of chicken in one sitting,* washing it down with a quart of whiskey and a handful of benzedrines, then shooting up before going onstage and playing like no one else on the scene.

Jazz musicians had long been fond of "tea" (marijuana), but few were interested in harder drugs. Parker's use of heroin gave the needle a new cachet. Many musicians emulated their idol by taking up his habit. And although bebop had begun in part as a reaction against the white-led swing bands, it soon became popular among white intellectuals. For those fans heroin provided an instant ticket to hipness; they could transcend the barriers of race and class by joining the brotherhood of junkies. (This was especially true as dope became increasingly popular

---

*Parker's fondness for chicken was the basis for his famous nickname, "Bird."

in the black ghettos, thanks to the new postwar flood of Corsican and Sicilian heroin.)

One study of forty jazz musicians of the bebop era found that more than 50% had been addicted to heroin at some point in their lives.[4] Many jazz junkies found themselves incarcerated. Dizzy Gillespie remembered "Cats were always getting busted with drugs by the police, and they had a saying, 'To get the best band, go to Kentucky.' That meant that the 'best band' was in Lexington, Kentucky, at the federal narcotics hospital."[5]

Billie Holiday and Chet Baker, among others, died of their habits, while Stan Getz, Miles Davis, and John Coltrane all spent years or decades battling addiction. And if the critics didn't get bebop, they could always write lurid tales about dope-addicted jazz musicians—and many did. As with early coverage of the rock and punk movements, mainstream journalists focused on the clothing and outlandish behavior rather than the musical innovations. This only served to perpetuate a vicious cycle of aspiring newcomers taking up syringes to become "cool." Heroin took an enormous toll on the jazz scene—and few paid a heavier price than Charlie Parker.

The Decline and Fall of Charlie Parker

Any musician who says he is playing better either on tea, the needle, or when he is juiced, is a plain, straight liar. When I get too much to drink, I can't even finger well, let alone play decent ideas. And, in the days when I was on the stuff, I may have thought I was playing better, but listening to some of the records now, I know I wasn't. Some of these smart kids who think you have to be completely knocked out to be a good hornman are just plain crazy. It isn't true. I know, believe me. That way you can miss the most important years of your life, the years of possible creation.

CHARLIE PARKER, 1949[6]

The instability and unreliability that had plagued Parker in Kansas City only got worse as his popularity increased. In 1942 he was fired from the Jay McShann Orchestra after falling asleep onstage during a performance in Detroit. When he was unable to get heroin he compensated by drinking Herculean quantities of alcohol, then swallowing handfuls of pills. He was notorious for showing up at gigs without his instrument, having pawned it to buy heroin, and many of his greatest recordings and performances were done using borrowed saxophones.

In early 1946 Parker and Dizzy Gillespie accepted a two-month engagement in Hollywood. Once the engagement ended, all the musicians returned to New York except for Bird, who cashed in his airplane ticket to buy drugs. By July he was a wreck, barely able to play at sessions. Things came to a head when he was arrested at LA's Civic Hotel for walking around the lobby nude, then setting his mattress on fire after the hotel manager locked him in his room. Charged with indecent exposure, resisting arrest, and arson, Parker was committed to Camarillo State Hospital for a six-month period.

Released in January 1947, Parker stayed in Los Angeles until April. The stay in the hospital had generally done him good: he was off drugs and alcohol and playing once again in top form. In 1948 he married his third wife, Doris Snyder (later the executors of his estate would discover that he had never divorced the first two). But soon after leaving the hospital he was once again drinking and using drugs. A gig in Chicago ended when he left the stage, stumbled into a phone booth, and urinated on the floor. Another gig, with Dizzy Gillespie's band in New York, was terminated after Parker nodded out during a performance.

Finally, in 1951, Parker's New York Cabaret Card was revoked upon the request of the Narcotics Squad. To play any New York venue that sold liquor, performers needed their card. Without it Parker was forced to play underground clubs and out-of-town gigs instead of the lucrative venues more fitting to a musician of his popularity and influence. This financial pressure, coupled with medical bills for Pree, his sickly infant daughter by his fourth wife, Chan, exacerbated Parker's other issues.

His drinking led to bleeding ulcers; to staunch the pain, he turned once again to narcotics.

When Pree died in 1954 Parker was inconsolable. Tensions between him and Chan grew, and at the beginning of September he locked himself in the bathroom and attempted suicide by drinking iodine. Doctors at Bellevue diagnosed his condition as acute alcoholism and latent schizophrenia. A Wasserman test revealed he had also been exposed to syphilis. Electroshock was suggested. When Chan expressed fears that it would effect his playing, the doctor asked, "Do you want a musician or a husband?"[7] Once sober and lucid, Parker was able to convince his doctors to release him on his own recognizance. Two weeks later, after another suicide attempt, he returned for another brief stay but was again released to his own custody.

Out on the streets it became increasingly clear that Parker's lifestyle had taken a toll on his body and his playing. A March 5, 1955, gig at Birdland ended in chaos as Parker clashed with Bud Powell and notoriously touchy bandleader Charles Mingus. Stumbling drunkenly away as he was ejected from the New York City club that bore his name, Parker said, "Mingus, I'm goin' someplace, pretty soon, where I'm not gonna bother anybody."[8]

A few days later Parker began vomiting blood at the New York apartment of Baroness Pannonica "Nica" de Koenigswarter, a wealthy arts patron and heiress to the Rothschild fortune. A doctor recommended hospitalization but Parker refused, hoping to travel to an upcoming gig in Boston. Finally a compromise was reached: Parker agreed to stay at Koenigswarter's apartment, with daily visits from her doctor, until he was well enough to travel. By Saturday he was well enough to sit up and watch television. During a comedy routine on the Dorsey Brothers show, Parker's laughter turned to choking, then silence. He was not yet thirty-five. Upon examining his body, the coroner attributed his death to a heart attack, pneumonia, stomach ulcers, and advanced cirrhosis and estimated the decedent's age as between fifty and sixty years old.

21

WILLIAM S. BURROUGHS

You see, a writer can profit from things that may be just unpleasant or boring to someone else because he uses those things subsequently as material for writing. And I would say that the experience I had with heroin as described in Junkie *later led to my subsequent books like* Naked Lunch, *so I don't regret it.*

WILLIAM S. BURROUGHS, 1978[1]

One might have expected the life of young William Seward Burroughs II to follow a predictable, even boring arc. His social credentials were certainly impeccable: his mother, Laura Lee, was a direct descendant of Confederate general Robert E. Lee, and his grandfather the inventor of the Burroughs adding machine. A future of genteel prosperity among his fellow bluebloods seemed inevitable.

But, alas, young William was ill suited to the life of a St. Louis socialite. Neighbors and fellow students didn't know what to make of the sickly, sepulchral boy with the dark sense of humor and fascination with crime, hoboes, and transgressive behavior. One of the respectable ladies on his block said he reminded her of a "walking corpse." (Upon later hearing of her death, Burroughs commented, "Well, it isn't every corpse can walk. Hers can't.")[2]

His parents sent William to the Los Alamos Ranch School in New Mexico in the hopes that fresh air and rigorous exercise would straighten him out. Unfortunately, their hopes were for naught. William developed a crush on another boy at the school and was expelled after an experiment with the sleeping drug chloral hydrate went awry.

Despite his best efforts to join the seedy set, Burroughs managed to graduate from Harvard University in 1936. Impressed with his achievement, his parents gave him a $200 monthly allowance—a decent but not enormous sum at the time. Freed from the necessity of earning a living, William was able to continue his explorations of the dark underbelly of American society. Moving to New York, he befriended a number of petty criminals and young intellectuals (and a few who could be classified in both circles). He was also introduced to the drug that would become a recurring theme in his later work and life.

> *You become a narcotics addict because you do not have strong motivations in any other direction. Junk wins by default. I tried it as a matter of curiosity. I drifted along taking shots when I could score. I ended up hooked. Most addicts I have talked to report a similar experience. They did not start using drugs for any reason they can remember. They just drifted along until they got hooked. . . . You don't decide to be an addict. One morning you wake up sick and you're an addict.*
>
> WILLIAM S. BURROUGHS, 1953[3]

Where once he could rely on money from home, Burroughs now found himself forced to support his habit. No longer just a visitor to the criminal world, he became involved in a number of illegal money-making schemes. His efforts at rolling drunks bore little fruit, and his attempts at dealing proved even less successful. Finally he was picked up for forging a narcotics prescription and sent home to his family in St. Louis. When his probationary period ended he returned to New

York long enough to pick up his common-law wife, Joan Vollmer, then headed to Texas for life as a gentleman farmer growing cotton, oranges, and marijuana. When that didn't pan out, the family moved to New Orleans. There he found himself once again in trouble with the law. Arrested for possession of marijuana and heroin, he decided to take his family and relocate to Mexico rather than face a potential sentence in Louisiana's notorious Angola prison.

Once ensconced in Mexico, Burroughs and Vollmer continued their descent into addiction. Her fondness for amphetamines matched his yen for opiates, and both began consuming large quantities of cheap Mexican booze. Then, on September 6, 1951, a drunken game of "William Tell" ended horribly when Burroughs missed the glass atop Vollmer's head and shot her between the eyebrows. His family was able to bail him out of jail, hire a lawyer, and bribe various witnesses and police officers. Burroughs left the country and returned to the United States, and from there he headed to Rome and ultimately to Tangier, Morocco.

Burroughs in the Interzone

There, alone in a foreign city, a guilt-ridden Burroughs tried to pick up the pieces of his life. Earlier, one of his friends, Beat poet Allen Ginsberg, nagged him into writing a short book about his life as a drug addict. Pulp publisher Ace Books picked up the manuscript and published it in 1953 (under the pen name "William Lee") as *Junkie: Confessions of an Unredeemed Drug Addict.**

Readers picking up *Junkie* might have expected yet another lurid tale of crime and punishment that ended with the antihero either changing his ways or dying, thereby proving that good always wins in the end. What they got instead was an anthropological study of junk and its users in Mexico and throughout the United States. Burroughs wrote with laconic detachment, drawing sharp portraits of himself, his habit, and his fellow junkies in spare, clean prose.

---

*Later editions have sometimes spelled the title *Junky*.

But Burroughs still had little interest in a writer's life. A sequel to *Junkie*, *Queer*, languished unpublished for decades after Burroughs lost interest in the manuscript. After a brief return to the United States (where efforts to get royalties owed on *Junkie* proved unfruitful), he returned to Tangier. He would remain there for the next four years.

Fueled by Eukodol (a German formulation of injectable oxycodone), Burroughs began writing snippets of fiction about the "Interzone," a dreamlike place-between-places where anything could happen and everything was for sale at the right price. His narrative introduced the reader to the sinister Dr. Benway, the political rivalries between the Factualists and Liquefactionists, and the ongoing saga of William Lee, a dope fiend on the run from police. But where *Junkie* had been a relatively straightforward tale of an addict and his circle, these Interzone narratives were a series of hallucinatory fragments with little in the way of a coherent plot.

While visiting Burroughs in 1957, Ginsberg made an effort to organize his filthy hotel room. Finding the pages of the Interzone narratives scattered about the floor, he compiled them into a manuscript and once again nagged Burroughs into submitting them for publication. In 1959 Olympia Press, a French publisher of erotica that had also published Henry Miller and other controversial authors, printed the Interzone narratives under the title *The Naked Lunch*.

> She seized a safety pin caked with blood and rust, gouged a great hole in her leg which seemed to hang open like an obscene, festering mouth waiting for unspeakable congress with the dropper which she now plunged out of sight into the gaping wound. . . . What does she care for the atom bomb, the bedbugs, the cancer rent, Friendly Finance waiting to repossess her delinquent flesh. . . . Sweet dreams, Pantopon Rose.[4]

As soon as it was released, the book attracted equal parts praise and condemnation. As a teenager Burroughs had burned the diary describing his romantic attraction to a fellow schoolboy, afraid someone might read it and discover his terrible secret. *Naked Lunch* explored his homosexuality in graphic detail: the narrator wanders amid a landscape of hustlers, queers, and sodomites of all stripes. And where *Junkie* had explored opiate addiction, *Naked Lunch* created a far more disturbing extended metaphor: all life is an addiction, and our continued struggle for existence no different from the junkie's efforts to acquire the next fix.

Naked Lunch was banned in Boston and prosecuted as obscene by the state of Massachusetts. In 1959 *Big Table,* a magazine, was deemed unfit for the U.S. mail because of excerpts from *Naked Lunch.* According to the postal inspector, these excerpts (and an article by Jack Kerouac titled "Old Angel Midnight")

> portray sexual matters and subjects in a most exacerbated, morbid and perverted manner. The language used exceeds any four letter Anglo-Saxon words which may be found in current contemporary novels. They discuss defecation, the genitals, sexual relations, perversions, and aberrations in the lowest type of language. I believe the publication appeals to prurient interest.[5]

Not until 1966 would the Massachusetts Supreme Judicial Court declare the work "not obscene," thanks to intensive lobbying efforts by writers like John Ciardi and Norman Mailer. This decision opened the door for works like James Joyce's *Ulysses,* D. H. Lawrence's *Lady Chatterley's Lover,* and Henry Miller's *Tropic of Cancer* to be published in the United States. *Naked Lunch* would become the last work of literature prosecuted for obscenity in the United States.

The Rise of a Counterculture Icon

Throughout the 1960s Burroughs continued publishing in literary magazines and through small presses. His friendship with British painter and intellectual Brion Gysin led him to the use of "cut-ups"—

arbitrary shuffling of texts to form new texts and escape the bonds of conventional language patterns. He also managed to break his opiate addiction, attributing his sobriety to a now-discredited cure using apomorphine, a powerful emetic that has no recreational value. Now dope-free, he cranked out novels like *Dead Fingers Talk, The Soft Machine, The Ticket That Exploded,* and *Nova Express.* He even covered the 1968 Democratic convention for *Esquire* magazine.

The mainstream still didn't know quite what to make of Burroughs, nor did much of the counterculture. His worldview was the polar opposite of the hippie ethos; instead of celebrating the body and the liberating power of sexuality, his writings reduced the human experience to secretions, intestines, and gibbering heaps of protoplasm seeking release in anonymous acts of sodomy. His fascination with guns and violence were at odds with the peace and love generation, as was his disinterest in LSD. ("It makes me nervous. My coordination isn't good and there's a metallic taste in my mouth and there's nothing I like about it.")[6]

But as Woodstock gave way to Altamont and the hippies were replaced by the punks, Burroughs found a whole new generation of fans. The leather-jackets-and-Mohawks crowd loved this child of wealth and privilege who rejected the system. His musings on shady interdimensional forces seeking control over a benumbed society no longer seemed so paranoid in the post-Watergate era, while his history of drug use and his open homosexuality added to his cachet of danger and mystery. The slender gentleman in a seersucker suit may have seemed an unlikely hero, but as he had done with the Beats, Burroughs became a mentor and father figure to younger artists seeking a voice.

To earn extra money ($200 a month not going as far in the 1970s as in the 1930s), Burroughs began giving readings at punk rock clubs. *Naked Lunch* and *Junkie* were no longer cult classics but Great Modern Literature. Critics compared him with poets of transgression like Rimbaud and Baudelaire, while fans hailed him as one of America's greatest writers. A few even reintroduced him to his old vice: in the 1970s he began using heroin once again and continued, with brief periods of sobriety, throughout the rest of his life.

By the 1980s he had become almost respectable. In 1981 he appeared on *Saturday Night Live,* reading excerpts from *Nova Express;* in 1989 he had a memorable cameo appearance as Tom the Priest in *Drugstore Cowboy,* a Gus Van Sant movie about a crew of pharmacy-robbing addicts. His "cut-ups" and philosophical ruminations influenced occultists like Genesis P-Orridge, Alan Moore, Robert Anton Wilson, and Peter Carroll (who initiated Burroughs into his order, the Illuminates of Thanateros). He also collaborated with artists like Tom Waits (the opera *Black Rider*), Kurt Cobain (*The Priest They Called Him*), Laurie Anderson ("Sharkey's Night" on *Mister Heartbreak*), and Ministry ("Quick Fix" on their *Just One Fix* album).

Burroughs also became an outspoken critic of the Reagan administration's War on Drugs. Some saw him as a primal force of liberation against the forces of fascism; others saw him as a wife-murdering heroin addict. He became an icon for prodrug and antidrug forces alike; depending on whom you asked, he was either a crusader for freedom or a cautionary tale. In all this his importance as an artist and thinker was sometimes lost or obscured—but then, Burroughs was well aware of the way language and the apprehension of the symbol could obscure or change meaning.

In 1981 he moved to the small college town of Lawrence, Kansas, with his secretary and partner, James Grauerholz. There he took up a life of gardening, hiking, and tending to his cats. Methadone maintenance helped him adjust to life in a city without a large heroin supply. One of his last art projects combined two of his loves: placing cans of paint before a canvas, he would then shoot them with one of his many guns to produce brightly colored random splatters. On August 2, 1997, he died in a Lawrence hospital. He was eighty-three years old.

Nothing is. There is no final enough of wisdom, experience—any fucking thing. No Holy Grail, No Final Satori, no final solution. Just conflict.

Only thing can resolve conflict is love, like I felt for Fletch and Ruski, Spooner and Calico. Pure love.

What I feel for my cats present and past.

Love? What is It?

Most natural painkiller what there is.

LOVE.

FINAL ENTRY IN BURROUGHS' DIARIES,
JULY 30, 1997[7]

22

LOU REED

California is full of meaningful causes. New York filled with meaningless noises, which could be its redeeming grace. . . . In New York a person is forced into the seclusion of his own individuality.

LOU REED, 1966[1]

Before he was a poster boy for intravenous drug abuse, Lou Reed was an English major at Syracuse University. There he met writer and fellow shock-therapy survivor Delmore Schwartz. The cantankerous professor and his notoriously difficult student bonded, and Schwartz encouraged Reed to be faithful to his art. Reed took his mentor at his word. He had played in a few doo-wop bands in high school and at college. He aspired to combine the dark, street-savvy worldview of writers like Nelson Algren (see chapter 19) with the doo-wop and garage rock he had played throughout his high school and college years. Arriving in New York, he hoped to find an audience for cheery tunes like "Heroin" and "I'm Waiting for the Man."

Alas, this wasn't exactly what Pickwick Records, Reed's first employer, wanted. The bargain-basement record company was looking for sound-alike tunes that capitalized on popular crazes. When Lou's dance parody "The Ostrich" garnered some airplay on local radio, Pickwick decided that the credited band, the Primitives, would have to go out on tour. But they needed someone to provide the right look. And so they hired a long-haired out-of-work artist—a classically trained Welsh violist and composer named John Cale—to play bass.

While rehearsing, Cale noticed Reed had tuned every string on his guitar to D, thereby creating an intriguing drone effect. Cale shared much of his own avant-garde work with Reed. They combined their musical sensibilities with Reed's gritty lyrics about New York street life. Sterling Morrison, a friend of Reed's from Syracuse University, joined them as a second guitarist and bassist; Angus MacLise, who played with Cale in La Monte Young's ensemble, accompanied on percussion. As the Warlocks, they played a number of underground clubs, galleries, and poetry readings throughout lower Manhattan.

Then, in the autumn of 1965, they received a $75 offer for their first paying gig. MacLise resigned, offended that they were commercializing their art. Drummer Maureen "Mo" Tucker stepped in, and the band renamed itself the Velvet Underground. On November 11, 1965, they played their first gig as the Velvet Underground, opening for the Myddle Class at a high school dance in Summit, New Jersey. Opening with "There She Goes Again," they then played "Venus in Furs," and ended with "Heroin." The students were reportedly shocked and confused; the reaction of the school administrators has not been preserved for history.

Undeterred, manager Al Aronowitz landed them a two-week gig in a more open-minded environment, Café Bizarre in Greenwich Village. But even New York's fringe wasn't quite sure what to make of this loud, aggressively atonal act whose subject matter was as black as their outfits. The Velvets' challenging work and Reed's even more challenging demeanor would bring their gig to a premature halt. Thankfully, one visitor at Café Bizarre, Andy Warhol, was more favorably disposed.

The thing is that Andy works very hard. One of the things you can learn from being at the Factory is if you want to do whatever you do, then you should work very, very hard. If you don't work very hard all the time, well then nothing will happen. And Andy works as hard as anybody I know. . . . Whenever he'd ask me how many songs I'd written that day, whatever the number was Andy would say, "you should do more."

LOU REED, 1966[2]

The association with one of America's most popular artists brought them new attention. On December 31, 1965, *The Making of an Underground Film,* hosted by Walter Cronkite, discussed an upcoming movie about the Velvets and featured "Venus in Furs." Then, in January, the Velvets became the house band for the Exploding Plastic Inevitable, a series of multimedia events that featured Warhol films, dancers, and other sensory stimuli combined with the Velvets' sinister songs about drugs, transvestites, and sadomasochism. With Germanic chanteuse Nico providing additional vocals and eye candy, the Velvets played at events around New York and a few other select cities.

Velvet Underground and Nico, released March 1967, featured a seven-minute version of their signature "Heroin." It gave listeners a taste both of Reed's ear for simple-but-tuneful melodies and the band's raw live power. The narrator croons sweetly of his plans to "nullify my life" and his dreams of escaping the places "where a man cannot be free / of all the evils of his town / and of himself and those around." The music builds to a crescendo, then returns to the elegiac structures of the beginning, with the sad refrain "I guess I just don't know."

And while "Heroin" might be suitably depressing to qualify as antidrug material, what were listeners to make of "I'm Waiting for the Man," a sprightly ode to the pleasures of copping dope in Harlem? There were no waggling fingers here, no condemnation of the Evils of Drug Abuse, just a celebration of that "sweet taste" that saves you from feeling "sick and dirty, more dead than alive."

The Velvet Underground is so far out that it makes the tremendous thumping beat of that great, groovy group the

*Modern Folk Quartet, which opened the program, sound
passé.*

KEVIN THOMAS, *LOS ANGELES TIMES*, MAY 5, 1966[3]

Even for 1967 this was too much to take. *Velvet Underground and
Nico* charted no higher than number 171 on Billboard's Top 200 and
received virtually no airplay. On its heels came an abrasive, searing fol-
lowup, *White Light White Heat* (1967). Its "Sister Ray" features a Bosch-
worthy gathering of sailors, drag queens, and junkies. Reed sings in his
flat, deadpan voice of an addict "looking for my mainline" and a murdered sailor ("Aw you shouldn't do that / don't you know you'll mess
the carpet"). Behind him the band produces a feedback-thick squall of
dirty, propulsive sound that drives the action along. It's a suburban kid's
most fervent dream of inner-city decadence, and one that would later
serve to increase the Velvets' reputation as poets of darkness.

Alas, upon release their second album received even less attention
than their first. In this era of "tuning in, turning on, and dropping out,"
LSD, psilocybin mushrooms, peyote, and other psychedelic substances
were the order of the day, and marijuana was becoming a valuable part of
many college students' breakfasts. But heroin was decidedly unfashion-
able, connected not with consciousness expansion but with crime and
degradation. Like crack in the 1980s and 1990s, heroin in the 1960s
was largely a poor man's drug, found more often in the ghetto than
among the jet set. Heroin would not become a media problem until it
began once again catching on among a wealthier and whiter clientele.

Reed would make several stabs at commercial success, cutting ties
with Warhol and Cale and trying to do a poppier, more radio-friendly
sound for *Velvet Underground* and 1970's *Loaded*. But it was no use.
On August 23, 1970, after performing his final show with the Velvet
Underground, Lou Reed's parents picked him up outside what would
later become a notorious punk club, Max's Kansas City. Returning to
their Freeport, Long Island, home he accepted a job working for his
father as a typist at $40 a week.

Nihilistic? The whole fucking country was nihilistic. What did we come out of? The lie of the Summer of Love into Charles Manson and the Vietnam War. Where is the positivity? I'm supposed to be fucking positive? Fuck you! You want positive, go elsewhere. Go find a different lie.

PERFORMANCE ARTIST AND MUSICIAN
LYDIA LUNCH DESCRIBING THE 1970s, 2008[4]

As Woodstock gave way to Altamont and the Vietnam conflict ground on, hope gave way to disillusionment. Angry artists were suddenly fashionable—and so too was heroin. The Rolling Stones included "Sister Morphine" on their 1971 *Sticky Fingers,* and guitarist Keith Richards would become one of the world's most famous addicts and debauchées. Heroin became the great demon queen of recreational psychopharmacology. People who happily snorted grams of cocaine and popped handfuls of pills solemnly warned against the dangers of the needle and the life-destroying power of even a single dose of smack. Janis Joplin's overdose in October 1970 helped cement heroin's reputation as a drug used only by the most insanely self-destructive.

But in the 1970s insane self-destruction, the stronger the better, was the order of the day. Heroin use became particularly prevalent among the gutter punks and countercultural musicians of New York. President Gerald Ford told the city to drop dead, and rising crime and white flight left many blocks deserted. On these dirty but cheap streets track marks vied with tattoos for most common body modification and sign of outsider status. A city that had always had an active heroin market now had a new generation of arty young kids fascinated with poppies. They not only emulated the Velvet Underground's musical stylings, they also practiced all its favored bad habits.

Meanwhile, after the job at his father's accounting firm failed to work out, Reed concentrated on his solo career. Moving to England to release *Lou Reed* (1971), he met yet another influential Velvets fan, David Bowie. Bowie offered to produce his second album, 1972's *Transformer.*

Its single "Walk on the Wild Side" took its title from a Nelson Algren novel; its plot was yet another Lou Reed story of homosexuality, transvestitism, prostitution, and various permutations thereof. But unlike his earlier efforts, this one garnered immediate airplay, reaching number 16 on the American charts and number 10 in the UK. It also helped introduce Americans to a movement that was growing fast across the pond—glam rock.

> INTERVIEWER: You want people to take drugs themselves? Is that perhaps why you sing about drugs?
>
> REED: Oh yeah. I want them to take drugs.
>
> INTERVIEWER: Why is this?
>
> REED: Because it's better than Monopoly.
>
> Lou Reed, 1974[5]

Reed would complain about fans who accosted him to say proudly, "I shot up to 'Heroin!'" Yet he would also mime the act of shooting up during many performances of the song. Reed chronicled the disintegration of two drug addicts in the 1973 album *Berlin*. A live show and subsequent album in 1974 gave us a glammed-up, drugged-out *Rock n Roll Animal*. On the title track of 1978's *Street Hassle*, he counsels a man whose girlfriend has just overdosed in an inconvenient location. His relationship with his adoring public was as thorny and complex as his dealings with record executives and journalists. He might be mocking, even hostile—but he always made sure to give the fans what they wanted.

While Reed certainly experimented with heroin, his more typical drugs of choice appear to have been amphetamines and alcohol. At the time "pep pills" were widely available and commonly used by touring entertainers and busy housewives alike. And Reed's partying was positively restrained next to Dionysian substance abusers like Iggy Pop or Keith Richards. The record suggests that Lou Reed generally showed up to his gigs sober enough to play, no matter what substances he might have enjoyed beforehand. His fans identified him as a junkie; he used that to his advantage, because he has always identified himself first and foremost as a working artist.

> *I haven't been near drugs for 30 years or so. Sobriety is a*
> *great gift. Better to be addicted to Martial Art or jogging.*
>
> LOU REED, 2007[6]

Many believe Reed is willfully self-destructive. He has frequently released a successful and commercially palatable album, then followed with a change-up that sent those new fans screaming for the exits. (*Metal Machine Music,* his 1975 double album of feedback noise, is probably the most notorious example of this.) But there has always been a certain calculation in Reed's approach. In the end his antics have generally served to enhance his career as much as they endangered it. When they did not, they were dropped from the repertoire.

Once Lou Reed the Drugged-Out BDSM Punk threatened to upstage Lou Reed the artist, it went back into the closet. As he had done with John Cale earlier, Reed got rid of heroin as soon as it looked like it might outshine him or demand equal billing. Heroin had been a prop in the Velvets' repertoire, but producers no more expected the original Velvets to be real junkies than they expected Bela Lugosi to be a real vampire. In 1981 Reed began attending AA and NA meetings; by the mid-'80s he was clean and sober and has by all accounts remained so since.

Some of Reed's followers and fellow travelers were not so fortunate. Nico battled a serious heroin habit for years. In June of 1979 original Velvets drummer Angus MacLise died in Kathmandu, Nepal, of complications of tuberculosis, malnutrition, and long-term heroin abuse. Earlier that year, in February, Sex Pistols bassist Sid Vicious died of an overdose. Vicious had been held for fifty-five days in connection with the murder of his girlfriend, Nancy Spungeon. Just released, he tried his usual shot but forgot to take his lowered tolerance into effect. Heroin was now part of punk's great Sacrificed King myth, and shooting up one of his sacraments.

Then, in 1980 Darby Crash, the twenty-two-year-old frontman for Los Angeles punk band the Germs, created a new benchmark for how not to use heroin for fame. Deciding to slough off this mortal coil and ensure his place in history as the American Sid Vicious, Crash opted for a lethal overdose. He signed a suicide pact with girlfriend Casey Cola, then they proceeded to split $400 worth of heroin between them. Cola lived. Crash died in his leather jacket, confident that he would now be a legend. Alas, his chosen date with death—December 7, 1980—meant that his obituary would not reach the papers before the December 8 murder of John Lennon.

> *Darby was known for not singing with the band during live performances. We played real fast and, if you were drunk, there's no way to keep up. When I heard about Lennon, I just thought, "Great timing as usual, Mr. Crash."*
> FORMER GERM PAUL BOLLES, 2000[7]

Ten years later and half a world away, the reunited Velvets performed "Heroin" at a 1990 Paris soiree honoring Andy Warhol. The setlist for their brief 1993 reunion included "Heroin" and "I'm Waiting for the Man," and Reed continues to play both songs live. In 2003 he also allowed Nissan to sample a riff from "Heroin" for an ad extolling the virtues of their Xterra SUV.

23

GIA CARANGI

Don't do it, even if she wants it, don't let her do it. I used to be a model. You don't want your kid to be a model.

GIA CARANGI, 1986[1]

"You should be a model" is one of the oldest pickup lines in the book. But Maurice Tannenbaum, a hair stylist and aspiring photographer, was completely sincere. Seventeen-year-old Carangi's look was like nothing else in 1977 Philadelphia. While the other members of her Bowie-loving clique were sporting sparkly glam-rock duds, Carangi was dressed in army fatigues, men's shirts, and cowboy boots. Her hard-edged androgyny was simultaneously intimidating and seductive, attracting the attention of men and women, straight and gay. But beneath her tough exterior lurked a vulnerable and insecure young girl. Flattered by Tannenbaum's interest, Carangi posed for her first photo sessions.

Tannenbaum's pictures paved the way for some local modeling jobs, allowing Carangi to quit work at her father's hoagie shop. The striking young beauty soon attracted the attention of Arthur Elgort, a photographer for Bloomingdale's. After working with Carangi, he introduced her to some of his friends, including famous photographers Richard Avedon, Francesco Scavullo, and Chris von Wangenheim. Within a few months she was in New York interviewing with the Wilhelmina Cooper Agency.

At 5 feet 8 inches, Carangi was a bit shorter than most runway models, and her brunette hair and brown eyes were a striking contrast to the blue-eyed blonde look that had been popularized by Cheryl Tiegs and Farrah Fawcett-Majors. But Cooper—who also represented several other "exotic" models—recognized Carangi's potential and signed her immediately. By the end of 1978, Carangi was already a well-established model, working for designers like Christian Dior, Diane von Fürstenberg, Giorgio Armani, Vidal Sassoon, and Yves Saint Laurent. The eighteen-year-old from northeast Philadelphia was now one of America's hottest models.

Gia Becomes a Star

She was looking for anyone's love, she would show up at my house sometimes in the middle of the night and I'd let her in and she just wanted someone to hug her.
JULIE FOSTER, GIA'S FRIEND AND FELLOW MODEL[2]

In the late 1970s, decadence was the order of the day, and celebrities flaunted their wealth and status in cocaine-fueled all-night parties. Carangi became a regular at hot spots like Studio 54 and the Mudd Club. Stories began to spread about this gorgeous bad girl. Some said she had carved her name in the receptionist's front desk at the Wilhelmina Cooper Agency with a switchblade. Others told lurid tales of her aggressive sexual advances toward her fellow models or talked about the time she walked out of an Avedon shoot after an argument with the famous photographer. These antics might have ruined the career of a lesser model, but they only added to the Gia mystique. She became an icon of the hard-partying '70s—gorgeous, sexually uninhibited, and ready for any kind of excitement that might come her way.

But while Gia's professional career was reaching new heights, her personal life was falling apart. An on-again off-again relationship with Sandy Linter, a makeup assistant Carangi met on a photo shoot, never became stable. And while just about everyone in the industry was fueling their hard-driven lifestyle with cocaine, amphetamines, and other prescription drugs, Gia was now flirting with heroin. Commanding as much as $10,000 a day for her photo shoots, she could easily afford any drug she wanted—and so long as she could show up to be photographed, the powers that be in the industry were inclined to look the other way at her misbehavior.

Then, in 1980, Wilhelmina Cooper died after a brief battle with lung cancer. Gia was devastated. Her relationship with her mother had always been troubled, and she had come to look upon Cooper as a maternal figure and an island of stability. Her use of heroin and other drugs escalated, and her charming quirks soon became liabilities. She walked off a Versace gig to score heroin and never returned. Other assignments were marked by violent temper tantrums or by Gia nodding off in front of the camera. In her shoots for the November 1980 issue of *Vogue,* the sympathetic photographer posed her to hide the weeping injection sores and swollen hands. Despite his best efforts and the work of makeup and airbrush artists, track marks are visible in several photos. By the beginning of 1981 she had been dropped by the Wilhelmina Cooper Agency. She then signed to the Eileen Ford Agency but was let go after three weeks.

Gia Goes to Rehab

INTERVIEWER: It almost destroyed you, didn't it? You thought more than once about packing it in, didn't you.

GIA: Yes I did. I guess you could say I did, yes I have. But I thought about that without drugs, too. Now I have a great lust for life, and it's a wonderful feeling.

GIA CARANGI, 1982[3]

In 1981 Gia signed up for a twenty-one-day detox program. But a relationship with a fellow heroin addict, college student Elyssa Golden, soon sent her back into drug usage. In the spring of 1981, twenty-one-year-old Gia was arrested for drunk driving. Later she was caught stealing from family and friends. Then yet another friend, photographer Chris von Wangenheim, died after an automobile accident. Despondent, Gia spiraled even further out of control, trying to numb her pain with ever-increasing doses of heroin.

By the fall of 1981 her looks were beginning to fade and the drug usage was taking its toll. In a 1982 appearance on *20/20* Gia claimed she was now clean, but her slurred speech and twitchy demeanor made it clear that she was still using. What was supposed to be a comeback appearance became instead a sad sign of how far Gia had fallen. Few American agencies were willing to work with her; a brief career modeling for European fashion designers ended in early 1983 when she was caught with drugs on a North African shoot. At the age of twenty-three Gia's modeling career was over. Cindy Crawford, another dark-haired sultry beauty, took Gia's place in photo shoots, earning the nickname "Baby Gia" before becoming famous in her own right.

Returning to Philadelphia, Gia entered a drug treatment program in Eagleville. Her modeling money had long since gone up her arm, and she entered the program as an indigent. She remained an inpatient there for six months, trying her best to overcome her addictions and get her life back. After release it looked briefly like she might succeed. She enrolled in a local community college, taking classes in cinematography and photography in an attempt to learn more about work on the other side of the camera. She got a job selling jeans at a local mall and worked as a cashier in a local supermarket. But three months after leaving rehab, the call of her addiction proved too strong to resist, and she vanished.

After relocating to Atlantic City and New York, she supported herself through prostitution and shoplifting. She was raped several times by dealers and fellow addicts. The face that had once graced fashion magazines was now covered with pimples and sores; her arms were covered with track marks, and she was alarmingly thin. When she collapsed with symptoms of pneumonia, her mother had her hospitalized yet again. There doctors made a grim discovery.

The Death of Gia Carangi

Life & Death
Energy & Peace
If I stopped today
it was fun

GIA CARANGI'S JOURNAL, 1986[4]

The "shooting galleries" where addicts gathered in the '80s generally featured an ample supply of used needles kept in containers of dirty water. For a fee an addict could "rent" one of these works to shoot up. Because syringes were hard to come by, many (including Gia) availed themselves of this "service." Unfortunately, this was also a prime vector for transmitting diseases, particularly AIDS.

In 1985 Ryan White, a thirteen-year-old hemophiliac, was barred from his school after developing AIDS from a tainted blood transfusion. In New York the Social Security Administration was interviewing AIDS patients by phone rather than risking face-to-face meetings.[5] The fashion industry had already lost many talented gay photographers and makeup artists to AIDS; when Carangi was diagnosed with the disease, she knew all too well what was in store for her.

After learning of Gia's disease, her stepfather refused to allow her to return home, fearing he would lose his job if it was discovered he was living with an AIDS patient. In Philadelphia's Warminster General Hospital, Gia was confined to an isolation ward; later she was transferred to Hahnemann University Hospital. There her mother kept watch by her bedside, allowing few visitors. Their relationship had always been tense and conflicted; now, as Gia lay dying, they were finally able to gain each other's affection and attention.

Despite the best medical care available at the time, Gia's condition continued to decline as opportunistic infections ravaged her body. By October she was breathing with the aid of a respirator; her liver and spleen were enlarged, and her kidneys had ceased functioning. On November 18, 1986, Gia Carangi died of complications from AIDS. Only family members and a few of her friends from rehab attended her funeral. Few in the modeling industry were even aware that she had been ill.

Carangi was the first high-profile IV drug user to fall victim to AIDS, but she was hardly the last. By June 1987, Dr. Don C. Des Jarlais of the New York State Division of Substance Abuse Services estimated that two hundred thousand IV drug users, mainly in New York and New Jersey, were infected with the AIDS virus.[6] An already stigmatized group came under even greater scrutiny, because it was believed that they were more likely to carry the "gay plague" into "normal" society through heterosexual contact. In the era of "Just Say No," there was little interest in funding needle exchanges or providing sterile syringes to addicts. Even today many cities and states ban needle exchanges and forbid the sale of needles without a prescription.

Gia might have been forgotten altogether, save as a cautionary tale about the dangers of drug abuse. But a decade later she would return as the patron saint of a new modeling movement, one for which she would serve not as warning but inspiration.

Heroin Chic

Fashion has always perceived boredom as cool. The goal is to look like you've seen everything, done everything, been everywhere. It's an intimidating look, and the drug thing is a continuation of all that.

TOM FORD, CREATIVE DIRECTOR, GUCCI, 1996[7]

In the mid-1990s a new look hit the runways. Waifish models with jutting bones, pale skin, and messy hair became all the rage, thanks to superstars like Kate Moss. Long sleeves and fingerless gloves (intended to cover real or imaginary tracks) became a fashion statement. Sexy come-hither stares were replaced by glazed detachment, with eyeliner and shadow used to provide that sunken-eyed addict look. A 1997 Jil Sander catalogue featured the model Guinevere van Seenus with knotted hair, clammy skin, and red-rimmed eyes; in one picture, the left sleeve of her sweater was pushed up.

Soon everyone was talking about the new "heroin chic." To celebrate this new movement, a few aspiring young models began declaring themselves "Gia's Girls." They emulated Gia's aggressive sexuality and open drug usage. As with Gia, many in the industry tacitly encouraged their abuses, telling them to inject in places where the marks would not be visible. (Under the tongue or between the toes were favorite spots.) They would warn the young models not to be "the next Gia"—meaning not that they should avoid heroin but that they should keep their usage discreet.

The look was not without controversy. Many critics blamed heroin chic for fueling the rise in heroin addiction among middle-class teenagers. Photographers blamed the modeling agencies for promoting the look, while the agencies pointed the finger at editors and stylists. Everyone insisted that heroin chic was strictly for the camera and that drug abuse was not a major part of the scene. Then, in 1997 Davide Sorrenti, a twenty-year-old photographer, died on his dealer's couch. His images of slender, pale, lethargic models had appeared in magazines like *Detour, Interview,* and *Ray Gun,* making him one of the fashion world's most widely emulated photographers. Although Sorrenti's death was actually caused by kidney failure exacerbated by Cooley's anemia, a genetic disease, his heroin usage was blamed—and suddenly heroin chic became decidedly less chic.

In May of 1997 President Bill Clinton issued a stinging rebuke of the movement, claiming, "You do not need to glamorize addiction to sell clothes" and stated, "The glorification of heroin is not creative, it's destructive."[8] In response, Fern Mallis, the executive director of the Council of Fashion Designers of America, said, "The fashion industry should not be the easy target to blame for society's woes."[9] Bridget de Socio, fashion editor of *Paper Magazine,* sniffed, "Clinton is irrelevant to what happens at a magazine like ours. . . . Heroin chic is ancient history anyway."[10] In 1998 HBO Pictures premiered *Gia,* a biopic based on the Gia Carangi story. It proved to be a major career milestone for its star, a then relatively unknown actress named Angelina Jolie.

24

LAYNE STALEY

Here's how my thinking pattern went: When I tried drugs,
they were fucking great, and they worked for me for years,
and now they're turning against me—and now I'm walking
through hell, and this sucks. I didn't want my fans to think
that heroin was cool. But then I've had fans come up to me
and give me the thumbs up, telling me they're high. That's
exactly what I didn't want to happen.

LAYNE STALEY, 1996[1]

On March 11, 1989, Andy Catlin's story, "Seattle, Rock City," appeared in Britain's popular *Melody Maker* magazine. A quirky mid-size city in the Pacific Northwest was suddenly a rock capital, and what had been a local movement was suddenly a hot new underground trend. A year earlier, Seattle's scene had been a small community of artists who communicated through mimeographed fanzines and independent LP releases. Now it was attracting a worldwide audience of both fans and record executives.

About this time Don Ienner, president at Columbia Records, was listening to a demo titled *The Treehouse Tapes*. Ienner was impressed by Jerry Cantrell's heavy, doom-laden guitar riffs and the hypnotic baritone wail of lead singer Layne Staley. The band Alice in Chains seemed a fitting example of the new "Seattle grunge" sound, with a hard, guitar-heavy edge that might also allow for crossover into the metal market. Accordingly, Ienner offered them a contract. In June of 1990 the Alice in Chains EP *We Die Young* was released, and in August their full-length debut, *Facelift,* hit record stores. It was the culmination of Staley's lifelong dream—and the beginning of the journey that would ultimately kill him.

The Beginning

I got [a] call saying that my dad had died, [but] my family always knew he was around doing all kind of drugs. Since that call I always was wondering, "Where is my dad?" I felt so sad for him and I missed him. He dropped out of my life for 15 years.

LAYNE STALEY, 2002[2]

When Layne Staley was seven his parents divorced, and his mother remarried. Taking his stepfather's name, Layne Elmer was remembered by most of his schoolmates as a quiet, introverted boy. While he excelled in classes he liked, he paid little attention to boring classes. And because he was one of the smallest boys in his class (until a growth spurt in his junior year), he became a frequent target for school bullies.

As an outlet for his frustration, the young Staley turned to music. At the age of twelve he began playing drums, but soon he switched to lead vocals, trading in his drum kit for a PA system. Later he would say that he hoped that becoming a rock star would bring his father back into his life. At sixteen, unbeknownst to his family, he began trying to find his long-lost biological father. What he found soon persuaded him that his father was a down-and-out junkie with little interest in his family.

Staley gave up on a reunion with his dad but not on his dream of stardom. Channeling his anger into his music, he developed an intense, scowling persona and a voice that ranged between down-in-the-gutter growls and out-of-the-depths shrieks. Taking his biological father's name, the quiet boy from the Seattle suburbs began the process of becoming Layne Staley the rock star.

In the summer of 1987, Staley met guitarist Jerry Cantrell at a Seattle party. The two hit it off immediately. When Staley found out Cantrell was homeless, he invited him back to his "residence"—a seedy rehearsal studio. The two would live there for the next year. Cantrell's musical vision was as despairing as Staley's and even more prolific. And Staley was the perfect singer to interpret his songs. As Cantrell later said, "I knew that voice was the guy I wanted to be playing with. It sounded like it came out of a 350-pound biker rather than skinny little Layne. I considered his voice to be my voice."[3]

Layne's tormented wail was now supported by a full band, as they recruited bassist Mike Starr and drummer Sean Kinney. Playing a few gigs as Alice N' Chains and Diamond Head, they settled on the final form of their name after signing a deal with Columbia. Along the way Layne ditched the blue satin jumpsuit and glam metal trappings of earlier performances, opting instead for the flannels and blue jeans that were fast becoming the Seattle bands' class uniform.

The Rise of Grunge

By the late 1980s glam metal (also known as hair metal) was foundering in a sea of sappy power ballads. Hair metal was looking as old and tired as the arena rock dinosaurs of a decade earlier. Talent scouts were looking for the new trend, and they found it in Seattle. The music coming out of there had an angrier, harder edge than the boisterous good times debauchery of the hair metal bands. Where they concentrated on speed and guitar pyrotechnics these Seattle bands played Black Sabbath–esque dirgelike jams, music that matched the endless gray skies and grayer economy of pre-tech bubble Seattle.

These dark, dissonant anthems found a willing audience among the children of the Reagan administration. They had seen the economic downturns of the early '80s and early '90s; they had come of age at a time when the rich were getting richer and the poor were forgotten. At a time when the first Bush administration continued Reagan's systematic sabotage of the Great Society, grunge spoke to a new generation of cynical and disaffected youth.

> *Coke (cocaine) has fallen so out of favor, heroin is more of a loser drug, like it fits in more with the grunge thing. Coke was the drug of the '80s, and everyone was all charged up. Heroin is the antithesis to that.*
>
> MARY TRUSCOTT,
> SEATTLE MUSIC EXECUTIVE, 1994[4]

The hair metal bands may have boasted of their fondness for various substances, but these Seattle musicians seemed to take their drugs a bit more seriously. Mother Love Bone, one of the first local bands to receive national attention, had their dreams of glory shattered in March 1990 when frontman Andrew Wood died of a heroin overdose. Wood had checked himself into rehab when they signed their contract so he could prepare for the inevitable nationwide tour but was unable to maintain sobriety.

But other Seattle bands stepped up to the plate, and MTV was ready to promote their sound. In January 1991, Alice in Chains drew attention for their existential bleakness and the creepy imagery of their debut video, "Man in a Box." The Grim Reaper/Christ figure with eyelids sewn shut and factory farming milieu made for a nightmare of angst and desperation, made watchable by the magnetic, charismatic frontman. In its first six months of release, *Facelift* sold forty thousand copies. After MTV put their video into rotation, they sold more than four hundred thousand. Then Nirvana's "Smells Like Teen Spirit" became wildly popular, and it was now official: Seattle grunge had become an American phenomenon.

Reunion, Triumph, and Tragedy

About this time Phil Staley, Layne's father, came back into the picture. As Layne had dreamed, his father had seen him on a magazine and decided to reestablish contact. "He said he'd been clean of drugs for six years," Stacy said bitterly. "So, why in the hell didn't he come back before?"[5] Layne's wariness about his father soon proved justified, as Phil lapsed and began using again. Before long father and son were bonding over injections. Layne made the first of many efforts to get clean, but found his father something less than supportive. "He started visiting me all day to get high and do drugs with me," he explained to an interviewer. "I was trying to kick this habit out of my life and here comes this man asking for money to buy some smack."[6]

By the time Alice in Chains stepped into the studio to work on their second album, 1992's *Dirt,* Layne was nursing a serious heroin habit. As his bandmates struggled with alcohol addiction and the perils of life as rock stars, Layne described his plight in songs like "Sickman," "Junkhead," and "Hate to Feel." It was difficult to miss the references to addiction, betrayal, and the desire for oblivion. While gossip about Staley's addiction swirled, it did nothing to discourage fans from purchasing three million copies of *Dirt.*

Dirt was hailed as an unsparing, cathartic exposure of the tensions within the group and the frontman's struggles with addiction. But brutal as the songs were, the private wars within the band were growing even worse. Bassist Mike Starr left in early 1993 and was replaced by Mike Inez from Ozzy Osbourne's backup band. Meanwhile, Staley enrolled in several rehab programs but failed to stay clean for long. Still, he continued to do his part to ensure the band's success. After breaking his foot before a winter 1992 tour opening for Ozzy, he made every date, performing on crutches or in a wheelchair.

A worldwide tour to support their new CD climaxed with triumphant performances at the summer 1993 Lollapalooza festival. Their grim tableaux of desperation and addiction provided a soundtrack for the new junkie chic. But unlike Lou Reed, Layne Staley was buying into his persona. Although the band was at the top of their game, Layne was growing increasingly unreliable, with frequent absences both at rehearsals and gigs. The demons that made him famous now threatened to destroy him. Although his bandmates were drinking copiously and using other substances, they still remained functional enough to play on the road. Layne made still more half-hearted attempts at rehabilitation but seemed unable to get clean long enough to take advantage of his success.

The April 1994 suicide of Nirvana frontman Kurt Cobain shocked Staley into a brief period of sobriety. Cobain had used heroin for both his stomach pain and his emotional issues. Unable to find a cure or to wean himself off opiates, Cobain shot himself. Shaken, Layne checked himself into yet another rehab and was able to stay clean for a while. He feared becoming another statistic in the growing list of Seattle casualties. But Layne's abstinence was brief and he was soon using again. By the summer of 1994, as the band prepared for a tour opening for Metallica, tensions had come to a head. When Layne arrived at practice high, not long after leaving rehab, drummer Sean Kinney threw down his sticks and vowed never again to play with Staley. The tour (which would have supported their number 1 EP release, *Jar of Flies*) was canceled, and Alice in Chains went on a six-month hiatus.

During their break, Layne continued recording with Mad Season, a supergroup founded after Seattle musicians Mike McCready and John Baker Saunders met in a Minneapolis rehab center. Mad Season allowed Layne to show a softer and more melodic side. The CD *Above* peaked at number 24, while the single "River of Deceit" reached number 2 on the Billboard Mainstream Rock charts and number 9 on the Modern Rock charts. But while Mad Season played a few Seattle gigs, it was never able to give *Above* the kind of touring support required. McCready's commitment to his other band, Pearl Jam, and Staley's increasingly fragile health meant Mad Season was to be a one-off project. In November of 1995 the band released *Alice in Chains*, a CD that debuted at number 1 but that again suffered from the lack of a promotional tour.

To journalists, Staley continued to be defensive about his habit. "Every article I see is dope this, junkie that, whiskey this—that ain't my title. Like 'Hi, I'm Layne, nail biter,' you know?" he told *Rolling Stone*'s Jon Wiederhorn in 1996. But if he would not acknowledge the severity of his problem, neither did he make much effort to hide it. In the same article Wiederhorn noted,

> When [Staley] returned from a trip to the bathroom, his sleeves were unbuttoned, exposing what appear to be red, round puncture marks from the wrist to the knuckles of his left hand. And as anyone who knows anything about IV drugs can tell you, the veins in his hands are used only after all the other veins have been tapped out.[7]

Perhaps the final nail in Layne's coffin was the October 1996 death of former lover Demri Parrott. Like Staley, Parrott had been struggling for years with her heroin habit. When she died of bacterial endocarditis (an infection of the heart valves spread by dirty needles), Layne was inconsolable. From this point forward he seemed resigned to his fate, expressing no interest in anything that might save him.

> *I was in San Francisco at Lollapalooza, and this girl walked up to me and stopped like she'd seen a ghost. And she said, "You're not dead." And I said, "No, you're right. Wow."*
>
> LAYNE STALEY, 1996[8]

Retreating to his Seattle condominium, Staley saw few people save his dealers. His days were spent in a haze of heroin and video games. Occasionally he walked down to the Rainbow, a nearby bar; there he would sit at a small table in the back corner and nod off. His arms were marked with scars and abscesses, and he had lost several teeth and weighed under 100 pounds. He remained in occasional contact with his mother and stepfather but greeted few other visitors.

Staley's fall from grace became a thrilling cautionary tale among a whole new generation of fans. Tales spread that the reclusive singer had AIDS, that he had hepatitis, that he had lost fingers or an entire arm to gangrene related to his incessant IV abuse. His management continued to deny reports of Staley's addiction, trying their best to play him as a suffering penitent trying to stay clean. Meanwhile, band members stopped coming around and began work on other musical projects. When they showed up at Layne's house he rarely answered the door anyway.

In early 2002 Layne spoke briefly to an Argentine journalist who had interviewed his family members for an upcoming biography. In an interview veering from hostile to confessional, he told her,

> I'm not using drugs to get high like many people think. I know I made a big mistake when I started using this shit. It's a very difficult thing to explain. My liver is not functioning and I'm throwing up all the time and shitting my pants. The pain is more than you can handle. It's the worst pain in the world. Dope sick hurts the entire body.
>
> I know I'm near death. I did crack and heroin for years. I never wanted to end my life this way. I know I have no chance. It's too late.[9]

On April 19, 2002, Seattle police made a routine "welfare call" to Staley's apartment after his mother called 911, claiming she had been unable to contact him for two weeks. The police forcibly entered and found the singer's body on the couch "in an advanced state of decomposition . . . the skin had a darkened, leathery appearance." Staley "was holding what appeared to be a loaded syringe in his right hand" and "had been sitting on numerous other syringes as well."[10] A toxicology report revealed acute intoxication from a speedball, the heroin-cocaine cocktail that killed (among others) John Belushi, Chris Farley, and River Phoenix.

25

ROBERT EARL
"DJ SCREW" DAVIS

*The Screw sound is when I mix tapes with songs that
people can relax to. . . . I make my tapes so everyone can
feel them. Some people may think that I make my tapes for
fryheads or something. My tapes are for everybody. . . . The
Screw sound is me hollering at my partners, shouting out
their neighborhoods and shit like that.*

ROBERT EARL "DJ SCREW" DAVIS, 1995[1]

When Robert Earl Davis Sr. first brought his teenage son to Houston, he
worried the boy might fall in with a rough crowd. Their gritty working-
class neighborhood near Hobby Airport was nothing like the small town
where young Robert Earl Jr. had grown up. As a long-haul trucker, the
elder Davis feared that he wouldn't be able to keep a close enough eye on
his son.

But as young Robert settled in to his new home, Davis Sr. relaxed.
When he left for work in the morning, Robert Earl was in his room
surrounded by his enormous record collection. When he returned at 4
a.m., his son was still listening to music in his room. Later Davis père
found that his son was staying out of trouble at school by avoiding it
altogether; by eighth grade he was rarely attending classes. "When he

dropped out in the eighth grade, I was scared," his father admitted. "If he didn't make it in music, where would he go? But he was blessed, and he made it."[2]

At seventeen young Robert Earl got his first DJ gig at the south side's Almeda skating rink. Soon he was working other clubs, where he mastered the fine art of turntablism. Instead of just playing back LPs for the crowd, today's turntablists use their records as the building blocks for their own art. Robert Earl learned how to scratch, repeat phrases, mix together beats from different records, and string songs together in a seamless whole. Playing to audiences taught him the fine art of improvisation; it allowed him to watch the dancers to see what worked. When he went home he continued his studies, listening obsessively to New York DJs and West Coast gangsta rappers like Ice Cube and Compton's Most Wanted.

Then, in 1989, or so the legend goes, the lucky accident happened. Robert Earl and some friends were making mixtapes while drinking and smoking some of the Mexican cannabis found throughout Texas. Robert Earl accidentally hit the turntable's pitch button, distorting the vocals and slowing down the beats. Everyone liked the resulting sound, and so Robert Earl began offering his "screwed down" mixes to an enthusiastic audience. A new career was born for DJ Screw*— and a new sound was born for Houston. Over his new "screwed and chopped" sounds Davis and his local friends would tell stories of life on Houston's south side. They offered shoutouts to area neighborhoods and celebrations of life on the Third Coast, where the good times included a popular local beverage known as "lean," "barre," or "purple drank."

---

*There are differing etymologies for DJ Screw's nom de turntable. One faction claims that he marked LPs he didn't like by scratching them with a screw; another swears it was due to his fondness for "screwing with the music."

Houston: City of Syrup

You people here drink cough syrup, you smoke weed, and you listen to slow music. You are crazy.

HOUSTON RAPPER MIKE D'S
OUT-OF-TOWN FRIENDS, 2001[3]

To make purple drank, one starts with a cup of Sprite, 7UP, or juice. To this is added prescription cough syrup, which is sold on the black market in baby food jars for as much as $20 an ounce. A fine evening can be had by "chunking up a deuce," or throwing two ounces of syrup and some Jolly Ranchers into your soda. Two ounces of syrup contain 120 milligrams of codeine, about the same amount found in two Tylenol 4s. But the syrup also contains 75 milligrams of promethazine, a powerfully sedating antihistamine. (A typical adult dose for nighttime, presurgical, or obstetrical sedation is 25–50 milligrams.)[4]

The promethazine also interferes with the metabolization of codeine, causing a larger percentage of the codeine (methylmorphine) to be demethylated by the body and converted into morphine. Like the "fours and doors" craze that plagued the East Coast in the 1980s, the drugs combine to produce a relaxed, warm high (which, as an added bonus, is largely free of opiate itching). Little known outside Houston and the surrounding areas, purple drank's active ingredient was easily available. Doctors hesitant to provide painkillers had no hesitation about prescribing codeine cough syrup, or even the more powerful Tussionex, a hydrocodone concoction used to make "mad yellow." And DJ Screw's slowed-down music was the perfect soundtrack to a drank-fueled evening.

Creating his bass-heavy mixes with his friends, he slowed down the final product before recording it onto a master cassette. Duplicate copies of this master, with names like *Tales from Tha 4th Ward* and *Let's Call Up on Drank,* were then sold to friends and fans. Before long the neighborhood phenomenon was known throughout Houston. Lines formed outside his door. On several occasions the police kicked in his door in search of drugs, unable to believe that Screw was attracting this kind of attention just for his music. Davis moved to another neighborhood and later opened Screwed Up Records and Tapes to distribute his mixes.

An appearance on a Screw mixtape could catapult a rapper to fame. MCs like Paul Wall, Big Moe, Lil Keke, Fat Pat, and Z-Ro became Houston celebrities after contributing to Screw projects. To DJ Screw's sluggish, hypnotic beats they sang the praises of Houston living, where they spent evenings "gripping the grain" (wood-grain steering wheels) driving down Houston freeways in their candy-painted vehicles. They sang about grills, the gold tooth jewelry popular among Houston's working-class black population. And they sang, and sang, and sang, about the pleasures of codeine. Screw made no secret of his fondness for the beverage, with mixtapes named *Codeine Fiend, Sippin Codeine,* and *Syrup Sippers,* among others.

Purple drank, and DJ Screw, became emblems of Houston hip-hop realness. Many local acts traced their roots to Davis. The Botany Boyz, members of Screw's Screwed Up Click (SUC), spoke of evenings spent "Smokin' N Lean' N," while fellow SUCer Fat Pat complained he had "Too Much Lean in My Cup." Kenneth "Big Moe" Moore, a gentle giant with a soulful delivery, got his start freestyling on Screwtapes. In 2000 he released *City of Syrup.* This concept CD about the codeine culture featured "Barre Baby," wherein Moe crooned, "I got the whole world sippin drank with me."

The Rise of the Screwed Up Click

He had guys calling him from prison. He would send them money. I'd say something to him and he'd say, "Mom, they just want to talk." He never said no to nobody.

IDA MAE DEARY, A.K.A. "MAMA SCREW,"
DAVIS'S MOTHER, 2001[5]

DJ Screw and the Screwed Up Click were hometown heroes, little known outside of Houston. But their local fans ensured the DJ Screw industry was a profitable one. In 2000 local fans purchased more than one million albums by Houston rap artists, and many of those were by members of the SUC (who also called themselves "Soldiers United for Cash"). *Ghetto Dreams,* released after Fat Pat's 1998 murder, sold more than twenty thousand copies during its first week in stores. Davis was now making more than $3,000 a week selling mixtapes. Combined with DJ gigs and other projects, this meant the country kid from Smithville, Texas, had achieved more financial success than he could ever have thought possible.

But rather than rest on his laurels, Davis increased his already formidable labors. At night he would spin for adoring crowds, earning as much as $1,500 a gig. After coming home, he locked himself in his studio to mix new tapes and produce new artists. His work ethic was reflected in mixtape titles like *You Don't Work You Don't Eat* and *All Work and No Play.* Davis would go for days on little or no sleep, fueled on cigarettes, drank, and restaurant take-out. Soon the once-slender Davis weighed well over 200 pounds. From 1998 on he was hospitalized several times with seizures and heart murmurs.

His friends and family urged him to take some time off, but he was single-minded in his efforts. "I'm married to my turntables," he once proclaimed, "and my records are my children."[6] Andrew "DJ Chill" Hatton, his first partner, said of Davis, "He was like a little ant, always working himself to death behind the turntables."[7] But if he was a driven musician, he was neither a ruthless nor an arrogant businessman. Davis was known for his generosity and his approachable demeanor. He was generally happy to chat with fans and fellow musicians alike. Screw had little interest in the limelight or stardom; he was content to make a living playing his music.

As the twentieth century ended, the "chopped and screwed" style was expanding beyond the city limits. Houston performers played to packed houses in Little Rock and New Orleans. In June 2000 Memphis rappers Three 6 Mafia had the biggest hit of their career with "Sippin on Some Syrup." Unfortunately, Davis would not survive to see his sound become a national phenomenon. On November 16, 2000, DJ Screw was found dead in his studio. Toxicology reports revealed codeine, alcohol, and marijuana in his system.

The Death of DJ Screw

Somebody gets shot, they don't say this father, this good man got shot. They're going to say a rapper got shot. So in terms of them trying to put a negative spin on it, I expected that. Because they don't understand the music, they don't understand the culture, they don't understand what we're doing.

DERRICK "D WRECK" DIXON,
WRECKSHOP RECORDS OWNER, 2008[8]

There is no question that Davis was a regular user of drank. According to one old friend, he had sipped syrup every day for the past decade.[9] Both codeine and promethazine tend to cause pulmonary edema (swelling and fluid in the lungs). In high doses, promethazine is also known to cause seizures. Davis reportedly had several seizures before his death. But while the syrup certainly did not help Davis's health, it was hardly the only factor contributing to his heart failure. A punishing workload combined with cigarette smoking and fatty fried foods also played a part in his demise.

But the circumstances of Davis's death fit all too neatly into a well-worn tale: the musician done in by drug abuse. Media outlets used his obituary as a cautionary tale about the powerful new opiate that was sweeping the region. Police and DEA agents arrested a few doctors for over-prescribing scheduled drugs, and a few pharmacies stopped carrying syrup after noting an increase in "thuggish" (read: black) customers buying codeine. Their efforts had only limited success. Because codeine syrup is available without a prescription in neighboring Mexico, syrup-sippers traveled south of the border or sent their friends on a syrup-buying vacation.

Houston's favorite beverage was now in the cup of many elsewhere. In 2006 Terrence Kiel, safety for the San Diego Chargers, pleaded guilty to felony drug charges resulting from an attempt to ship two cases of codeine-based cough syrup to a friend. While the felony charges were later dropped after he completed community service, Kiel was dropped from the team and later died in an alcohol-fueled car accident. New Orleans rapper Dwayne Michael "Lil Wayne" Carter frequently sings of his fondness for syrup. On his 2008 Grammy-winning *Tha Carter III* he claims he is "used to promethazine, in two cups, I'm screwed up," while on the 2007 video for Playaz Circle's "Duffle Bag Boy," he holds a Styrofoam drank cup with the words "RIP DJ Screw" written on it.

Davis had been accused of fueling a rising tide of codeine abuse. Studies in 2003 and 2004 by the University of Texas School of Public Health found that 25% of at-risk Houston teenagers had used cough syrup, with 10% claiming they had used the drug within thirty days of being questioned.[10] This is another common narrative seen when dealing with hip-hop. Hip-hop chronicles urban life, sometimes accurately and sometimes in broadly drawn cartoonish strokes. But instead of being treated as an exposé of preexisting conditions, it is instead stigmatized for causing them. Instead of listening to the message, people find it easier to blame the messenger. Hip-hop may have promoted purple drank, but it did not create it. OxyContin abuse became a national emergency without a backing soundtrack.

If the drank phenomenon was unstoppable, so was DJ Screw. While it is America's fourth-largest city, Houston has always been seen as a bit of a cultural wasteland. Not only is it less exciting than Philadelphia, the fifth largest, it doesn't even measure up to smaller Texas cities like Dallas and Austin. Today Houston rappers and musicians can be found in record stores around the country. Like Seattle grunge or New Orleans zydeco, Houston hip-hop has become a recognizable symbol of the city—and SUC alumni are now famous not just in Texas but around the United States.

But while codeine-sipping remains fashionable, it has come under growing scrutiny after still more fatalities. In 2002 Big Moe's *Purple World* reached number 3 on Billboard's R&B/Hip-Hop charts, thanks largely to its single "Purple Stuff" and the *Willy Wonka*–inspired promotional video. In October 2007 he died of a heart attack at age thirty-three. While many linked Moe's death to codeine, evidence suggested his weight of more than 350 pounds was more to blame. Then, in December 2007 Chad "Pimp C" Butler of legendary Texas rap group UGK (Underground Kings) was found dead in his hotel room. The LA coroner attributed his death to a codeine and promethazine overdose exacerbated by a preexisting sleep apnea condition.

> *We all know that in Houston, Texas, we have a problem now with the cough syrup epidemic. And while it wasn't solely the cause of his death, we have to be very real about the consequences to some of these things. . . . To anyone out there thinking about sipping syrup or currently abusing syrup, you may want to take a very good look at yourself, a long look at yourself.*
>
> BERNARD "BUN B" FREEDMAN,
> PIMP C'S PARTNER IN UGK, 2007[11]

PART FOUR

TECHNIQUES AND CONUNDRUMS

Now that you have read about poppies and their magical chemicals, you may want to experience them for yourself. You may be unable to get medical help for your chronic pain condition; you may seek dreams and visions; you may just want to get high. Poppy does not care why you come to her. She offers her gifts and her bargain to all who ask.

Presumably you know the laws of your jurisdiction. You are also aware that opiates are addictive and that an overdose can be fatal. You have been apprised of some of the worst side effects and have heard about the suffering opiates can cause. If you choose to take this risk, you presumably do so as an informed and responsible adult. I cannot be held responsible for how you use this substance.

Perhaps you started *before* you were responsible or an adult. Now you're trying to figure out how to manage your habit. Alternately, you have no habit at all. You are confident that you will never become one of the statistics; after all, you're now an experienced user. You're probably right. But consider the consequences if you are wrong.

Should you insist on using illicit opiates, there are safer ways of ingesting them. They will minimize your risk for some of the worst damage. I have also included tips for those who want to break their habits. Kicking will suck; you'll have to decide if staying addicted sucks worse. And if you don't already have a habit, I've offered some pointers on how to avoid full-blown addiction.

But these are no guarantees that you will not wind up a casualty. You might not become a homeless junkie spare-changing for your next fix. But you may have to plan your schedule around opening time at the local methadone clinic. You might be forced to postpone vacations because you couldn't guarantee a supply of your medicine. Or you might become a convicted felon. If you wish to claim her as an ally, you need to understand her dangers. Poppy has captured many who swore they could avoid her snares.

26

CULTIVATION

Human beings have been growing poppies for at least 7,500 years. Even today they are cultivated and harvested by people using hand tools and rudimentary technology. Without the benefit of agricultural corporations, *P. somniferum* has spread far beyond its original home in southeastern Europe. Poppy has relocated many times during her history. The great Egyptian and Persian opium fields are but a memory, and several millennia have passed since the Italian peninsula has seen widespread poppy cultivation. But each field eradicated has only led to new fields sown elsewhere as Poppy's siren song draws in new devotees.

The Golden Triangle—a mountainous area overlapping the borders of Myanmar (Burma), Laos, Vietnam, and Thailand—has long been a hotbed of poppy cultivation. During the Vietnam conflict American forces made deals with opium-cultivating warlords, offering them arms and tacit support in exchange for their assistance in dealing with Communist rebels. In return they provided American and European junkies with an ample supply of heroin. The infrastructure the war created continues to produce opium today. In the late 1980s Burmese warlord Khun Sa controlled some three hundred thousand acres of poppy fields and twenty heroin factories, producing an estimated annual revenue of $1.5 billion, and in Rangoon banks offered (and still offer) money laundering services for a 40% fee. In 1990 the U.S. Embassy in Burma stated, "exports of opium appear to be worth as much as all legal exports."[1]

Today, although much of Asia's heroin and opium come from the Golden Triangle, Afghanistan has surpassed it as the major heroin supplier to Europe and the eastern United States. An estimated 95% of the world's heroin is produced from opium grown in this remote and mountainous country. At first the devoutly Islamic Taliban forces declared a moratorium on poppy cultivation in regions under their control and enforced it by killing growers. But as the war against American forces ground on, they discovered they could make more money (and accumulate more arms) by taxing poppy fields. Today many regions under Taliban control have a thriving industry in *P. somniferum* and its derivatives.

International forces have attempted to limit Afghanistan's poppy production by various means. Efforts to encourage alternate crops have not been particularly successful. As Arghandi Gul, a farmer and village elder living in the poppy-producing Nagahar province, complains, "[In 2007] they told us they would provide an alternative livelihood if we agreed to eradicating the poppy. So people happily agreed. In return for this, we got 400 bags of fertilizer for 4,000 homes. This year, we got sixty 20 kg bags of flour for our village. That was their 'alternative livelihood'!"[2] Water shortages and a long-standing drought have not helped the cause. While wheat and other crops require irrigation to grow in Afghanistan, poppies can be sown with little preparation. And every burned poppy field means more farmers unable to support their families—and likely to turn to the Taliban for aid.

But while Afghanistan continues to be the world's major heroin producer, it has some competition on the other side of the globe. In 1983 poppy plantations were first observed in Colombia, and in 1988 two laboratories for processing heroin and morphine were discovered, one in Bogotá and the other in Barranquilla. By 1991 Colombia's Anti-Narcotics Police noted a startling increase in the number of poppy plantations in the main Colombian mountain ranges.[3] Growers capitalizing on America's opiate craving filled the western United States with crudely cooked but powerful "black tar heroin."

The Colombian government, with U.S. encouragement, has engaged in a campaign of defoliation against the poppy and coca plantations. The main ingredient used in these efforts, glyphosate (sold in the United States as Roundup), has been shown to be hazardous to animals, humans, and the environment. It was designed to be applied manually in small doses, not aerially by the hundreds of gallons. Doctors in sprayed regions have reported a drastic increase in health complaints, mainly respiratory, skin, and gastrointestinal problems, particularly in children. These health problems are compounded by malnutrition. In many cases legal crops have been destroyed and livestock (particularly chicken and fish) killed by the spraying. Aerial eradication also threatens aquatic life in Amazon waterways and encourages destruction of the rain forest. Each acre sprayed leads growers to more remote areas.

A study by the conservative RAND Corporation in Washington found that crop eradication was the least effective way to lower drug use in the United States and estimated that drug treatment was actually twenty-three times more cost effective.[4] But despite this evidence, chemical warfare against poppy and coca growers continues with United States funding and support.

Growing Your Own

While commercial production of opium poppies requires a fairly large patch of isolated land, it is possible to grow small quantities of *P. somniferum* in your garden. Indeed, many people do; opium poppy seeds are easily available and widely grown. By cultivating Poppy, you may be able to make her acquaintance without running the risks of getting to know her through consumption. If you are so inclined, you may even be able to experience opium, something that is uncommon in most parts of the world. Thanks to law enforcement, most opium is today converted into more potent heroin, which is easier to smuggle and transport.

If you live in a region that is classified as USDA Zone 7 or above (in other words, if your climate is similar to or warmer than New York City;

St. Louis, Missouri; or Tulsa, Oklahoma), you can scatter poppy seeds on the ground in the fall, even in the winter if your region's climate is particularly mild. If you live in a cooler region, you should scatter them in the earliest part of spring, after the last frost. They will require a lot of sunlight—at least six hours a day—so make sure you plant them in well-lit ground. It is also important that you plant them in their final home from the start. Because they have long taproots, poppies do not transplant well.

But once those conditions are met, you should have little problem growing poppies. While they need a well-drained soil, they will grow in heavy clay, medium loam, or light sandy dirt. They grow like wild-flowers (which they are) and are easy to maintain. They can tolerate heat and dry conditions (although they can be sensitive to overwater-ing), and their bitter foliage is rarely targeted by deer or other her-bivores that might invade your flowerbed. Indeed, you will probably have to thin your crop when your poppies grow into seedlings. The adult plants will need to be at least four and preferably as much as ten inches apart.

Within sixty days after sprouting, the plant will grow from one to two feet in height, with one primary, long, smooth stem. The leafless upper portion of this stem is called the peduncle. One or more second-ary stems, called tillers, may grow from the main stem of the plant. The main stem of a fully matured *P. somniferum* plant can range between two and five feet in height.

As the plant grows, the main stem and each tiller will terminate in a flower bud. The peduncle portion of the stem elongates, forming a distinctive hook that causes the bud to be turned upside down. As the flower develops, the peduncle straightens and the buds point upward. A day or two later the two outer segments of the bud, called sepals, fall away, exposing the four petals (which may be single or double and may be white, pink, reddish purple, crimson red, or variegated).

The petals last two to eight days and then drop to reveal a small, round, green fruit, which continues to develop. This pod produces the cherished opium alkaloids. The skin of the poppy pod encloses the wall of the pod ovary. The ovary wall consists of an outer, middle, and inner layer; the cells of the middle layer secrete more than 95% of the opium latex.

Once the poppies are blooming, the flowers will last two to eight days before the petals drop off, leaving behind a poppy pod capsule. Those wishing to harvest opium will take a small knife and score the capsule with three or four shallow cuts. The next day the harvester will scrape off the extruded opium latex. This is a labor-intensive and delicate process. If the capsule is cut too deeply, the latex will drip into the pod and be lost; too shallow, and little or no opium will be produced. Yields of raw opium vary according to the size of the pod and the efficiency of the farmer. The average weight of raw opium collected per pod is 80 milligrams, and a good crop will produce 10 to 50 kilograms per hectare (2.47 acres) planted.

Talking to Your Plants

When a spirit speaks to you, the voice comes from outside your physical and spiritual boundaries to communicate with your awareness and soul matrix on various levels; when the physical herb speaks to you, it speaks from inside your body to communicate with your cells and organs. Learning to listen with subtle senses and with your physical body are important skills in this path; they warn of danger and gauge the intensity of experience.

SPIRIT-WORKER AND PLANT SHAMAN
SILENCE MAESTAS, 2009[5]

You may feel a bit self-conscious talking with your flowers. Those feelings will go away once they start answering you back. Shamans have long known that sentience is not reserved to humanity, or even to the animal kingdom. Among plant spirits, Poppy is more chatty than most, and you should have little difficulty opening up lines of communication with her.

As with any sort of communication, listening is as important as talking. Sit quietly with your Poppies and let them talk to you. Don't try to engage in creative visualization, guided meditation, or anything that involves you taking control of the interactions. Instead aim for a zen awareness of the Poppies; pay keen attention to the way they move in the breeze, the way their petals and leaves change color as shadows pass over them, the changes they go through between sunrise and nightfall. You will find many messages there, just waiting for you to notice them.

You may want to avoid ingesting Poppy, but you can still seek her aid in magical work. A pillow made with poppy petals can become a powerful tool for dream work. You may also find it useful to place poppy flowers by your nightstand or over your bed. (Author Christopher Penczak uses this approach when working with Datura, a powerful deliriant ingested only by the very brave or very foolish.)[6] This may be as much work as you need to do with Poppy—and when dealing with this particular spirit, caution and moderation is well advised. Even if you wish to experiment further with Poppy, you may wish to approach her first in this fashion. Getting to know her beforehand may help you to choose wisely when (not if) she tries to seduce you.

Poppy is a powerful spirit, but she is also a demanding one. You may find yourself devoting ever more time to your garden and your conversations. Learning to set boundaries now will serve you well if you wish to go further in your work. Alternately, it may convince you that she is too high-maintenance for your tastes. That is also a wise decision; many who have become ensnared by Poppy wish they had made that choice.

Legal Issues

Depending on your jurisdiction, the cultivation of *P. somniferum* in a personal garden may or may not be legal. Whatever the status, these rules often go unenforced. Opium poppies are a popular garden plant, cherished for their hardiness and their spectacular blooms. But despite this tolerance, harvesting controlled substances from your flowers is unquestionably illegal. If your local police department hears that you are harvesting opium, you are likely to receive a visit from unsmiling people bearing badges. (And keep in mind that sliced pods are prima facie evidence that you were growing your poppies for illicit purposes.)

It is highly unlikely that you will be able to grow enough poppies to yield any significant quantity of opium. Based on the yields previously stated, a ten-meter-square patch of poppies would produce 10 to 50 grams—and because a smoker can easily consume several grams in one session, that's not so much as you might think. It may, however, be enough to get you slapped with some very serious felony charges, especially if the law in your state makes no distinction between opium and heroin.

As is often the case when dealing with Poppy, discretion is in order. Those sweet old ladies who appreciate your lovely flowers need not know they are oohing and aahing over *Papaver somniferum.* You can even find safety in gardening aesthetics. While poppies are lovely, they only bloom for a few days. Their flowers are also very delicate, liable to damage from wind or even heavy rain. Hence, many gardeners plant them in a bed containing other annuals, so that there is an ever-changing show of blossoms to entertain the eye and divert the attention of the curious.

27

POPPY TEA

In the swampy fen country of Cambridgeshire and Lincolnshire, doughty locals have long warded off ague, rheumatism, and winter coughs with *P. somniferum* tea. For variety they sometimes boil fresh poppy heads in beer.[1] At Middle Eastern funerals, mourners are sometimes offered glasses of iced poppy tea as an antidote to their sorrow, and in Afghanistan cranky children are soothed with a beverage of black tea and poppy heads.[2] Before them the ancient Greeks drank *mekonion* (see chapter 2), a potent poppy-head tea that was used by physicians as a mild painkiller and cough suppressant. Poppy tea has a long history—and it certainly isn't because of the notoriously foul taste!

The DEA is aware that many of the poppy pods on the market today are not being sold to flower arrangers. There have been occasional letters to flower wholesalers and seed companies.[3] In March 1996, Jim Hogshire, editor of *Pills-a-Go-Go* and author of *Opium for the Masses,* was charged with cultivation and possession of a Class Two felony drug after a King County (Washington) SWAT team raided his home and found dried poppy pods. The charge was ultimately dismissed. Had he been found guilty, he could have faced as much as ten years in prison. In 2003 an eBay poppy pod seller, Krsna Lev-Twombley, was arrested by the DEA after selling pods to an undercover officer. Lev-Twombly eventually pled guilty to one count of felony distribution of poppy straw and served time in a California federal prison.

Still, pods remain widely available, with a few caveats. Dried poppies are perfectly legal if you put them in a vase. Turn them into poppy straw and put them into a tea and you have a Schedule II substance on your hands. Few sellers will answer questions about the morphine content of their pods, offer you tea recipes, or in any way acknowledge that you may be abusing them. That being said, they will happily provide you with enough poppy heads to make fifty wreaths, and even ship them overnight if your crafting addiction demands immediate attention.

An opiate-naive person who chokes down enough tea to "catch a nod" can get lucid dreams that will rival anything you'll get from psychedelics. When used occasionally in a religious context, there is little danger of physical addiction and a lesser (but still very real) risk of becoming psychologically dependent on that warm glow of pleasure. You must decide if that risk is worth taking before incorporating poppies into your spiritual toolkit.

Poppy Tea Brewing

A quick online search will reveal a number of recipes for poppy pod tea and poppy seed tea (commonly known by the acronyms PPT and PST). Both pods and seeds can be used to make tea, but the treatment differs. Poppy pods contain the various active alkaloids within their cells and must be subjected to an *extraction*. Poppy seeds have a coating of alkaloids on their surface and must be *washed*.

To make seed tea, a quantity of seeds (300–1,000 grams, approximately 12–32 ounces) is placed in a bottle. Cool or room temperature water is added and the seeds are shaken for one to three minutes. At the end of that time, the seeds are strained out and the alkaloid-filled tea is consumed. The end result is unpredictable. If the seeds are "dirty" or covered with a large amount of morphine and codeine, the brew will be dark, bitter, and euphoric. If they were prewashed, like most of the seeds sold in the spice aisle of grocery stores, the tea may be useless.

And if they soaked too long, the water will draw out a large quantity of poppy seed oils, resulting in a nauseating, soapy glop.

Pod tea is made by grinding the dried pods using a coffee or a spice grinder. It is important they be powdered as finely as possible to provide a greater surface area for the extraction. The ground pods are then placed in hot water and simmered (not boiled) for ten to thirty minutes. Properly prepared, 10 to 15 grams of dried pod material will produce a strongly analgesic and trance-inducing cup of tea. Those who already have an opiate tolerance may need to take more; those who are slender or small may need to take a bit less. The drink also produces the warm prickly itches of morphine intoxication and the long-lasting glow of pleasure that characterizes the opium mix of alkaloids.

To this basic recipe tea-makers add their own special touches. Some add lemon or cranberry juice to their simmering water, believing that more acidic water results in better morphine extraction. Others use calcium carbonate (antiheartburn tablets) to make the morphine more water-soluble and bioavailable. Some swear by extractions using cool water and say boiling destroys morphine, while others state you can boil your tea with no ill effects. Arguments about the best way to make tea can be as heated as any amateur brewer's forum—especially when people are waiting for an overdue pod delivery.

Poppy Tea, Overdose, and Addiction

Estimates on the amounts of morphine and codeine in a glass of poppy tea vary, but anecdotal evidence suggests that the punch they pack is greater than can be accounted for with any single specific alkaloid. Drinkers have reported signs of miosis (pinpoint pupils) and feelings of opiate intoxication for eight to twelve hours or longer after taking a dose. Morphine has a low oral bioavailability (approximately 75% is metabolized in the "first pass" through the liver before ever reaching the body) and a short half-life (two to three hours). The DEA's analysis of Lev-Twombley's pods found a typical pod contained 1.72 milligrams of morphine.[4] This would mean a tea made with five of his pods would have less than 10 milligrams of morphine, a barely psychoactive dosage.

Although some have given bigger estimates of poppy straw's morphine content (as high as 1% or higher), evidence suggests the lower rather than the higher counts may be correct. To date there are few medical reports of overdose as a result of drinking tea. One website, poppyseedtea.com, provides the medical files for a seventeen-year-old who died after drinking 2 liters of poppy seed tea. According to toxicology reports, the brew he consumed had 259 micrograms of morphine per milliliter, or 500 milligrams—well over a toxic dose for someone who did not already have a serious opiate tolerance.[5]

In March 2009 Alexander McGuillan, a twenty-year-old college student in Boulder, Colorado, died of a morphine overdose after consuming poppy tea and Xanax. In July another Boulder student, nineteen-year-old Jeffrey Joseph Bohan, was found dead after drinking poppy tea with his brother. In the wake of the bad publicity, eBay banned the sale of poppy pods, because both had bought their supplies on the popular auction site. (As of 2010, pods and bulk quantities of poppy seeds are still available on many other online sites.)

Getting even a nonlethal quantity of poppy tea down requires a cast-iron stomach. The taste is unbelievably grassy, dirty, and bitter, and no amount of sugar or instant lemonade can kill that foul flavor. And if you get it down, there is no guarantee it will stay there. Many tea drinkers report nausea after dosing, and vomiting is not uncommon. But while it may be difficult (although not impossible) to overdose on poppy tea, it is not at all hard to become dependent on it.

> *Poppy tea is the fucking devil.*
> *I started experimenting with poppy pods recently, not much,*
> *cup of tea here and there, pretty soon once a day, then 3–4*
> *times a day, now I'm trying to get off these fuckers and its*

hell, I've had withdrawals from heroin that weren't like
this . . .

NOCTURNAL, MARCH 20, 2008,

FROM BLUELIGHT "OTHER DRUGS" FORUM[6]

Because of its long half-life, the various alkaloids build up in your system. Using the same dose every day for three days could leave you seriously high by your third day. But this also means that taking a few days off between doses is no guarantee that you will not develop a habit. It also results in withdrawal from poppy tea being more drawn-out than with shorter-acting opioids that are more quickly metabolized. Some have compared poppy tea withdrawal to methadone: a lengthy period of illness followed by a lengthier period of severe depression.

If you are using pods recreationally, you should avoid using them more often than bimonthly and preferably less frequently. If you are taking these for a chronic pain condition, you need to concentrate on analgesia rather than euphoria. The idea is to keep your intake as low as possible while getting the desired amount of relief. Analgesic and other therapeutic properties can be enjoyed well before the Warm Fuzzy Blanket of Unconditional Love descends. Once you have tasted the tea, you will be happy to drink as little as possible . . . and you can soon build a tolerance requiring you to drink pitchers of the stuff!

Pods and poppy seeds are relatively inexpensive and widely available. When one is first using them this is a bonus. Later, it can make it very difficult to get clean during periods of tea-sickness. When you're feeling ill and know your local spice store or favored online vendor can make you better, it's hard to resist. It's nothing like using heroin—you can buy your drug of choice retail, right? So it can't be that bad. Besides, you aren't using that much. (And those sniffles are probably just a summer cold or a winter flu, there's no reason to panic. You can't really get dope sick on this stuff, it's just seeds and dried flowers, it can't be that bad, you can't be an addict . . .)

If you find yourself with a poppy tea habit, you should read chapter 33 for some pointers on getting off and staying off opiates. Don't fool yourself into thinking you don't have a "real" addiction. You do. If you are unable or unwilling to address the issue at present, here are some things to watch out for while feeding the monkey on your back.

Living on Poppy Tea

Regular users get accustomed to being irregular; poppy tea is notorious for causing constipation. Perhaps you snigger now. When you are dealing with hemorrhoids, rectal prolapses, and exquisitely painful experiences that many pod users call "shitting a pineapple," you may not be so amused. Gastric distress is also common, and you may find yourself unable to eat for hours after taking tea. When you can, a high-fiber diet with lots of liquid will help keep your bathroom from becoming a torture chamber. Also avoid sugary junk food. Anecdotal evidence suggests there is something to the legend of the opiate user's "sweet tooth."

Some longtime opiate addicts have used pod tea as "homemade methadone." By dosing with the tea they were able to wean themselves off oxycodone, IV heroin, or other considerably riskier means of ingestion. Most people with a serious opiate tolerance require excessive amounts of tea to produce euphoria comparable to their drug of choice. Some use it for maintenance between bouts of heavier use. Given the shortage of effective drug choices, it may be their best available treatment for their condition.

Many with irritable bowel syndrome and other intestinal conditions have said small doses of poppy tea kill two birds with one stone: the combined analgesic and antidiarrheal effects are particularly suited to their needs. But care must be taken. If the pods were sprayed with pesticides or the seeds have grown moldy, your daily dose could exacerbate your condition. The cure can easily go too far in the opposite direction; the line between alleviating diarrhea and stopping you up altogether is fine, and the grass really isn't greener on the other side.

Poppy tea occasionally causes intense itching, thanks to the histaminic release that is familiar to many junkies. Many take antihistamines before indulging in the beverage. Others come to enjoy the tingling sensation, associating it with the "come-up" of the alkaloid high. However you feel, be sure to keep an eye on your skin. Poppy tea doesn't produce the obsessive "face-picking" of methamphetamine or other stimulants— but when you're warm, happy, and itchy you might not feel those cuts and scratches until you awaken from your reverie. And if you start having difficulty breathing or enormous hives, get to a hospital fast. An allergic reaction can kill just as quickly as an overdose.

Mixing alcohol and opiates can lead to dangerously shallow breathing and increased sedation. Those two or three beers you used to throw back with your buddies after work may now put you on the floor. (This is true even if you haven't had any tea for a couple days. Remember that long half-life?) Be especially careful about using other opiates on top of your regular dose of tea. They might interact unpredictably and hit you harder than you were expecting.

After reading about Kompot (chapter 11), you may be tempted to try making your own homemade heroin with poppy pods. Unless you have a very large supply (as in several bales of the stuff), combined with access to at least one scheduled chemical, you are not likely to succeed. And if you are entertaining the notion of injecting poppy pod tea, you can expect anaphylactic shock and pulmonary edema (fluid in the lungs), leading to death or serious injury, probably combined with an abscess at the point of injection. Note that the words "great rush" do not appear in that description.

You might be tempted to make laudanum by using vodka or grain alcohol to extract the morphine from your pods. It won't work. Laudanum was a suspension of opium in wine or distilled spirits. It did not dissolve into the alcohol, but was suspended in it—it was more like mayonnaise or Hollandaise sauce than an opium-flavored drink. You will get a much better alkaloid extraction from water than any adult beverage. And while an alcohol extraction will not have a higher percentage of morphine, it will contain more fats and other noxious substances that might not leach out in water.

Ultimately, poppy tea requires discretion. Keep your intake to the bare minimum required for your purposes. The more you use, the more likely you are to have unpleasant side effects. Your tolerance for increasing doses will grow rapidly with regular usage. This does not mean that your euphoria will get higher; quite the opposite, in fact. If you start using regularly, the dose that once made you feel good might not even make you feel well.

28

PILLS, TABLETS, AND CAPSULES

Among the 875 prescriptions and 700 drugs recorded in the Ebers Papyrus, a 4.5-meter scroll that originated in Egypt circa 1500 BCE, is a remedy for roundworm. Salt and *silphium* (a now-extinct species of giant fennel) were mixed with honey, made into balls, and swallowed. Another prescription, for "dejection," involves finely ground malachite put into bread dough, made into pills, and gulped down with sweet beer.[1] This, according to Egyptian mythology, was part of the wisdom handed down by Thoth, who was known by the praise name Ph-ar-imki (Warrant of Security)—a word that would come down to us as "pharmacy."

From Egypt this form of dosing came to Greece, where physicians provided chunks of medicine called *katapotia* (something to be swallowed). Centuries later the Roman scholar Pliny (23–79 CE) coined the word *pilula* (literally "little ball"). The British Museum contains a Roman-era pill-making stone. The pharmacist pressed the substance into the grooves to form long, snaky strings. These were then cut into disks, much as one cuts cookie dough, to form pills.[2]

Many of the earliest pills contained opium. Its tarry consistency made it well suited for rolling into lentil-size doses. To mask its bitter taste, other flavorings were often added; cinnamon, nutmeg, and honey were among the favorites. Pharmacists also discovered they could get better effects by blending active substances. *Catapotia,* an early sleeping pill, contained a mix of ingredients that typically included mandrake, henbane, rue, and opium powdered and then beaten into a paste. A bean-size lump was generally sufficient to induce somnolence.[3]

Pills (opiated and otherwise) remained popular for millennia. The technology used for making them was essentially unchanged. The active ingredients were thoroughly mixed using a mortar and pestle. An excipient (inert binding substance), generally liquid glucose, was then added until a stiff but still workable mass was formed. This was then rolled into a tube and cut into appropriately sized doses. By the eighteenth century pill machines allowed for more accurate cutting of the pills, and pill rounders ensured the doses would have an aesthetically pleasing spherical shape. Pharmacists might then roll the finished pills in talcum powder to give them a pearlescent finish or in varnish to give them a sheen. Extra special (and costly) formulations might even be coated with gold or silver leaf.

Although pills allowed pharmacists to compound weighed medicaments into single doses of medicine, they had a drawback: their preparation required moisture. This could inactivate the drugs contained therein. Then a new method of preparing medicine was created, one that would soon overtake the more cumbersome method of rolling and cutting: the tablet.

Tablets

William Brockedon was a man of many talents. The son of a clockmaker, he showed early promise as a draftsman and artist and was sent to London's Royal Academy. In 1816 he received 100 guineas as a prize for his painting *Christ Raising the Widow's Son.* In 1822 his *Vision of the Chariots to the Prophet Zechariah,* painted in Rome during his first tour of Italy, was exhibited in the Pantheon. Later he retraced Hannibal's campaign in his 1828–1830 two-volume work *The Passes of the Alps,* which became a bestseller and is considered one of the first illustrated travel guides.

His artistic skill was matched by an innovative mind. By the 1830s the Borrowdale black lead (graphite) mine was failing, and pieces suitable for sketching were becoming harder to find. He invented a process by which waste graphite could be compressed into cakes of "Brockedon's Compound Plumbago" and used for pencils. The invention was a great success, and Brockedon became a wealthy man. But not content to rest on his laurels, Brockedon realized his process could be used to make pills as well. In 1844 he was awarded a patent for a machine that could produce pills and lozenges. The ingredients to be compressed were placed in a die. A punch was then inserted and struck with a heavy hammer. Brockedon's sodium bicarbonate and potassium bicarbonate tablets* became popular.

Soon other pharmacists discovered how to produce tablets of other medication by mixing binders and pressing them into shape. Then, in 1872, American pharmacist and inventor John Wyeth invented a rotary tablet press that allowed for mass production of tablets. This set the stage for large pharmaceutical companies to provide the medications that had originally been compounded down at the local apothecary. Tablets containing morphine (and later heroin) would become among the most popular drugs in the patent medicine salesman's cabinet.

Within a few years the old method of making pills was obsolete. Tablet presses allowed faster production of pills, more accurate dosing, and greater uniformity in the weight and appearance of doses. Tablets also generally dissolved more quickly than pills, resulting in a quicker onset of action when taken. But tablets soon faced competition as an even faster means of getting medication into a patient's system came on the market.

---

*Although the words are often used interchangeably, a pill is produced by mixing the ingredients, while a tablet is made by compressing them.

Capsules

In 1834 French pharmacists Mothes and DuBlanc patented a one-piece soft gelatin capsule. This soon became a popular method of administering copaiba balsam, an unpleasant-tasting drug used at the time to manage venereal disease. In 1846 another Frenchman, J. C. Heuby, patented a hard, two-piece capsule made of starch or tapioca combined with carrageenan. In 1847 an Englishman, James Murdock, patented a means of making these capsules out of gelatin, a substance that is still used today in most capsules. (Some scholars believe that Murdock, a patent agent by trade, was merely acting as the English patent agent for Heuby.)[4]

The Murdock/Heuby process involves dipping metal rods in molten gelatin solution. Before use, the two halves are separated, the capsule is filled with powder (either by placing a compressed slug of powder into one half of the capsule or by filling one half of the capsule with loose powder), and the other half of the capsule is pressed on. The advantage of inserting a slug of compressed powder is that control of weight variation is better, but the machinery involved is more complex. The output of even the fastest modern capsule-filling machines is about one-fifth that of modern tablet presses, making them more expensive to produce.

Gelatin capsules break down rapidly in the stomach, allowing for quick delivery of their payload. It is also easier to formulate capsules than tablets, because there is no need to be concerned about making the powders stick together under pressure. But there are also some disadvantages to capsules. The rapid dissolution of capsules can be a drawback as well as an advantage. It can result in gastric or esophageal irritation from high concentrations of the drug in a localized area. Capsules are also more sensitive to environmental humidity than tablets; when they get too dry they become brittle, and when damp they can become sticky and soft. And vegetarians and those wishing to observe religious dietary laws might not want to consume a substance made from the collagen of pig skins and bones. (Carageenan and other vegetarian and kosher capsules are available, but they are still the exception rather than the rule.)

Despite these drawbacks, the smooth surface and oblong shape of capsules makes them easier to swallow than comparably sized tablets, and many patients prefer them. A brief setback in their popularity occurred in 1982, after a person or persons unknown replaced Tylenol Extra Strength capsules with cyanide-laced capsules and deposited them on the shelves of several food stores and pharmacies in the Chicago area, causing at least seven deaths. But that (and several later copycat poisonings) did little to slow the growth of the capsule market. Today many pharmaceutical companies produce oblong "caplets," which combine a tablet's ease of production with a capsule's shape and ease of consumption.

Enteric Coatings and Time-Release Formulations

There are times when quick dissolution of the medicine is not helpful. When a tablet or capsule is introduced into the stomach, it is immediately soaked in stomach acids, which attack the ingredients and break them down into smaller pieces. Much of the medicine may be destroyed in this hostile environment, with only a small percentage making it to the small intestine where it can be absorbed.

Enteric coatings—inactive, nonabsorbable pH-sensitive polymers—are used to ensure that the medication survives its trip through the stomach. These polymers remain intact in the stomach's acidic environment. But when the tablet reaches the pH-neutral region of the duodenum and small intestine, they break down rapidly. Within an hour of leaving the stomach, the coating and tablet are completely disintegrated. Aspirin, ibuprofen, and other NSAID (nonsteroidal anti-inflammatory drugs) are frequently covered with this coating to reduce their risk of stomach upset and provide maximal pain relief.

To increase the useful life of a tablet or capsule, many companies have developed various timed-release technologies. Some incorporate the medication in a matrix of acrylics or other slowly digested substances;

others place it in tiny beads that are released when the capsule is digested and gradually release the medication; still others combine an instant release of medication with a more gradual supply of the same or a different drug. Purdue Pharma's Contin system, used with morphine (MS Contin) and oxycodone (OxyContin; see chapter 12) are among the most famous examples of these technologies applied to opiates.

Suppositories

Patients who suffer from severe nausea and vomiting may be unable to keep oral medication down long enough to reap any benefit from it. In those situations a suppository may prove useful. Suppositories are inserted into the anus,* and as they dissolve, their medicinal payload is absorbed by the rectum's vascular and lymphatic system. This is typically a faster and more efficient way of getting a drug into the system, because it avoids having the medicine pass through the entire gastrointestinal tract and allows more to reach the bloodstream.

Among the painkillers given through suppository are morphine, oxymorphone, and hydromorphone. Opioid suppositories are especially useful in alleviating the pain of cancer patients undergoing chemotherapy. They produce less of the nausea that is often associated with opiates and offer quick relief from suffering. Unfortunately, many patients are concerned with the stigma of inserting things in their rectum and are reluctant to use these forms of medication.

Other users have found that rectal application gives them the quick come-up and "rush" more typically associated with shooting up, while avoiding many of the health risks of intravenous usage. The drug of choice is mixed with water and placed in a small syringe (without a needle; we are seeking to irrigate the rectum, not puncture it with a sharp object!). The syringe is then inserted past the sphincter and the water is

---

*While vaginal suppositories are also produced, these are intended for topical relief of the immediate area (e.g., for vaginal yeast infections), not as a delivery system by which medicines can reach the body.

squirted into the colon. Assuming the colon is empty (post bowel movement and/or enema) this mode of delivery is one of the most efficient and relatively safe ways of using opiates. Alas, the stigma that bothers many pain patients is not lost on many male recreational users. Afraid they might be considered "gay" for inserting their drugs in their ass, they instead engage in risky but more socially acceptable behaviors.

Dangers

Be they tablets, capsules, or other forms, we have grown accustomed to oral medications. This makes many users complacent. They feel there is little or no risk in taking prescription medication according to the instructions—or even in taking it for recreation. People who wouldn't dream of using heroin or "street drugs" will happily gobble painkillers for relief and entertainment. This is a dangerous misconception that has led to many casualties among patients and recreational users alike.

As has been the case since the dawn of history, many pharmacists compound drugs to maximize their effect. Today many opiates are mixed with acetaminophen, an NSAID, a febrifuge (antifever medication), and a mild painkiller. Acetaminophen is combined with oxycodone in Percocet, with hydrocodone in Vicodin, and with codeine in a variety of formulations. Taken in excess, acetaminophen is extremely dangerous and can cause liver failure. Those who wish to take large quantities of these compounded opiates are advised to consider a cold-water extraction (chapter 9) to minimize their acetaminophen dosage.

Users should also be careful about combining prescription drugs to increase their high. Mixing benzodiazepines like Valium, Klonipin, or Xanax with opiates can result in dangerous suppression of breathing and heartbeat; the drugs potentiate each other, increasing their effect and lowering the threshold for an overdose. Those who regularly take anti-anxiety drugs may not think they will pose a problem when taking a couple of painkillers. Alas, ignorance of the laws of pharmacology is no defense against serious medical complications. (This applies to physical dependence and addiction as well. One can get hooked on prescription medication as surely as on heroin and suffer from equally painful withdrawals and cravings when the substance of choice is withdrawn.)

Finally, tablets and capsules are meant to be ingested orally. Many IV users have come to believe that shooting prescription drugs is somehow "safer" than using heroin or illicit opiates. Tablets allow for more precise dosing than street drugs (which can vary widely in purity). But they also contain binders and fillers that can wreak havoc with an abuser's circulatory and pulmonary systems. Using a micron filter can remove many but not all of the non-water-soluble binders from a prepared shot. Using cotton or cigarette filters will allow a significant percentage of microscopic fragments of talc, starch, or other inert ingredients to pass into your shot—and from there into your body. The consequences of this can be severe, ranging from thrombosis and gangrene to granulomas forming in the lungs. Amputation and even death can result.

29

SMOKING

At first the Chinese couldn't figure out what those Dutch sailors were doing. They combined opium pills, a common Chinese dysentery treatment, with tobacco. They then put the mixture in their pipes, lit it on fire, and inhaled the smoke from the *doop*—a Dutch word for a thick, viscous sauce (and the root of the English word *dope*). But soon the practice caught on among sailors, merchants, and laborers who were in frequent contact with foreign sailors. From there, opium and tobacco smoking soon became popular throughout China, and later in much of Asia.

In 1638 the Chongzhen emperor made tobacco use a crime punishable by decapitation. This edict was repealed in 1644 with the Chongzhen emperor's overthrow and the rise of the Manchu Dynasty. But by that time the edict had changed China's smoking habits forever. Instead of smoking opium with tobacco, many Chinese began smoking their opium "neat," both at home and in "opium dens."

This new method necessitated some changes in the mode of smoking. While a mixture of tobacco and opium smokes relatively easy, opium alone cannot come in direct contact with the flame lest it burn too fast and ooze away. The Chinese opium smokers used an oil lamp set in the middle of the floor. A pea-size pill of opium was placed in the clay bowl of a special pipe with a tiny smoke hole. The bowl was then brought near the heat above the lamp. As the opium was warmed, it began to sizzle and give off fumes. The smoker would then inhale.

But as smoking opium became more popular, many authorities began to lobby for stricter controls. Opium smoking became associated with gambling, crime, and other vices. In the late eighteenth century court official Yu Jiao said of the *yangui* (addicted smoker, or "smoke ghost"):

> When craving hits, his eyes water and his nose runs; he can barely lift his hands and feet. Even if a bare blade were applied to his neck or if a ferocious tiger jumped out in front of him, he would simply surrender and submit to his death.[1]

In 1729, when two hundred chests of foreign opium were imported, Emperor Yung Ching enacted severe penalties on the sale of opium and on running public opium-smoking houses. This had little effect on the practice. By 1790 more than four thousand chests were arriving in China annually. In 1796 opium smoking was again prohibited, and in 1800 the importation of foreign opium was again declared illegal. But all this had little effect: imports rose to five thousand chests in 1820, sixteen thousand chests in 1830, twenty thousand chests in 1838, and seventy thousand chests in 1858, after the Second Opium War forced the Chinese government to legalize the sale of opium.[2]

Opium Smoking Comes to America

During much of the nineteenth century, China was wracked by civil wars and famine. Desperate peasants signed on as "coolies"—contract laborers—and made their way to worksites around the world. After the Gold Rush of the 1840s and 1850s and the subsequent efforts to build a transcontinental railroad, many Chinese laborers found their way to the United States. There they found work—but also vicious racial prejudice. Chinese immigrants were forced to pay special taxes, forbidden to marry white European partners (or to bring their wives and children to the United States), denied any chance at citizenship, and herded into "Chinatowns." But this racism also served to create a cohesive Chinese community in America, one that preserved many Chinese customs, including opium smoking.

At first opium dens in America catered exclusively to a Chinese clientele. But by the 1870s the "Oriental vice" had begun attracting a growing number of white smokers. In 1877 Dr. Winslow Anderson of San Francisco reported that as many as ten thousand white San Franciscans, including a surprising number of wealthy and otherwise respectable citizens, were frequenting opium dens. In horrified tones he denounced the opium dens where one could find "young white girls from sixteen to twenty years of age, lying half-undressed on the floor or couches, smoking with their 'lovers.'"[3] In 1892 a Butte, Montana, newspaper declared:

> White men and even white girls cannot make an honest living with the Chinese around. They have their own opium dens and sell opium and smoke it, and when apprehended as criminals, escape into their underground dens, which are of mammoth proportions and cannot be found.[4]

Opium dens came to be seen as havens for the worst sort of white people: gamblers, prostitutes, and other ne'er-do-wells. The divans on which opium smokers reclined while consuming their drugs led to opium houses being called "dives," a word that would become synonymous with low-class establishments of all sorts. Meanwhile, wealthy whites fascinated with Eastern decadence began slumming in these establishments for kicks, and bans and crusades against the dens only made them more alluring. Some rich users purchased their own opium pipes and set up "smoking rooms" complete with pillows, carpets, and "Orientalist" decorations.

Buddhas of gigantic size . . . swinging banners with fringes
of many-coloured stones, lanterns with glass sides on which
are painted grotesque figures. The air is full of the scent of
joss-sticks. The wizard reclines on a divan, inhaling opium
slowly, clothed with the subdued gorgeousness of China. . . .
He has the appearance of a pickled walnut. His forehead is
a lattice-work of wrinkles. His pigtail, braided with red, is
twisted round his head. His hands are as claws. The effect
is weird, unearthly.

OSCAR WILDE, 1894[5]

At this time opium was available in most pharmacies, and morphine and syringes could be purchased through the Sears Roebuck catalogue. But opium smoking became stigmatized as a Chinese habit, one that destroyed the health and, worse, promoted race-mixing in opium dens. Much as later lawmakers would treat crack cocaine (most commonly used and sold by black smokers) more harshly than the sniffed powder, nineteenth-century demagogues railed against opium dens as part of their larger campaign against the "yellow peril."

Most opium smokers, like most opiate users, ultimately reached a set preferred dosage (typically seven to fifteen pills a day). But Chinese missionaries and temperance activists suggested that a single puff of the pipe would lead to lifelong addiction and financial and moral ruin; some even suggested that opium smoking was part of an insidious Chinese plot to corrupt white Christian society. Their propaganda would later expand to include all opiates and opioids.

The Physiology of Smoking

While Chinese opium smoking is of relatively recent vintage, there is some evidence that devotees of the Cretan poppy goddess at Gazi used a simple smoking apparatus to inhale opium fumes. The Greek historian Herodotus described a Scythian custom of throwing hemp on red-hot stones and inhaling it in an enclosed tent. Indigenous tribes in the Americas were long accustomed to smoking tobacco and other substances wrapped in leaves, in cow horns, or in clay pipes.

One might wonder who first came up with the idea of inhaling smoke. Bob Newhart has a hilarious sketch wherein he envisions Walter Raleigh explaining tobacco to his bosses in England.

> You set fire to it, and then what happens, Walt? You breathe in the smoke. (LAUGHTER) Well, it seems to me you could stand in front of a fireplace and get the same thing goin' for you. I don't think we'll be able to move that, Walt.[6]

When smoke is inhaled, it fills the alveoli, tiny sacs found throughout the tissues of the lung. These alveoli are lined with a mesh of capillaries. They draw in carbon dioxide from the blood, which then takes up oxygen and carries it (along with anything else inhaled) through the body. There are some three hundred million alveoli in an adult's lungs, with a total surface area of around seventy-five square meters— approximately the size of a tennis court. This means that any substance inhaled will quickly reach the bloodstream and be carried through the body. While it can take an hour or more for eaten opium to take effect, an opium smoker will start to feel the effects almost instantly.

But though smoking gives a more immediate effect, it is also a more wasteful mode of consumption. The smoker must not burn the opium, lest the morphine and other alkaloids break down in the heat. Instead, it must be warmed until it vaporizes. Even then, much of the opium will remain on the pipe as tarry dross. An estimated 80% to 90% of the active compounds are lost from fumes that either escape the pipe or are exhaled unabsorbed by the smoker.[7] This means it is more difficult to overdose from smoking opium than eating it, but it also means that a greater amount of opium is required to produce the same effect. But those seeking a "rush"—a quick blast of euphoria as the substance of choice floods the body—are willing to trade efficiency for pleasure.

While the rush from smoking is not so strong as that experienced by intravenous usage, there is today less social stigma attached with smoking than injection. (This is in marked contrast to the nineteenth century, when respectable users injected morphine and smoking was reserved for loose women, criminals, slumming tourists, and "heathen Chinamen.") As a result, many of today's heroin users choose to smoke their drug of choice rather than shooting it.

Chasing the Dragon

In the 1950s heroin addicts in Hong Kong began using a new method of ingesting their heroin. Placing a mixture of one part heroin and four parts *daii fan,* a barbiturate sleeping powder, on a piece of creased tin foil, they then heated the mixture until smoke began to rise. To ensure the mix vaporized and didn't burn, they moved the heat source, then "chased the dragon" (*chui lung*) by inhaling it through a thin tube. This technique enabled them to feed their habit without carrying pipes, needles, or other incriminating paraphernalia and quickly spread as the Hong Kong and Chinese governments began cracking down on opiate users.

Unlike opium, heroin hydrochloride does not smoke well. The addition of the barbiturate powder increases the amount of vaporization. Later the technique was improved by replacing the barbiturate powder with caffeine, creating a smokable mix called "Chinese no. 3." By the 1970s Chinese no. 3 was available in Thailand, Singapore, and Malaysia, and by the 1980s it had reached India and Pakistan. "Brown sugar"—Iranian heroin consisting of heroin base mixed with caffeine— became available in Europe in 1975, and by the 1980s many European heroin addicts had replaced injection with smoking. (Others added citric acid or lemon juice to their "brown sugar," thereby converting the base to a water-soluble salt and making it suitable for injection.)

Heroin smoking came later to the United States. Legal pressure on traffickers and importers meant that most American heroin was of low purity. As a result, American heroin addicts preferred injection as the most efficient delivery system. This changed with the advent of "black tar heroin" in the 1980s. Black tar heroin is easy to smoke, although the burning vinegar taste (a by-product of excess acetic acid used in production) leaves much to be desired. Many young users began smoking black tar thinking they were using opium. Others considered it safer than injecting. And with the advent of fentanyl patches (chapter 14), some users have taken to splitting open patches and then smoking the gel found therein. This is extremely dangerous, given fentanyl's potency; a sufficiently large hit may be the last thing you ever inhale.

While smoking is less hazardous than injecting, it is not without its risks. Many regular heroin smokers report impaired lung function, chronic bronchitis, and emphysema. (This danger is compounded if the user also smokes tobacco, cannabis, or hashish.) Physical dependence can develop quickly, and many addiction specialists believe the quick rush produced by smoking causes an increased risk of psychological addiction. The intense cravings associated with crack smoking can also occur in heroin smokers. And because smoking is comparatively inefficient, many users find their tolerance rises to a point where economics force them to inject their drugs.

A number of heroin smokers develop toxic leukoencephalopathy. The white matter of their brains begins breaking down, resulting in loss of coordination, slurred speech, and cognitive impairment. This condition has a fatality rate of approximately 25%, while many who survive suffer permanent brain damage. Between January and July 2003, seventeen cases of heroin-related toxic leukoencephalopathy were confirmed in British Columbia. Seven of these were fatal.[8] Similar cases have been recorded in New York, Los Angeles, the Netherlands, and Taiwan. The toxin that causes this has not yet been identified, and there is little information on how many heroin smokers may presently suffer from mild forms of this condition.

30

INSUFFLATION

During the 1970s most American heroin was of dubious quality. As a result, users injected it to get the most out of their investment. This meant that heroin was used only by the hardest of hard-core drug users. Respectable folks might smoke some grass with their friends—but only gutter punks and junkies shot up. While this made heroin a status symbol among certain countercultural types, most considered it the most addictive and dangerous drug known to man—certainly nothing that would interest a typical recreational user.

Meanwhile, like mirror balls and gold chains, cocaine sniffing became an emblem of disco decadence. A few lines of Peruvian marching powder up the nostrils made the smart set smarter, the beautiful people more beautiful, and the suffering artists even more insufferable. Cutting lines of cocaine with an Amex card and sniffing them through rolled-up $100 bills was a way of flaunting your wealth. Snorting became a sign of one's sophistication, conspicuous consumption for an age of excess.

Even after leisure suits and coke-spoons fell out of fashion, America's fondness for cocaine continued. Snorting coke was a popular pastime among many middle- and upper-income Americans. While crack was stigmatized as a "ghetto drug," powder cocaine remained a status symbol favored by the rich and bored. And while many authorities urged everyone to "just say no" to cocaine—and many snorters wound up in rehab after their usage spiraled out of control—there was a basic idea that sniffing was safer than smoking, and definitely safer than the needle.

Then, in the 1990s, the purity of street heroin began increasing dramatically, as South American smugglers increased the competition in the black market. In 1973 the average bag of street heroin contained less than 10% diacetylmorphine; by 1998 it was over 60% pure.[1] A $10 bag of heroin was now enough to provide a potent high to a novice sniffer. And while cocaine was becoming passé, heroin was chic. A generation of wealthy and middle-class youths who would never dream of using needles began experimenting with heroin. And in time the aficionados grew younger and younger.

"Cheese" Comes to Dallas

To market heroin to kids you've got to get rid of the needle, because even the hardcore cheese users have said, "I wouldn't stick a needle in my arm to get high, but I'll snort it up my nose." So you've got to get rid of the needles and you've got to make it cheap enough for kids to afford.

JEREMY LIEBBE, NARCOTICS OFFICER,
DALLAS INDEPENDENT SCHOOL DISTRICT POLICE, 2007[2]

In 2005 a new drug began appearing in Dallas middle and high schools. Dubbed "cheese" because of its resemblance to powdered parmesan cheese, it was being sold for as little as $1 a dose or $10 a gram. Young users would snort it through rolled-up bills or ballpoint pen cases for a drowsy, euphoric high. When analyzed in labs, cheese was found to consist largely of acetaminophen combined with diphenhydramine (Benadryl) and small quantities of heroin. For many Dallas law enforcement officials, the cheese crisis recalled an earlier epidemic. Between 1996 and 1999 the affluent Dallas suburb of Plano saw more than twenty fatal heroin overdoses. Most of the victims were teenagers. But these users were even younger. Between August 15, 2005, and March 1, 2006, Dallas Independent School District police recorded seventy-eight drug-related cases involving cheese. The youngest user was thirteen.[3]

To make cheese, dealers (typically older students) dissolve black tar heroin in water. This "monkey juice" is then mixed with crushed Tylenol PM (acetaminophen and diphenhydramine) tablets. After this is dried, the end result is a cream-colored powder. Folded up in scraps of paper (typically torn notebook paper), this cheese is then sold to fellow students. This technique has been used for years by black tar consumers wishing to snort their drug of choice, although they typically used a lower percentage of pills in their final mixture.

In large enough quantities, diphenhydramine can cause hallucinations and delirium; in smaller quantities, it is a strong sedative. Like promethazine and glutethimide, it also interferes with the CYP2D6 enzyme that breaks down opiates, thereby prolonging and strengthening their effects. Dealers have long used diphenhydramine as a "cut" for their product, while recreational opiate users frequently take Benadryl before dosing to increase their high and prevent the notorious opiate itches. Although the heroin content of cheese is low (typically 3%–10%), the diphenhydramine synergizes with the heroin to provide greater sedation and euphoria. When used by opiate-naive youths, the combination can prove lethal.

On January 3, 2005, sixteen-year-old Brandi Nolen died at Doctor's Hospital in Dallas. Tests showed she had methamphetamine, heroin, and diphenhydramine in her system. Three weeks later, seventeen-year-old Garrett Hill died of a cheese heroin overdose in his mother's house in north Dallas. Later that year, eighteen-year-old Lorenzo Ontiveros, sixteen-year-old Nicholas Cannata, and eighteen-year-old Hugo Rivera died of cheese.[4] In 2006, eleven more students at Dallas-area high schools would join them in death, thanks to what law enforcement and journalists were now dubbing "starter heroin."

Those who had solemnly reported urban legends of "Blue Star Acid" marketed on playgrounds and strawberry-flavored methamphetamine now had a real high school drug crisis on their hands. Anti-immigration advocates began telling tales of shadowy Mexican gangs creating cheese to lure youngsters into lives of addiction, prostitution, and crime. Around the country school officials and parents were warned that cheese might be showing up in their community Any Day Now. Robert Lubran, director of the Division of Pharmacologic Therapies at the federal Substance Abuse and Mental Health Services Administration, said, "The people who market these drugs are very savvy, and if there's profit to be made by moving to another community, we know they'll do that."[5] Meanwhile, Zachary Thompson, director of the Dallas County Health and Human Services, said, "The cheese heroin has been the most instantly addictive and deadliest drug . . . that we have seen since the crack cocaine epidemic,"[6] and the DEA warned that their investigations of cheese "revealed a complicated web of gangs and drug dealers linked with several powerful Mexican drug cartels."[7]

While so far cheese seems largely confined to the Dallas area, it remains a persistent problem there. On January 24, 2009, seventeen-year-old Kathleen Arendt died after taking cheese,[8] and on April 6, nineteen-year-old Alexander Dubrocq, who had been battling an addiction to cheese for months, was found dead by his parents of an apparent heroin overdose.[9] And as the market for cheese has grown, it has become available outside schools as well. In February 2009, Barbara Sims, a sixty-year-old grandmother in the quiet Dallas suburb of Rowlett, was charged with possession with the intent to distribute controlled substances after police arrested her with 9 ounces (250 grams) of Mexican black tar heroin and several cases of antihistamines. Police claimed she was distributing cheese to drug houses throughout the Dallas area.

Insufflation and the Blood-Brain Barrier

In the late nineteenth century, German bacteriologist Paul Ehrlich found that colored dyes injected into the bloodstream would travel through the body and stain most tissues. The brain, however, remained unstained. Ehrlich assumed that the brain had a low affinity for the dyes. But later one of his students, Edwin Goldman, injected dye into cerebrospinal fluid. This stained the brain but no other tissues. This was the first discovery of the blood-brain barrier.

All blood vessels have an endothelial lining composed of flat cells that lie close together like paving stones and provide a smooth surface for the flow of blood. The endothelial lining of most vessels is relatively porous, allowing gases and some fluids to pass through. But the endothelial cells that line the capillaries around the brain and central nervous system are very tightly sealed. Lipid-soluble substances like alcohol, caffeine, and THC can reach the brain through the cell-membranes, and special mechanisms allow glucose and other critical molecules (including most opiates) to enter. But most larger molecules (as well as most toxins and bacteria) will be blocked from entering the brain.

While most of the brain and central nervous system is protected by this barrier, there are a few exceptions. The area postrema, or "vomiting center," has direct access to the bloodstream. When it detects a toxic substance it sends a signal that causes the stomach to regurgitate its contents, thereby protecting the body from further damage. The pineal gland pumps melatonin into the body to induce drowsiness and sleep. And insufflation is effective because the blood-brain barrier is not so tight near the olfactory nerves, which are responsible for our sense of smell.

When a water-soluble powder is inhaled through the nostrils, it comes to rest on the mucous membranes of the sinuses. From there much of it is absorbed into the bloodstream and the brain via the many capillaries that are entwined through the nasal mucosa. (Hence the profuse bleeding that can result from a blow to the nose.) Carried along the pathway of the olfactory nerves, some goes directly to the brain. The remainder is bound up in mucus, a thick, gelatinous fluid that is produced to protect the sinuses from foreign particles (like inhaled powders). This may be removed by sneezing or blowing your nose. If it is swallowed as postnasal drip it will ultimately land in your stomach and be ingested there.

The Greek physician Galen used a tube of bronze or horn to inject liquid medicine into a patient's nostrils and draw out pus from sinuses.[10] Today doctors are finding that nasal delivery of analgesics can be as quick as and less invasive than injection. A 2002 Australian study of twenty-four patients receiving postoperative patient-controlled analgesia found that nasal fentanyl spray produced equally rapid onset of analgesia as intravenous administration, with no significant difference in side effects (although four patients experienced mild nasal stinging).[11] Cambridge, Massachusetts, biotechnology firm Javelin is developing an intranasal formulation of morphine, Rylomine. By combining morphine with ChiSys, a carbohydrate polymer, Rylomine enhances absorption across nasal membranes and achieves many of the benefits of intravenous morphine without the need for needles. As of August 2010, Rylomine is in Stage III clinical trials in the United States.[12]

The Dangers of Snorting

Opiates are not so damaging to the nose as cocaine or methamphetamine (both of which can literally eat holes in your septum if snorted too frequently). Still, when snorting crushed tablets, the user is also ingesting binders and fillers like talc, silicone, wax, and other substances that can cause damage to sensitive mucous membranes. Street heroin is also cut with substances that are not intended for intranasal use. Long-term snorting of any substance can cause permanent damage to the cilia, which filter out foreign particles, leaving the user more vulnerable to colds and respiratory infections.

The risk of AIDS and hepatitis transmission from dirty needles is well known. But these diseases can also be passed through snorting utensils. Prolonged intranasal drug use erodes mucous membranes and causes bleeding. When straws are shared, traces of bodily fluids and infectious diseases can be passed between users. A study of drug-using clients with active chronic hepatitis C revealed trace amounts of blood on 8% of plastic soda straws used in the test; 5% of the straws also had detectable levels of hepatitis C virus (HCV).[13] This may come as a shock to those who regularly pass around mirrors and rolled-up bills, but it is a very real danger. For safety's sake, it is best to use your own bill rather than sharing it with someone else.

Heath Ledger died after snorting oxycodone combined with oral ingestion of several other benzodiazepines and opiates, and Chris Farley died after snorting heroin and smoking crack cocaine. And even comparatively low-potency cheese has been implicated in dozens of deaths, especially when mixed with alcohol or other drugs. Although insufflation carries less risk of overdose than intravenous injection, it is not necessarily safe. Caution and discretion are advised when using street opiates or when combining opiates with other prescription or nonprescription substances.

31

INJECTION

You may not think that you will ever need this chapter. For many IV users, the needle was originally their line in the sand. So long as they took their opiates any other way, they didn't have a drug problem; they were junkies only when they started shooting up. Ultimately they found other methods too expensive and inefficient. When it costs you $200 to snort or swallow your daily habit versus $25 to inject it, you may also cross that line.

Alternately, you may be intrigued by the idea of joining the Order of the Hypodermic. You may see the needle as the Ironman Triathlon of drug use, the tool by which poseurs are separated from the Truly Hard Core. You have probably heard stories about how the heroin rush is like an orgasm all over your body and how nothing will ever feel as good as that first intravenous experience. Or you've heard that it's a sure ticket to degradation and ruin, and your self-destructive streak just can't resist finding out more.

Intravenous usage of drugs is extremely dangerous, but it can also be extremely pleasurable. That is why so many people get past their innate fear of needles and social stigma and begin shooting up. That intense rush of good feeling is a powerful behavioral reinforcement, strong enough to overcome many adverse stimuli and deeply conditioned behaviors. Indeed, many addicts say that opiates were made for the needle. They are at least partially right; the modern-day use of syringes began as a method of delivering morphine.

The Hypodermic Syringe

In 1845 Irish physician Francis Rynd introduced a solution of 15 grains of morphine (approximately 970 milligrams) dissolved in creosote to a patient with tic douloureux. To alleviate his patient's suffering, Rynd made four punctures with a hollow needle, inserting the morphine/creosote solution directly into the supraorbital nerve and along the temporal, malar, and buccal nerves.[1] While Rynd wrote of his experiments, he did not describe the means by which the morphine solution was administered (a small glass bottle that emptied into the puncture via gravity). It would be left to Scottish and French surgeons, Alexander Wood and Charles-Gabriel Pravaz, to perfect the modern-day hypodermic syringe.

Pravaz developed a novel method of treating aneurysms in 1853: he injected a solution of ferric chloride directly into the aneurysm, thereby causing the bulging wall to swell and thicken and the blood to clot. Over time, the damaged blood vessel turned into scar tissue that faded from view. This technique (known as sclerotherapy) is still used for varicose veins.

Instead of relying on gravity to carry the substance into the patient's body, Wood's syringe (designed by a Mr. Daniel Ferguson of 21 Giltspur Street, London, maker of surgical instruments and trusses) featured a plunger that allowed him to control the amount of material inserted. Wood reported the successful results from nine cases in an 1855 paper and in a second paper in the *British Medical Journal* in 1858.

Wood saw his invention as a treatment for opium addiction. He believed that the act of taking opiated medicines through the mouth caused patients to develop an appetite for them. By injecting the drug rather than swallowing it, Wood hoped his patients would not become addicted. He was quickly disappointed, as several of his patients became dependent on morphine injections. (An oft-repeated urban legend claims that Wood's wife, Rebecca, died of a morphine overdose after becoming addicted to his new invention. In reality, she outlived Wood by ten years, dying in 1894.)[2] But others were not so quickly convinced. In his 1868 *Hypodermic Injection of Remedies,* Dr. Francis Anstie claimed:

> of danger, there is absolutely none. . . . The advantages of the hypodermic injection of morphia over its administration by mouth are immense. . . . The majority of unpleasant symptoms which opiates can produce are entirely absent. . . . It is certainly the fact that there is far less tendency with hypodermic than with gastric medication to rapid and large increase of the dose, when morphia is used for a long time together.[3]

The hypodermic gets its name from the Greek *hypo* (beneath) and *dermis* (skin). The needle pierces the top layer of the skin, and the material in the syringe is injected into the subcutaneous layer below. From here most injected materials are quickly accepted into the bloodstream and then circulated throughout the body. While there have been numerous modifications that improved the safety and efficiency of the hypodermic, Wood's basic design is still in use. Fluid is drawn up through a hollow needle into the main tube when the plunger handle is pulled back, and the liquid is dispensed out through the needle when the plunger handle is pushed back down. Graduated markings on the cylinder allow the user to control the dosage of each shot.

The hypodermic quickly became a status symbol among physicians, a sign that they had the finest and most modern medical equipment at their disposal. Wealthy clients learned how to inject themselves or trained their servants in the technique. Well-bred ladies could purchase jeweled syringe cases for traveling. Soon mass production allowed social climbers to purchase their own hypodermics. The 1897 Sears Roebuck catalog featured hypodermic kits (a syringe, two vials of cocaine or morphine, two needles, and a carrying case) for $1.50. Additional needles could be had for 25 cents each or $2.75 a dozen.[4]

The Intravenous Discovery

For decades needles were used only for subcutaneous injections. Then, in the early 1920s, an anonymous heroin addict in Terre Haute, Indiana, accidentally struck a vein while shooting up. At first he was terrified, certain he would die as the effect hit him. But when he survived he remembered the intense euphoria and let his fellow addict friends know about it. By 1935, 42% of addicts admitted to a government drug hospital were taking heroin intravenously.[5]

A subcutaneous or intramuscular shot takes some time to be absorbed into the bloodstream. Intravenous injections, by contrast, result in an immediate delivery of the whole payload into the system. This causes the "rush" that IV drug addicts crave. It also results in a more efficient use of the substance, because it avoids the "first pass" metabolism of the digestive system and liver. As black market heroin and morphine became more expensive and less pure, users found it more cost-effective to shoot their drug than eat, sniff, or smoke it.

But because hypodermics were hard to come by, users were forced to improvise. In an effort to stop intravenous drug abuse, laws were passed making the sale of needles and syringes illegal without a prescription. Unauthorized possession of a syringe was grounds for arrest and, in many states, incarceration. A long-time Baltimore addict describes one technique used by addicts who had no access to syringes.

In those days, you could go into a drugstore and buy needles for, like, 25 cents apiece. And then you had to have an eyedropper. You would tear the white edge off a dollar bill, wet it, and wrap it around the eyedropper. They called that the "collar." Then [you put] the needle in the eyedropper, screwing the needle into the dollar bill. It's really better than using a syringe because . . . as you put it in your vein, blood would roll up into the eyedropper. Then you squeeze the bulb, and it would go into your arm. Then when you let the bulb go, [blood] would flow back into the eyedropper.[6]

Scarcity also led addicts to share their "works," even after it became apparent that this was a prime vector for the spread of various diseases. In 1929 many Egyptian addicts came down with malaria transmitted through shared equipment; in 1933 the same disease occurred among IV users in New York City.[7] And because needles were frequently used repeatedly, users' veins would quickly become damaged by the blunt tips. This led to scars or "tracks" along the inner arms, feet, hands, or other injection sites. As these abused veins collapse, the hands and feet can become chronically puffy and swollen due to circulatory and lymphatic damage. Ultimately necrosis (tissue death) can result.

These issues were of little concern to most health officials. Most intravenous drug users came from lower socioeconomic backgrounds, and a disproportionate number were minorities. They had chosen to use illegal drugs (or so the conventional wisdom went), and so they were responsible for any damage they might incur thanks to their unwholesome behavior. But then, in the 1980s, a new disease threatened to spread from the addict community into the law-abiding population.

The Birth of Needle Exchanges

In October 1981 Dr. Mary Guinan of the Center for Disease Control was examining the cases of GRID (gay-related immune disease) among patients who claimed to be heterosexual. Although they had no history of attendance at bathhouses, they all acknowledged use of intravenous heroin.[8] By March of 1982 Guinan had found ten women who had contracted GRID (now called acquired immune deficiency syndrome, or AIDS). Nearly all of them had had sex with bisexual men or, more commonly, intravenous drug users. Junkies became part of the notorious "4-H Club" (homosexuals, hemophiliacs, Haitians, and heroin addicts)—and AIDS became yet another excuse for escalating the War on Drugs.

In 1986 Jon Parker, a recovering heroin addict, was earning a master's degree in public health at Yale University. In one of his courses, the professor commented that there was no reason to make addicts the focus of HIV prevention efforts, because they would not change their behavior. Angered by this nonchalant dismissal, Parker began meeting with IV drug users to warn them about the dangers of HIV transmission. In November 1986, Parker began distributing—and later exchanging—needles and syringes on the streets of New Haven, Connecticut, and Boston, Massachusetts.

Similar programs already existed in Europe. Since 1984, Amsterdam Junkiebond had been exchanging needles and syringes with aid from the Municipal Health Service. But Parker's needle exchange received no government backing; instead, he was arrested dozens of times in eight different states as he sought to challenge laws requiring prescriptions for needle purchases.[9]

In April 1988 Dave Purchase, an activist in Tacoma, Washington, informed the mayor and other public officials that he planned to begin a program. In August of that year he set up a table in downtown Tacoma to exchange needles and syringes. Despite support from the Tacoma chief of police and county public health commissioner, the state district attorney argued that the program violated the state's drug paraphernalia act, thus making the county public health commissioner file a suit seeking a judgment that the exchange was lawful.[10]

> *I do not favor needle exchange programs and other so-called harm reduction strategies to combat drug use. I support a comprehensive mix of prevention, education, treatment, law enforcement and supply interdiction to curb drug use and promote a healthy drug free America, not misguided efforts to weaken drug laws—and needle exchange programs signal nothing but abdication.*
>
> GEORGE W. BUSH, 2000[11]

Today intravenous drug users still make up a disproportionate number of new AIDS and hepatitis C infections, thanks to sharing needles.

Despite this, there remains considerable resistance to needle exchange programs. In January 2001 a federal judge ruled that Bridgeport, Connecticut, police were contravening the Connecticut needle exchange law by arresting and harassing needle exchange clients. In February of 2004 officials from the Bridgeport needle exchange reported that police had not only continued but escalated their harassment since the court ruling.[12] In November 2005 Shoshanna Scholar, executive director of Bridgeport's Clean Needles Now, made an official complaint about alleged police harassment, stating her site had been targeted by police three times in a five-week period, resulting in six searches, an arrest for a parole violation, and the confiscation of one man's needles.[13] As of May 2009, no federal funding exists for needle exchange programs, despite numerous studies suggesting they could save thousands of lives and millions of dollars in health care costs.

Safe(r) Injecting

The greatest immediate danger of intravenous drug usage is the increased risk of overdose. IV heroin hits the body all at once, which results in the euphoric rush but can also lead to respiratory depression and death. (And, unlike swallowed pills, vomiting will do nothing to lower the level of toxic chemicals in your body.) If you choose to inject, dose conservatively. You can always take more, but once you push the plunger, you can't take less. Be especially careful about shooting up after you have been drinking or taking other drugs. Most "heroin overdoses" are really polydrug overdoses that result from various respiratory depressants potentiating each other.

Do not share your needles with anyone and do not reuse your needles. This may be easier said than done. If you are dope sick and out of syringes, you may decide to use your friend's works just this once. If you do this, you should first wash out the needle and syringe by filling them completely several times with clean water. After each time, shoot the water into the sink or onto the ground. Do not shoot the water back into your clean water supply. Then completely fill the needle and syringe with full-strength household bleach several times. Leave it in the syringe at least thirty seconds each time. Then rinse the syringe and needle by once again filling them several times with clean water. This will not eliminate your risk of disease, but it will reduce it.

Clean your "cooker"—the surface on which you mix your opiates with water—with alcohol before you begin mixing. Try to use distilled sterile water if at all possible. Abscesses—inflammations and collections of pus beneath the skin—can occur at the site of a missed injection. If left untreated, they can lead to gangrene and ultimately amputation of the limb. If you see a red, swollen sore near an injection site, get to an emergency room. And even if you don't miss your shot, you may still be at risk of endocarditis, infection of the heart valves caused by injection of nonsterile substances. (Unless you are using ampules prepared specifically for injection, there is a 100% chance that your drug is nonsterile.) Micron filters can also help to remove bacteria and nonsoluble foreign substances from your shot, although they will be of little help against viruses.

The rush caused by intravenous injections can provide a powerful reinforcement for continued needle usage. Many IV addicts who have weaned themselves off heroin spend months injecting sterile water because of an overwhelming compulsion to use the needle. Others find themselves unable to stop because the pleasurable sensations from their shot override any efforts at self-preservation.

You may think these dangers outweigh any possible reward. If so, you are absolutely correct. There is no safe way to inject street drugs; there are only ways of minimizing the risk. Indeed, this attracts many people to intravenous drug usage. It appeals both to the Eros drive for pleasure and the Thanateros urge to die. Consider this well before taking that first shot. You may have a hard time remembering the glamour of self-destruction when you are dealing with oozing sores, necrotic fingertips, and other damage caused by your habit.

32

DEPENDENCE, ADDICTION, AND TOLERANCE

It is the iron fist inside Poppy's warm velvet glove. It is our justification for sending out armies to uproot her and putting up legal hurdles for those wishing her services. We have called it a disease and a moral failing; we have created industries to punish and to cure those who suffer from it. But how much do we *really* know about addiction?

Among celebrities, addiction has become a badge of honor—so long as one finally gets clean and sober and mouths the proper recovery slogans. Being a party animal in a twelve-step program gives one the street credibility of substance abuse without the pesky side effects that come with active addiction. Like 1930s exploitation films, we seek titillation in the guise of stern warning. We enjoy the tales of fun and sleaze, so long as they come with the morally uplifting endings of abstinence or death.

Those of us who are not so famous need not fear. We can be chocoholics, adrenaline junkies, compulsive shoppers, or gambling addicts. The language of addiction is frequently evoked in our culture, and not always in an entirely negative way. The "news junkie" who obsessively watches CNN is one thing; the "drug addict" quite another. Before we try to understand addiction, we might benefit from considering the various conditions falling under that rubric.

Physical Dependence

Opiates work by attaching themselves to opioid receptors located at various points in the body, especially the central nervous and gastro-intestinal systems. When they are used regularly, the body lowers its own production of the endogenous opioids and endorphins that would normally attach to those receptors. So long as the body is being supplied with an appropriate dose of opiates, all is well. But when those chemicals are withdrawn, the body goes through a period of readjustment. During that time, the classic symptoms of withdrawal come into play.

The physical signs resemble a bad case of the flu, with teary eyes, joint and muscle aches, and a runny nose. The skin grows clammy and is covered with goose pimples (hence the expression "cold turkey"). Nausea, vomiting, and diarrhea are common; so is restless leg syndrome ("kicking the habit"). The withdrawing addict normally suffers from insomnia, with brief periods of fitful sleep interrupted by nightmares. Profuse sweating is accompanied by hot and cold flashes. Blankets are uncomfortably warm and scratchy, but the addict may feel bitterly cold when uncovered. This is accompanied by intense feelings of fear, shame, anxiety, and sadness along with an increased sensitivity to light, pain, and other stimuli.

These symptoms are almost clichés at this point, memorialized in antidrug pamphlets and in movies like *Trainspotting* and *The Man with the Golden Arm*. Less known but no less real are the profound feelings of depersonalization, anhedonia, and depression that come after the most obvious physical symptoms are gone. This post acute withdrawal syndrome (PAWS) can last anywhere from a few weeks to a year or more. While the body can return to baseline in fairly short order, putting the psyche back in order after addiction takes a bit longer.

Opiates have become notorious for causing physical addiction.

Doctors who prescribe painkillers too liberally are regularly accused of turning their patients into junkies. According to one commonly cited myth, the American Civil War produced hundreds of thousands of addicts thanks to overuse of morphine and opium. In 1915, as pressure mounted to regulate and control opiate usage, Yale professor Jeanette Marks suggested that World War I would create a whole new generation of dope fiends.

> Did you know that there is practically no old American family of Civil War reputation which has not had its addicts? . . . It was the "army disease" because of its prevalence? . . . With the war that hangs over us, the drug evil will spread into a giantism of even more terrible growth than the present? . . . There are something like 4,000,000 victims of opium and cocaine in this country today?[1]

Then, in 1971, with the country facing yet another "drug crisis," yellow journalist Gerald Starkey provided even more juicy details:

> In 1865 there were an estimated 400,000 young War veterans addicted to Morphine. . . . The returning veteran could be . . . identified because he had a leather thong around his neck and a leather bag (with) Morphine Sulfate tablets, along with a syringe and a needle issued to the soldier on his discharge. . . . This was called the "Soldier's Disease."[2]

While this "Soldier's Disease" has been referenced in many medical journals and popular texts, sociologist, statistician, and historian Jerry Mandel has suggested it owes more to antidrug propaganda than actual history. Syringes did not come into common use in American medicine until the 1870s.[3] And contemporary reports from the battlefield do not mention soldiers suffering from opiate withdrawal or becoming addicted to opium or morphine—a condition that was well-known to physicians of the time. David F. Musto, a renowned drug historian and professor at the Yale University School of Medicine, noted, "The Civil War, far from initiating opiate use on a large scale in the United States, hardly makes a ripple in its constantly expanding consumption" and observed that the rapid rise in American opium and morphine imports does not begin until the 1870s.[4]

Today many pain patients are undermedicated, despite evidence that opiates are not a sure ticket to a life of addiction. Most patients who are prescribed opioids for pain do not become addicted to the drugs. Studies have shown that the abuse potential of opioid medications is generally low in healthy, non-drug-abusing volunteers. One study found that only four out of about twelve thousand patients who were given opioids for acute pain became addicted. In a study of thirty-eight chronic pain patients, most of whom received opioids for four to seven years, only two patients became addicted, and both had a prior history of drug abuse.[5]

No one would deny that opiates can cause physical dependence and psychological addiction—but other regularly prescribed substances can also produce habituation. Benzodiazepenes like alprazolam (Xanax), clonazepam (Klonopin), diazepam (Valium), and lorazepam (Ativan), which are listed among the top one hundred most commonly prescribed medications, are also extremely addictive. Abrupt cessation of therapeutic levels after several months of use can result in withdrawal symptoms including increased heart rate and blood pressure level, insomnia, panic attacks, sensory hypersensitivity, and seizures. These symptoms can continue for months and even years.[6] Antidepressant withdrawal after six or more weeks of usage can cause irritability, anxiety, sadness, insomnia, headaches, dizziness, fatigue, and nausea.[7] And heavy drinkers who try to quit without medical supervision can die or suffer brain damage from delirium tremens, colloquially known as the "DTs."

Psychological Addiction

But even substances that do not cause physical dependence can produce powerful psychological addiction. Cocaine and methamphetamine do not produce the spectacular withdrawal symptoms of an alcohol, benzodiazepine, or opiate "kick." Users can quickly become accustomed to the pleasure and well-being their use engenders. Before long, they may start seeking those feelings to the exclusion of everything else and despite negative reinforcement like loss of friends and family, health issues, and even prison.

In 1954 researchers James Olds and Peter Milner implanted electrodes into the pleasure center of the hypothalamus of various male rats. By tramping on a pedal, the rats could receive direct stimulation to the center via an electrical current. This resulted in strong repetitive behavior. The rats would stimulate themselves up to five thousand times a day until they fell down unconscious from exhaustion, and they showed no interest in drinking, eating, or nearby females in heat.[8] This has become one of the standard models for psychological addiction: a pleasurable behavior that can override even natural drives for food and reproduction.

The line between "physical" and "psychological" addiction may not be so clear-cut as once believed. Many neuroscientists believe psychological addiction is associated with the dopaminergic system of the brain's reward system. Pleasurable activities result in elevated dopamine levels in the brain. Chronic elevation of dopamine will result in a decrease in the number of dopamine receptors available, or downregulation. When addicts abstain from the dopamine-elevating activity (be it drug usage, sex, shopping, gambling, or other addiction), they experience depression, discomfort, and anhedonia until their brains readjust to a life free of that stimulus.

A great number of pain patients become physically dependent on opiates. But once they are weaned off the drug—or get over the immediate withdrawal symptoms—they have no desire to use again. When the pain goes away, so does their desire to take painkillers. By contrast, those who take their medication not for analgesia but for the euphoria it brings may find themselves craving another dose long after their recovery. Pain patients who begin abusing their drugs for recreation run a high risk of becoming addicted to their medication.

This same risk can affect "chippers"—people who occasionally use opiates for recreation but who take steps to avoid becoming physically dependent. By using only on weekends or other set dates, they hope that they won't become "junkies" who must take their drug to stay well. But while these steps may help avoid dependence, they do little to avoid psychological addiction. A chipper who counts the days between doses and spends most of the "down time" thinking about the last dose and the dose to come is already psychologically dependent and likely to become a full-fledged addict sooner rather than later.

Those who become physically dependent on opiates can get powerful positive reinforcement for continued usage during withdrawals. In the midst of their suffering, they can suddenly begin feeling better with a "fix." Because addicts frequently wake up in the morning feeling the first signs of dope sickness, they have many chances to reinforce the idea that sobriety equals pain and opiates equal freedom from pain. This idea may persist even after the addict has "kicked the habit" and is no longer physically dependent.

Tolerance

Opiate users can rapidly develop a physical tolerance to their medicine, consuming doses that would incapacitate or even kill an opiate-naive person. After decades of use, the English author Wilkie Collins (*The Moonstone*) required heroic doses of laudanum to treat his rheumatism and gout. His 1889 obituary stated that he "was in the habit of taking daily . . . more laudanum than would have sufficed to kill a ship's crew or company of soldiers."[9]

Addicts who abstain for a period of time will sometimes overdose on amounts they would have tolerated in the past. Former users who return to their habit are advised to dose very conservatively. Indeed, many addicts will take time off in an effort to lower their tolerance and the cost of their habit. But they generally find their financial relief is only temporary as their tolerance quickly returns to its former levels.

The mechanisms by which this develops are poorly understood. Several theories exist involving cellular and molecular changes caused by long-term exposure to opiates. Some anecdotal evidence suggests that small quantities of dextromethorphan (DXM, found in many cough syrups) can help slow the development of tolerance, although it does not seem to be useful in reversing tolerance that has already developed. Studies also found that very low doses of the opiate agonist naltrexone can increase the analgesic potential of opiates while slowing and possibly even reversing the development of tolerance.[10]

Along with this physical tolerance comes a psychological acclimation to the drug's effects. Regular users become accustomed to the side effects of the drug. Much as tobacco users learn to smoke cigarettes without choking and drinkers learn to tolerate and even enjoy the taste of beer, users of opiates become less prone to nausea and discomfort as they continue taking the same dosage. This allows them to handle greater doses to alleviate their pain—or, if they are recreational users, to take more in search of a better high.

Alas, as regular users get accustomed to the side effects, so too do they become accustomed to the euphoria. The bliss they felt upon consuming a small dose of their opiate of choice soon fades. This tempts them to increase their consumption—and because they have also become accustomed to some of the drug's unpleasant effects, they are capable of taking a greater amount. Tolerance develops quickly, especially among recreational users who are likely to consume far more than would be necessary to alleviate pain. This can lead to a large and expensive habit, and one that will increase until the user either finds a plateau dosage based on finances or decides to break the cycle once and for all.

33

GETTING CLEAN AND STAYING CLEAN

Persons who become drug dependent are those who are markedly lacking in pleasurable sensory awareness, who have lost the child-like ability to create natural euphoria through active play, including recreational sex, and who, upon experimentation with drugs, tend to employ these agents in large quantities as a passive means of euphoria, or at least as a means of removing some of the pain and anxiety attending a humorless, dysphoric life style.

PSYCHOTHERAPIST GEORGE B. GREAVES, 1980[1]

Perhaps your experiments with opiates have led you to psychological addiction or physical dependency. You may have decided that your spirit allies are too demanding and their price too high. Your efforts to use in moderation have failed repeatedly, and you keep stepping over every boundary you set for your usage. As a result, you have decided to cut your ties with Poppy. Alas, you will soon find that this is easier said than done. Poppy releases her devotees with great reluctance. But while this poses a serious problem, it also offers you an opportunity for growth.

Once upon a time, life passages were celebrated by ordeals. Acolytes were removed from their old lives, and after enduring various trials and tribulations, they were reborn as adults, shamans, or initiates. Their sufferings helped mark the passage between profane and sacred status. In prevailing through them, they proved their worth to the community and to themselves. For many today, addiction and recovery can serve a similar purpose. After hitting rock bottom and losing the trappings of their previous existence, addicts are forced to reconstruct themselves and learn to live a drug-free life.

Needless to say, this initiation is a perilous one. Those who fail this vision quest may die or be permanently scarred. But those who triumph frequently find themselves much stronger for the experience. If Poppy did not work for you as a spirit ally, perhaps you will gain wisdom in treating her as an opponent you must conquer.

Tapering

Depending on your opiate of choice, the first phase of withdrawal may take anywhere from several days to several weeks. Shorter-acting opiates like heroin or oxycodone are metabolized more quickly. The withdrawal will come on within six to eight hours after your last dose, and the worst physical symptoms will be over within five to seven days. Methadone or poppy tea withdrawals may not begin until several days after your last dose, but because the drug stays in your system longer, the withdrawal will be more protracted.

To avoid this lengthy misery, many opiate users prefer to taper their dosage. A small dose in the morning can stave off most of the withdrawals; by cutting that back until the habituation is negligible, they are able to function (if not necessarily at 100%) through their daily routine. This tapering is generally useful with long-lasting opiates like poppy tea or methadone, which require daily or less frequent dosing.

If you decide to taper, stick to your schedule. The temptation will be great to increase your dosage just this once. If you do that, you're likely to find your tapering plans go to naught. If you cannot renew your supply, you'll be facing "cold turkey" withdrawal; if you can, you're likely to go back to using as much or more than you were before you tried to quit. And if you are tapering to reduce your tolerance, be advised that any gains you make are likely to be short-lived. Most users who chase euphoria find it increasingly difficult to obtain. If possible, put someone else in control of your tapering supply and have them provide the medication. This will help you maintain the schedule and resist temptation.

You may also wish to speak to a doctor about buprenorphine, sold as Subutex or Suboxone. Unfortunately, you cannot take buprenorphine until you are experiencing mild to moderate withdrawal symptoms. Buprenorphine competes with other opioid molecules and knocks them off the receptors. If you still have opiates in your system, it may induce precipitated withdrawal. If you are already in the first stages of withdrawal when you take your first dose, buprenorphine will relieve your suffering.[2] Some people use buprenorphine to taper off their drug of choice, while others use it as part of a maintenance plan. Your physician can help you to determine which course will be right for you.

"Cold Turkey"

Users of shorter-acting opiates often find that the extended low-grade sickness is worse than biting the bullet and stopping use abruptly. While the suffering can be intense, the worst of it will be over quickly enough. And while opiate withdrawal is undoubtedly unpleasant, it is almost never fatal. (That being said, addicts with preexisting medical conditions are urged to consult a doctor before attempting to quit.)

There are several things you can do to alleviate some of the worst symptoms. Many addicts have reported that loperamide (Immodium) helps not only with diarrhea but also with much of the gastric upset and nausea that often accompanies withdrawal. (This is not surprising, because loperamide relieves diarrhea by acting upon the opioid receptors in the gastrointestinal tract.) And while you are likely to have little appetite during the worst of withdrawal, you should try to stay hydrated at the very least by drinking plenty of fluids. Multivitamin supplements are also a good idea, especially if you haven't been eating well during your period of addiction.

The restless leg syndrome (RLS) is considered by many to be one of the worst parts of opiate withdrawal. The constant fidgeting, kicking, and cramping are exhausting and make the insomnia that typically accompanies opiate withdrawal even worse. Clonidine, a prescription medication commonly used for high blood pressure, has also shown promise in reducing RLS, as well as withdrawal-related hot-and-cold flashes and sweating. Many addicts also find that hot baths help with the cramping and muscle aches. If you have access to a Jacuzzi or a bathtub, soaking may make you feel better.

Anything that causes a release of endorphins will help your body readjust to an opiate-free existence. It may be difficult to imagine working out when you're in the throes of dope sickness, but even basic stretching exercises may improve your mood. Orgasms with a partner or by yourself are also an excellent way to get those endorphin levels up. (Many addicts report feelings of extreme arousal during withdrawal. This is not surprising since opiates often reduce or suppress the sex drive altogether.)

Some withdrawing addicts use benzodiazepines to cope with the anxiety and insomnia. While they may help, caution is advised. If you decide to use benzodiazepines as part of your withdrawal regimen, medical supervision is strongly advised. At the very least, be conservative in your dosing. While benzos may help you feel a bit better, they will not relieve all of the unpleasant mental symptoms, no matter how many you take. Trading one addiction for another is never a good idea, especially when the withdrawals from your new drug are considerably more harsh and long-lasting.

Ibogaine

To join the Bwiti religion of Gabon, one ingests large quantities of the root bark of *Tabernanthe iboga*. This perennial rainforest shrub contains a number of psychoactive alkaloids, most notably ibogaine. In small doses ibogaine works as a stimulant; hunters and warriors chew *T. iboga* root to reduce hunger and fatigue. But in larger doses it becomes a powerful hallucinogenic, sending initiates into a deep sleep that may last four to five days. During this time they see fantastic apparitions of God and the ancestors, and when they return to consciousness they have died on this earth and been reborn closer to the divine.[3]

In 1962 a nineteen-year-old college dropout named Howard Lotsof acquired some ibogaine from a friend. Lotsof was no stranger to drug experimentation; he had already acquired a heroin habit and a fondness for cocaine. But nothing prepared him for his ibogaine trip.

> I saw what might be construed as either experiencing my birth or a form of an oedipal connection. I found myself on stage under spotlights and suddenly a ladder appeared and I began to climb the ladder and as I did my clothes vanished. I reached the top of the ladder and a diving board appeared and I walked out to the end of the diving board and I looked down and a swimming pool appeared. And in the swimming pool I saw my mother, naked. As I dived toward her she changed into my sister who changed into a female infant and at the moment my fingers touched her vagina the image disappeared and another image, which I don't remember, superseded it.[4]

After his trip was over, Lotsof felt no desire to use heroin. In his words,

> Where I had viewed heroin as comfortable, I now viewed heroin as emulating death. Where I had a previous physiological need for heroin, the need completely vanished. I felt my basic change was I chose life over death, and that heroin represented death.[5]

Since that time, many other addicts have reported that ibogaine journeys helped them to overcome their habit. At a 1995 meeting of the

National Institute on Drug Abuse (NIDA), Lotsof presented a collection of case reports showing that ten of fifty-two treatments (19%) led to cessation of heroin or cocaine use for a year or longer; fifteen treatments (29%) led to two months or less of sobriety; and the remaining treatments were followed by sober periods of two months to one year.[6]

Despite these and other promising studies, ibogaine remains a Schedule I controlled substance in the United States (like LSD and heroin), and pharmaceutical companies have shown little interest in researching its ability to help addicts. A number of offshore clinics offer ibogaine therapy for addiction and psychological trauma. There are also several underground "ibogaine evangelists" who provide ibogaine to those in need.

If you choose to treat your addiction with ibogaine, caution is advised. A number of deaths have resulted from ibogaine treatment. Ibogaine is generally contraindicated for those suffering from high blood pressure, liver disease, or a preexisting heart condition. You should also be aware that ibogaine is not a "quick fix." While it appears to ameliorate many withdrawal symptoms and to lessen postwithdrawal cravings, it should be used as an adjunct to counseling and therapy. An ibogaine vision may show you the areas of your life that need work, but it will not heal all the underlying problems. Those who are trying to sell ibogaine as a quick cure-all for addiction are doing a disservice to the treatment and to their clients.

After Withdrawal

Drug usage can become a large part of the user's identity and a badge of membership in a social group. Giving up the drug can mean losing that membership and that identity. Now that you have recovered, you may find that many of the addicts you considered friends are barely acquaintances. When you no longer have your drug of choice in common, you may have very little else to talk about. You may also discover that your old friends are less than supportive of your decision. By quitting you have cast their willpower into question; your ability to get clean makes their excuses ring hollow.

Post acute withdrawal syndrome is a very real and poorly understood part of recovery. Instead of feeling happy about your triumph, you may find yourself stuck in a black pit of gloom and numb despair. The temptation to relieve your misery by going back to your old regimen may be overwhelming, but don't give up hope just yet! You may find that antidepressant supplements like 5-HTP, St. John's wort, or SAM-e improve your mood. You may also get some relief from prescription antidepressants.

Find some ways to reward yourself for your sobriety. Now that you are not using, you have more time and money to spare. Pursue an old hobby or develop a new one. Find a cause you believe in or a wrong that needs to be righted. For a recovering addict, idleness is a bad thing. Sobriety is not all grim and humorless. You have new opportunities for joy.

If you choose to get clean through a drug rehabilitation center (or are sent there by court order), your therapy will almost certainly be directly or indirectly inspired by the twelve steps of Alcoholics Anonymous. For many people, twelve-step programs like Narcotics Anonymous are an invaluable aid to maintaining sobriety. Others chafe at the insistence on giving up control to a "Higher Power" and claim that many twelve-step groups are cults in which members are expected to toe the Big Book party line. Whatever issues they may have, twelve-step groups can provide you with a network of sober friends and acquaintances.

Above all else, understand that learning to live without drugs is a process. You are likely to relapse multiple times before you finally are able to get clean once and for all. Don't use this as an excuse to use Just This Once, but don't beat up on yourself too badly if you slip up. Remember that there's no better time to get sober than right now. Every day you continue using will just make it that much harder to stop again. Your opponent is patient. She will wait years or decades to welcome you back.

AFTERWORD

*For it is in the power of all so-called intoxicating drugs
to reveal a man to himself. If this revelation declares
a Star, then it shines brighter ever after. If it declares a
Christian—a thing nor man nor beast, but a muddle of
mind—he craves the drug, no more for its analytical but
for its numbing effect. . . . We of Thelema think it vitally
aright to let a man take opium. He may destroy his physical
vehicle thereby, but he may produce another Kubla Khan.
It is his own responsibility.*

ALEISTER CROWLEY, AUTHOR, OCCULTIST,
"GREAT BEAST," AND HEROIN ADDICT, 1912[1]

Current governmental attitudes toward drugs are based on mistrust.
The Powers That Be have determined that we are incapable of using
Poppy and her derivatives responsibly. To protect us from ourselves, they
have put up a variety of barriers designed to keep us safe from her siren
song. I have assumed that my readers are capable of making an appropriate decision if given the proper information. I have not glossed over
the risks attendant upon her usage, but neither have I felt it necessary to
exaggerate Poppy's dangers or minimize her gifts. Those suffering from
pain (physical or psychological) may find she gives them solace; those
seeking visions may find dreams in her embrace.

Some believe that spirit allies are entirely benevolent figures who exist only to lead us to enlightenment. Shamans have long known better. Spirits have their own agendas and demand payment for their services. If you treat your work with Poppy as a business proposition rather than a love affair—if you call on her only when you need her services and leave her alone when you do not—you will find yourself less indebted to her. And if you remember that she is by nature a seductress who will try to tempt you into using just a little bit more, you may be better able to resist her wiles.

Perhaps you have come to opiates seeking self-destruction. Many users are enamored of Poppy's fruits because they bring oblivion. It is your body and you are (or should be) free to do with it as you will. If you wish to experience slow suicide, Poppy will happily provide that for you. She will take away the pain of existence as surely as she will take away the pain of injuries. Before you choose to go down that path, be advised that you may not be able to turn back should you change your mind. Falling into the abyss is easier than climbing out.

An important part of risk reduction involves understanding that there are risks. You may be convinced that you will never become a junkie. There are many junkies who used to feel that way, until Poppy proved them wrong. Be aware that addiction generally involves a good deal of self-delusion. Addicts are typically the last person to realize there is a problem with their drug usage. Those who work with spirit allies, particularly one as unforgiving as Poppy, cannot afford self-delusion.

I do not complain here about "abuse." Poppy *wants* to alter your consciousness; that is one of the major means by which she encourages human cultivation. Euphoria is not a side effect of Poppy's alkaloids but one of the main reasons she generates those substances. You may accept that gift if you will. But be advised that Poppy has her own best interests at heart, not yours. We may believe that Poppy is a tool that suits our purposes. Be advised that Poppy feels the same way about us.

The door stands open before you. Here you may find dreams and nightmares, wisdom and oblivion, healing and harm. Those who are worthy may learn, but those who are not may be destroyed. The shaman's path has always been a road filled with traps and pitfalls, a steep ascent littered with the corpses of those who tried and failed. The strongest allies may also become the deadliest enemies—and vice versa. The wise will tread cautiously. The foolish will do as they will. Choose wisely while you still can.

NOTES

Chapter 1. In the Beginning

1. Leendert P. Louwe Kooijmans, "The Mesolithic/Neolithic Transformation in the Lower Rhine Basin," in *Case Studies in European Prehistory*, Peter I. Bogucki, ed. (Boca Raton, La.: CRC Press, 1993), 130.

2. C. C. Bakels, "Abstract: *Papaver somniferum* Culture in Prehistory and Early History," Symposium: Plants in Health and Culture, Leiden, February 16–17, 2004, www.plantsinhealthandculture.nl/plantsinhealthandculture/Abstracts/AbstractBakels.html (accessed January 13, 2009).

3. Gill Campbell and Mark Robinson (with Polydora Baker, Simon Davis, and Sebastian Payne), "Environment and Land Use in the Valley Bottom," English Heritage, www.english-heritage.org.uk/upload/pdf/018-036_Chapter2_FINAL.pdf (accessed January 14, 2009).

4. Graeme Baker, *Prehistoric Farming in Europe* (Cambridge: Cambridge University Press, 1985), 123.

5. Robert Kunzig, "La Marmotta," *Discover,* November 1, 2002, http://discovermagazine.com/2002/nov/cover (accessed January 13, 2009).

6. C. C. Bakels, "Fruits and Seeds from the Linearbandkeramik Settlement at Meindling, Germany, with Special Reference to Papaver Somniferum," *Analecta Prehistorica Leidensia* 25 (1992): 66.

7. Thomas W. Kavanagh, "Archaeological Parameters for the Beginnings of Beer," *Brewing Techniques* (September/October 1994), www.brewingtechniques.com/library/backissues/issue2.5/kavanagh.html (accessed January 14, 2009).

8. Bronislaw Szerszynski, *Nature, Technology and the Sacred* (New York: Blackwell Press, 2005), 17.

9. Graham Harvey, *Animism: Respecting the Living World* (Kent Town, Australia: Wakefield Press, 2005), 68.

Chapter 2. The Bronze Age World

1. Richard Effland, "The Hunter-Gatherers of Modern Times," Mesa Community College Anthropology, 2003, www.mc.maricopa.edu/dept/d10/asb/anthro2003/lifeways/diasporas/modern.html (accessed January 15, 2009).

2. William A. Emboden, Jr., "Art and Artifact as Ethnobotanical Tools in the Ancient Near East with Emphasis on Psychoactive Plants," in *Ethnobotany: Evolution of a Discipline*, Richard Evans Schultes and Siri Von Reis, eds. (Portland, Ore.: Timber Press, 1995), 98.

3. Paul Collins, "Vessel Fragment with an Image of a Goddess," Metropolitan Museum of Art Special Collections, 2000, www.metmuseum.org/special/First_Cities/firstcities_stop4.htm (accessed January 15, 2009).

4. Emboden, "Art and Artifact," 98.

5. Ibid., 101–2.

6. L. D. Kapoor, *Opium Poppy: Botany, Chemistry and Pharmacology* (Binghamton, N.Y.: Haworth Press, 1995), 2.

7. Emboden, "Art and Artifact," 104.

8. Margaret Serpico and Raymond White, "Oils, Fat and Wax" in *Ancient Egyptian Materials and Technology,* Paul T. Nicholson and Ian Shaw, eds. (Cambridge: Cambridge University Press, 2000), 404.

9. P. G. Kritikos and S. P. Papadaki, "The History of the Poppy and of Opium and Their Expansion in Antiquity in the Eastern Mediterranean Area," first published in the *Journal of the Archæological Society of Athens,* 1967. Available at Poppies.org, www.poppies.org/news/99502023966018.shtml (accessed January 16, 2009).

10. Ibid.

11. Rodney Castleden, *Mycenaeans* (London: Routledge, 2005), 158.

12. Ivan Valencic, "Has the Mystery of the Eleusinian Mysteries Been Solved?" *Yearbook for Ethnomedicine and the Study of Consciousness* 3 (1994): 325–36. Available at Schaffer Library of Drug Policy, www.druglibrary.org/schaffer/lsd/valencic.htm (accessed January 16, 2009).

13. Homer, *Odyssey,* book 4, Samuel Butler, trans. Available at Online Literature, www.online-literature.com/homer/odyssey/4/ (accessed January 16, 2009).

14. Homer, *Iliad,* book 8, Samuel Butler, trans. Available at The Internet Classics Archive, http://classics.mit.edu/Homer/iliad.8.viii.html (accessed January 16, 2009).

15. Homer, *Iliad,* book 14, Samuel Butler, trans. Available at The Internet Classics Archive, http://classics.mit.edu/Homer/iliad.14.xiv.html (accessed January 16, 2009).

16. See http://web.archive.org/web/20031003171025/http://home.att.net/~hagardorn/images/epidaurus_museum2.jpg (accessed September 10, 2010).

17. Martin Booth, *Opium: A History* (New York: Macmillan, 1999), 17.

Chapter 3. Rome

1. Aelius Donatus, "Life of Virgil," David Wilson-Okamura, trans.Virgil.org, 1996, http://virgil.org/vitae/ (accessed January 20, 2009).

2. Virgil, *Aeneid,* book 4, 483–990, A. S. Kline, trans. Available at Poetry in Translation, http://tkline.pgcc.net/PITBR/Latin/VirgilAeniedIV.htm (accessed January 20, 2009).

3. Shane Blackman, *Chilling Out: The Cultural Politics of Substance Consumption, Youth and Drug Policy* (New York: McGraw-Hill, 2004), 131–32.

4. Virgil, *Georgics,* book 4, 543–46, A. S. Kline, trans. Available at Poetry in Translation, http://tkline.pgcc.net/PITBR/Latin/VirgilGeorgicsIV.htm (accessed August 3, 2010).

5. Virgil, *Georgics,* book 1, 78, A. S. Kline, trans. Available at Poetry in Translation, http://tkline.pgcc.net/PITBR/Latin/VirgilGeorgicsIV.htm (accessed August 3, 2010).

6. Hesiod, *Theogony,* Hugh G. Evelyn White, trans.

7. Horace, *Satires,* book 1, satire 8, C. Smart, trans. Available at Project Gutenberg. www.gutenberg.org/files/14020/14020-h/14020-h.htm (accessed January 20, 2009).

8. Ovid. *Fasti,* Book 4, A. S. Kline, trans. Available at Poetry in Translation, www.poetryintranslation.com/PITBR/Latin/OvidFastiBkFour.htm (accessed August 3, 2010).

9. Ovid, *The Metamorphoses,* Horace Gregory, trans. (New York: Signet Classics, 2001), 316.

10. Mary Ann Dwight and Tayler Lewis, *Grecian and Roman Mythology* (New York: Putnam, 1849), 58–59.

11. "Galen the Physician," Hellenica, www.mlahanas.de/Greeks/Galen.htm (accessed January 20, 2009); J. M. Scott, *The White Poppy: a History of Opium.* London: Heinemann, 1969. 5.

12. Marcus Aurelius, *Meditations,* book 2, George Long, trans. Available at Internet Classics Archive, http://classics.mit.edu/Antoninus/meditations.2.two.html (accessed January 20, 2009).

13. Thomas W. Africa, "The Opium Addiction of Marcus Aurelius," *Journal of the History of Ideas* 22, no. 1 (January–March 1961): 99.

Chapter 4. The Islamic World

1. Ustadha Zaynab Ansari, "Does the Koran Teach to Kill, Tax or Convert Infidels?" SunniPath, June 13, 2006, http://qa.sunnipath.com/issue_view .asp?HD=7&ID=9801&CATE=1426 (accessed January 21, 2009).

2. Zachariah Matthews, "The Golden Age of Islam," *Salam Magazine* (September–October 2004), www.famsy.com/salam/GoldenAge1004.htm (accessed January 22, 2009).

3. Selma Tibi, "Al-Razi and Islamic Medicine in the 9th Century," The James Lind Library, 2005, www.jameslindlibrary.org/trial_records/9th-15th-century/ al-razi/al-razi-commentary.html (accessed January 22, 2009).

4. Ibid.

5. Walter Sneader, *Drug Discovery* (New York: John Wiley & Sons, 2005), 25.

6. L. D. Kapoor, *Opium Poppy: Botany, Chemistry and Pharmacology* (Binghamton, N.Y.: Haworth Press, 1995), 3.

7. Monzur Ahmed, "Ibn Sina" at Ummah.com, www.ummah.com/history/scholars/ ibn_sina (accessed August 3, 2010).

8. George Watt, *The Commercial Products of India: Being an Abridgement of "The Dictionary of the Economic Products of India"* (London: John Murray, 1908), 846.

9. Kapoor, *Opium Poppy,* 11.

10. Maneka Gandhi and Yasmin Singh, *Brahma's Hair: On the Mythology of Indian Plants* (New Delhi, India: Rupa & Company, 2007), 57–58.

11. Karl Vick, "Opiates of the Iranian People: Despair Drives World's Highest Addiction Rate," *Washington Post,* September 23, 2005, www.washingtonpost .com/wp-dyn/content/article/2005/09/22/AR2005092202287.html (accessed January 22, 2009).

12. Cedric Gouverneur, "Iran Loses Its Drug War," *Le Monde Diplomatique,* March 2002, http://mondediplo.com/2002/03/13drug (accessed January 22, 2009).

13. Vick, "Opiates."

14. Google AFP, "Iran Nabbed 900 Tonnes of Afghan Drugs in 2007," *Google News,* June 23, 2008, http://afp.google.com/article/ALeqM5g6EKMkDXcY-ltSPXlI6yhuToHDJA (accessed January 22, 2009).

15. Michael Theodoulou, "Iran Warns of 'Drug Tsunami' if UN Cash for Patrols Is Cut," news.scotsman.com, June 25, 2008, http://news.scotsman.com/world/ Iran-warns-of-39drug-tsunami39.4218442.jp (accessed January 22, 2009).

16. Vick, "Opiates."

17. Gouverneur, "Iran Loses Its Drug War."

18. Vick, "Opiates."

19. Bijan Nissaramanesh, Mike Trace, and Marcus Roberts, "The Rise of Harm Reduction in the Islamic Republic of Iran," Beckley Foundation, 2005, http://beckleyfoundation.org/pdf/paper_08.pdf (accessed January 22, 2009).

20. Nasser Karimi, "Iranian AIDS Doctors Get Several Years in Jail," *Washington Post,* January 22, 2009, www.washingtonpost.com/wp-dyn/content/article/2009/01/22/AR2009012201529.html (accessed January 22, 2009).

Chapter 5. The Return to Europe

1. Dirk Hoerder, *Cultures in Contact* (Raleigh, N.C.: Duke University Press, 2002), 55.

2. Ibid., 47.

3. Piers D. Mitchell, *Medicine in the Crusades* (Cambridge: Cambridge University Press, 2002), 200.

4. Paracelsus, *The Book Concerning the Tincture of the Philosophers,* A. E. Waite, trans. Available at Sacred Texts Online, www.sacred-texts.com/alc/paracel2.htm (accessed August 3, 2010).

5. Thomas Dormandy, *The Worst of Evils* (New Haven, Conn.: Yale University Press, 2006), 94.

6. Richard P. T. Davenport-Hines, *The Pursuit of Oblivion: A Global History of Narcotics* (New York: W. W. Norton & Co., 2002), 32.

7. Allen G. Debus, "Paracelsus: The Medical Chemistry of the Paracelsians," National Library of Medicine, www.nlm.nih.gov/exhibition/paracelsus/paracelsus_4.html (accessed January 25, 2009).

8. Martin Booth, *Opium: A History* (New York: Macmillan, 1999), 24–25.

9. William Shakespeare, *Othello,* act 3, scene 3, lines 331–34.

10. Davenport-Hines, *Pursuit of Oblivion,* 32.

11. Ibid.

12. Booth, *Opium,* 25.

13. Davenport-Hines, *Pursuit of Oblivion,* 36.

14. Dormandy, *Worst of Evils,* 130.

15. Verner Stillner, "Dover's Powder," Encyclopedia of Drugs and Addictive Behavior, 2001, www.bookrags.com/research/dovers-powder-edaa-01 (accessed January 26, 2009).

Chapter 6. The Colonial Era: 1500–1900

1. George Hubbard Blakeslee, *China and the Far East* (New York: Thomas Crowell & Co., 1910), 173.

2. Martijn Burger, "The Forgotten Gold? The Importance of the Dutch Opium Trade in the Seventeenth Century," *Eidos* 2 (2003): 19.

3. George Bryan Souza, "Opium and the Company: Maritime Trade and Imperial Finances on Java, 1684–1796," *Modern Asian Studies* 43, no. 1 (2009): 124.

4. E. M. Jacobs, *Merchant in Asia* (Leiden, Netherlands: CNWS Publications, 2006), 129.

5. Burger, "The Forgotten Gold?" 20.

6. Jacobs, *Merchant in Asia,* 130.

7. "Cultural and Intellectual Life of Armenians in India: Armenian Scholars in India," MENQ.AM, www.menq.am/history/chap4_part02.htm (accessed February 20, 2009).

8. "China: Controlling the Opium Trade," John V. O'Brien Pages, http://web.jjay .cuny.edu/~jobrien/reference/ob56.html (accessed February 21, 2009).

9. Wang Ke-Wen, "Opium War," in *Modern China: An Encyclopedia of History, Culture, and Nationalism,* Wang Ke-Wen, ed. (London: Taylor & Francis, 1998), 252.

10. Frank Sanello, *The Opium Wars* (Naperville, Ill.: Sourcebooks, 2004), 21.

11. Ibid.

12. Karl Meyer, "The Opium War's Secret History," *New York Times,* June 28, 1997. Available at www.nytimes.com/1997/06/28/opinion/the-opium-war-s-secret-history.html (accessed August 3, 2010).

13. Lin Tse-Hsü, "Letter of Advice to Queen Victoria," 1839. Available at Brooklyn College Chinese Cultural Studies, http://acc6.its.brooklyn.cuny.edu/~phalsall/ texts/com-lin.html (accessed February 20, 2009).

Chapter 7. The War on Drugs

1. Frank Sanello, *The Opium Wars* (Naperville, Ill.: Sourcebooks, 2004), 74–75.

2. Ibid.

3. Richard P. T. Davenport-Hines, *The Pursuit of Oblivion: A Global History of Narcotics* (New York: W. W. Norton & Co., 2002), 100.

4. Ibid.

5. Ibid., 86.

6. John Strachan, "For the Ladies," *History Today* (April 2004). Available at http:// goliath.ecnext.com/coms2/gi_0199-204548/For-the-ladies-John-Strachan.html (accessed February 22, 2009).

7. Anthony S. Wahl, "Opium and Infant Mortality," Victorian Web, www
.victorianweb.org/science/health/health4.html (accessed February 22, 2009).

8. Friedrich Engels, *The Condition of the Working Class in England,* Otto
Henderson, trans. (Palo Alto, Calif.: Stanford University Press, 1958), 118.

9. Virginia Berridge and Griffith Edwards, "The 1868 Pharmacy Act," chap. 10
in *Opium and the People: Opiate Use in Nineteenth-Century England* (1987).
Available at Drugtext, www.drugtext.org/library/books/opiumpeople/pharmact
.html (accessed February 25, 2009).

10. Edward M. Brecher and the Editors of *Consumer Reports* Magazine,
"Nineteenth-Century America—A 'Dope Fiend's Paradise,'" chap. 1 in *The
Consumers Union Report on Licit and Illicit Drugs* (1972). Available at Schaffer
Library of Drug Policy, www.druglibrary.org/schaffer/Library/studies/cu/cu1
.html (accessed February 27, 2009).

11. Kathleen L. Lodwick, *Crusaders against Opium: Protestant Missionaries in
China, 1874–1917* (Louisville: University of Kentucky Press, 1996), 30.

12. Edward M. Brecher and the Editors of *Consumer Reports* Magazine, "Opium
Smoking Is Outlawed," chap. 6 in *The Consumers Union Report on Licit
and Illicit Drugs* (1972). Available at Schaffer Library of Drug Policy, www
.druglibrary.org/SCHAFFER/library/studies/cu/cu6.htm (accessed February
27, 2009).

13. Harrison Act, Sec. 2(a).

14. Hans A. Baer, Merrill Singer, and Ida Susser, *Medical Anthropology and the
World System: A Critical Perspective* (Westport, Conn.: Greenwood Publishing
Group, 2003), 188–89.

15. David T. Courtwright, "Morality, Religion and Drug Use," in *Morality and
Health: Interdisciplinary Perspectives,* Allan M. Brandt and Paul Rozin, eds.
(London: Routledge, 1997), 243.

16. Dan Russell, "Prohibition Is Treason," in *Under the Influence: The Disinformation Guide to Drugs,* Preston Peet, ed. (New York: Disinformation Company,
2004), 56.

17. Harry Anslinger, "Hemp Around Their Necks" (1961). Available at Drug
Library, http://druglibrary.net/schaffer/History/murd3.htm (accessed August
4, 2010).

18. Radley Balko, "Bush Should Feel Doctors' Pain," *Cato Institute,* April 5, 2005,
www.cato.org/pub_display.php?pub_id=3727 (accessed February 28, 2009).

19. Eric C. Schneider, *Smack* (Philadelphia: University of Pennsylvania Press,
2008), 23.

20. Rufus King, "The Drug Hang-Up, America's Fifty Year Folly, The Narcotic

Control Act of 1956." Available at Schaffer Library of Drug Policy, www
.druglibrary.org/special/king/dhu/dhu16.htm (accessed August 4, 2010).

21. Maia Szalavitz, "Drug Laws," *Gotham Gazette,* August 19, 2002, www
.gothamgazette.com/iotw/prisons/szalavitz.shtml (accessed February 28,
2009).

Chapter 8. Morphine

1. Ursula Klein, "Not a Pure Science: Chemistry in the 18th and 19th Centuries,"
Science 306 (5 November 2004): 981.

2. Friedrich Sertürner, "Darstellung der reinen Mohnsäure (Opiumsäure) nebst
einer Chemischen Untersuchung des Opiums mit vorzüglicher Hinsicht auf
einen darin neu entdeckten Stoff und die dahin gehörigen Bemerkungen,"
Journal der Pharmacie fuer Aerzte und Apotheker 14 (1806): 47–93, in Ryan
J. Huxtable and Stephan K. W. Schwarz, "The Isolation of Morphine—First
Principles in Science and Ethics," *Molecular Interventions* 1 (2001): 189–91,
http://molinterv.aspetjournals.org/cgi/reprint/1/4/189 (accessed September 19,
2007).

3. Friedrich Sertürner, "Ueber das Morphium, eine neue salzfähige Grundlage,
und die Mekonsäure, als Hauptbestandtheile des Opiums," *Annalen der Physik*
55 (1817): 56–89, in Ryan J. Huxtable and Stephan K. W. Schwarz, "The
Isolation of Morphine—First Principles in Science and Ethics," *Molecular
Interventions* 1 (2001): 189–91, http://molinterv.aspetjournals.org/cgi/
reprint/1/4/189 (accessed September 19, 2007).

4. Martin Booth, *Opium: A History* (New York: St. Martin's Press, 1998),
69–70.

5. Richard P. T. Davenport-Hines, *The Pursuit of Oblivion: A Global History of
Narcotics* (New York: W. W. Norton & Co., 2002), 100.

6. Donald G. McNeil Jr., "Fear of Morphine Dooms Third World Poor to
Die Painfully," *New York Times,* September 10, 2007, www.nytimes.com/
2007/09/10/health/10pain.html?ex=1347163200&en=6b9e294119deb150&ei
=5124 (accessed February 4, 2009).

7. International Council on Security and Development: Poppy for Medicine,
"Global Need for Morphine," 2007, www.poppyformedicine.net/modules/
need_morphine/html_met (accessed February 4, 2009).

8. Nell Muirden, "Report on IAHPC Traveling Fellowship to Papua New
Guinea," International Association for Hospice & Palliative Care, 2001, www
.hospicecare.com/travelfellow/tf2001/papuanewguinea.htm (accessed February
4, 2009).

9. News-Medical.net, "Morphine for Cancer Pain Relief," December 11, 2007, www.news-medical.net/?id=33381 (accessed February 4, 2009).

10. Sydney Speisel, "Your Health This Week," *Slate,* October 16, 2007, www.slate .com/id/2176013/ (accessed February 4, 2009).

11. Carl Sherman, "Adjunctive Oral Morphine Effective For Refractory OCD," *Clinical Psychiatry News* (July 2001). Available at FindArticles, http://findarticles .com/p/articles/mi_hb4345/is_7_29/ai_n28856777/pg_1 (accessed February 4, 2009).

12. Michael Feinberg, Jean-Paul Pegeron, and Meir Steiner, "The Effect of Morphine on Symptoms of Endogenous Depression," *NIDA Research Monograph Series* 43 (1982): 245–50. Available at http://opioids.com/antidepressant/history .html (accessed February 4, 2009).

13. Edward M. Brecher and the Editors of *Consumer Reports* Magazine, "Opiates for Pain Relief, for Tranquilization, and for Pleasure," chap. 2 in *The Consumers Union Report on Licit and Illicit Drugs* (1972). Available at Schaffer Library of Drug Policy, www.druglibrary.org/SCHAFFER/library/studies/cu/cu2.html (accessed February 28, 2009).

14. Ibid.

Chapter 9. Codeine

1. W. Hale White, "Codeina. Codeine. Methyl Morphine," in *Materia Medica, Pharmacy, Pharmacology and Therapeutics* (1911). Available at Chest of Books, http://chestofbooks.com/health/materia-medica-drugs/Pharmacy-Pharmacology-And-Therapeutics/Codeina-Codeine-Methyl-Morphine.html (accessed February 9, 2009).

2. Paul Schiff, "Opium and Its Alkaloids," *American Journal of Pharmaceutical Education* 66 (2002): 186–94. Available at http://findarticles.com/p/articles/ mi_qa3833/is_200207/ai_n9107282/print (accessed September 25, 2007).

3. John R. Horn and Philip D. Hansten, "Narcotic Analgesics Metabolized by CYP2D6," *Pharmacy Times,* www.pharmacytimes.com/issues/articles/ 2005-05_2238.asp (accessed February 9, 2009).

4. Gideon Koren, James Cairns, David Chitayat, Andrea Gaedigk, and Steven J. Leeder, "Pharmacogenetics of Fatal Morphine Poisoning in a Breastfed Neonate of a Codeine Using Mother," Motherrisk, 2003, www.motherisk.org/documents/ Codeine-Breastfeeding-Lancet_Case_Report.doc (accessed February 9, 2009).

5. Lauren Neegard, "Most Popular Painkiller Is Lead Cause of Acute Liver Failure," *Associated Press,* December 25, 2005, www.natap.org/2006/HCV/013006_04 .htm (accessed February 5, 2009).

6. Ibid.

7. Maren Mayhew, "Acetaminophen Toxicity," *Journal for Nurse Practitioners* 3, no. 3 (May 30, 2007): 186–88. Available at Medscape, www.medscape.com/viewarticle/557074 (accessed February 6, 2009).

8. K. R. Bedford, S. L. Nolan, R. Onrust, and J. D. Siegers, "The Illicit Preparation of Morphine and Heroin from Pharmaceutical Products Containing Codeine: 'Homebake' Laboratories in New Zealand," *Forensic Science International* 34, no. 3 (1987): 197–204. Available at www.erowid.org/archive/rhodium/chemistry/codeine.homebake.labs.html (accessed September 25, 2007).

9. Ibid.

10. "Waiting Lists Send Addicts Back to a Life of Crime," Stuff, www.stuff.co.nz/national/600628 (accessed August 8, 2010).

11. Editorial, "Glutethimide—An Unsafe Alternative to Barbiturate Hypnotics," *British Medical Journal* 1, no. 6023 (June 12, 1976): 1424–25.

12. Poison Control Center/Children's Hospital of Philadelphia, "Loads," 1996, www.chop.edu/consumer/jsp/division/generic.jsp?id=72607 (accessed February 10, 2009).

13. News-Medical.net, "Noscapine Effective against Prostate Cancer," February 18, 2007, www.news-medical.net/?id=21951 (accessed February 10, 2009).

14. MedInsight Research Group, "Noscapine: A Safe Cough Suppressant with Newly Discovered Effects in Treating Cancer and Stroke," February 2007, www.pcref.org/MedInsight%20-%20PCREF%20Noscapine%20Review.pdf (accessed February 10, 2009).

15. Ibid., 5.

Chapter 10. Heroin

1. Namit Verma Delhi, "The Dope on Dope," *Hard News*, July 2006, www.hardnewsmedia.com/2007/10/1582 (accessed March 1, 2009).

2. "Heroin Hydrochloride" in *Bayer Pharmaceutical Products and Technical Preparations* Cincinnati, Ohio: Dow's Anti-Trust Drug Stores, 1900. Available at Sure Cure Antiques, www.surecureantiques.com/items/700152/en2store.html (accessed August 8, 2010).

3. Tom Carnwath and Ian Smith, *Heroin Century* (London: Routledge, 2002), 54.

4. Alfred W. McCoy, "Luciano Organizes the Postwar Heroin Trade," in *The Politics of Heroin in Southeast Asia* (1972). Available at Drugtext, www.drugtext.org/library/books/McCoy/book/09.htm (accessed March 5, 2009).

5. Jorrit Kamminga, "The Political History of Turkey's Opium Licensing System for

the Production of Medicines: Lessons for Afghanistan," International Council on Security and Development: Poppy for Medicine, www.poppyformedicine .net/documents/Political_History_Poppy_Licensing_Turkey_May_2006.pdf (accessed March 6, 2009).

6. Sidney Cohen, *The Substance Abuse Problems,* vol. 1 and 2 (Binghamton, N.Y.: Haworth Press, 1985), 180.

7. Alfred W. McCoy, "The Consequences of Complicity: A Generation of Junkies," in *The Politics of Heroin in Southeast Asia* (1972). Available at Drugtext, www .drugtext.org/library/books/McCoy/book/48.htm (accessed March 6, 2009).

8. Mark Jacobson, "The Return of Superfly," *New York Magazine,* August 14, 2000, http://nymag.com/nymetro/news/people/features/3649/ (accessed March 6, 2009).

9. Jennifer Lloyd, "Heroin," *Almanac of Policy Issues* (June 2003), www.policyalmanac .org/crime/archive/heroin.shtml (accessed March 6, 2009).

Chapter 11. Kompot

1. E. A. Babaian, "Drug Addiction Control in the USSR," *Bulletin on Narcotics* (1971/01/01), www.unodc.org/unodc/en/data-and-analysis/bulletin/bulletin _1971-01-01_1_page002.html (accessed January 7, 2009).

2. Jennifer Hull, "Eastern Europe Shooting Up Under a Red Star," *Time,* June 24, 2001, www.time.com/time/magazine/article/0,9171,145798,00.html (accessed January 6, 2009).

3. Drug Law and Health Policy Resource Network, *Drug Law and Policy in Poland* (Drug Law and Health Policy Resource Network, 2002). Available at Drug Policy Alliance, www.drugpolicy.org/docUploads/POLAND.pdf (accessed January 7, 2009).

4. Klemens Ochel, "Introduction: HIV/AIDS and Human Development in Central and Eastern Europe and the Commonwealth of Independent States" (2004). Available at Caritas Europa, www.caritas-europa.org/module/FileLib/ PresentationHIVTrendsResponses-DrKlemensOchel.pdf (accessed January 7, 2009).

5. Zofia Smardz, "The Crisis of Polish Drug Abuse," *Alicia Patterson Foundation* 10, no. 2 (1987), www.aliciapatterson.org/APF1002/Smardz/Smardz.html (accessed January 7, 2009).

6. P. C. van Duyne, *Cross-Border Crime in a Changing Europe* (Huntington, N.Y.: Nova Science Publishers, 2001), 80–82.

7. Jane Narvilene, "Open Borders: Threats and Opportunities" (address to the Conference of the European Cities against Drugs, April 25, 2002), www.ecad .net/conf/conf2_8.html (accessed January 7, 2009).

8. Smardz, "Polish Drug Abuse."

9. Drug Law and Health Policy Network, *Drug Policies = Death: HIV/AIDS in Central and Eastern Europe* (Drug Law and Health Policy Network, 2002). Available at www.drugpolicy.org/docUploads/drugpolicies_death.pdf (accessed January 7, 2009).

10. Ochel, "Introduction."

11. Smardz, "Polish Drug Abuse."

12. Tom Carnwath and Ian Smith, *Heroin Century* (London: Routledge, 2002), 158.

13. Michael Schwirtz, "Russia Scorns Methadone for Heroin Addiction," *New York Times*, July 22, 2008, www.nytimes.com/2008/07/22/health/22meth.htm.

14. Human Rights Watch, "Russia: Drug Addiction Treatment Requires Reform," November 22, 2007, http://thinkweb.hrw.org/en/news/2007/11/07/russia-drug-addiction-treatment-requires-reform (accessed January 7, 2009).

15. Human Rights Watch, "Rhetoric and Risk: Human Rights Abuses Impeding Ukraine's Fight against HIV/AIDS," March 1, 2006, www.hrw.org/en/reports/2006/03/01/rhetoric-and-risk (accessed January 7, 2009).

16. Peter Baker, "Russia Sees an AIDS Explosion," *Washington Post,* June 13, 2004.

17. Martin Jelsma, "Learning Lessons from the Taliban Opium Ban," *International Journal on Drug Policy* 16, no. 2 (March 2005). Available at Transnational Institute, www.tni.org/detail_page.phtml?page=archives_jelsma_taliban (accessed January 6, 2009).

Chapter 12. Oxycodone

1. Department of Health and Human Services Tasmania, "Thebaine," www.dhhs.tas.gov.au/service_information/information/thebaine (accessed January 29, 2009).

2. Robert D. Johnson, Russell J. Lewis, and Rachael Hatrap, *Poppy Seed Consumption or Opiate Use: The Determination of Thebaine and Opiates of Abuse in Postmortem Fluids and Tissues* (Washington, D.C.: Office of Aerospace Medicine, 2005). Available at www.faa.gov/library/reports/medical/oamtechreports/2000s/media/0511.pdf (accessed September 25, 2007).

3. Barry Meier, *Pain Killer: A "Wonder" Drug's Trail of Addiction and Death*, rev. ed. (New York: Rodale Publishers, 2003), 93.

4. Ibid., 73.

5. Ibid., 94.

6. Ibid., 97.

7. Paul Tough, "The Alchemy of OxyContin," *New York Times,* July 29, 2001, http://query.nytimes.com/gst/fullpage.html?res=9403E2DF113AF93AA1575 4C0A9679C8B63 (accessed February 28, 2009).

8. Ronald T. Libby, *The Criminalization of Medicine* (Westport, Conn.: Greenwood Publishing Group, 2008), 10.

9. Tough, "Alchemy of OxyContin."

10. Fox Butterfield, "Theft of Painkiller Reflects Its Popularity on the Street," *New York Times,* July 7, 2001, http://query.nytimes.com/gst/fullpage.html?res= 980CE6DE1238F934A35754C0A9679C8B63 (accessed February 28, 2009).

11. Dave McDaniel, "Local Pharmacist Pulls OxyContin from Shelves," MSNBC .com, February 18, 2009, www.msnbc.msn.com/id/29245824/ (accessed March 1, 2009).

12. Tina Rosenberg, "When Is a Pain Doctor a Drug Pusher?" *New York Times Magazine,* June 17, 2007, www.nytimes.com/2007/06/17/magazine/17pain-t .html?pagewanted=all (accessed February 28, 2009).

Chapter 13. Methadone

1. Ralf Gerlach, "A Brief Overview on the Discovery of Methadone," INDRO Online, www.indro-online.de/discovery.pdf (accessed January 10, 2009).

2. G. Gazelle and P. G. Fine, "Fast Fact and Concept #75: Methadone for Pain," End of Life/Palliative Education Resource Center, 2002, www.eperc.mcw.edu/ fastFact/ff_75.htm (accessed January 10, 2009).

3. Joyce H. Lowinson, et al., "Methadone Maintenance," in *Substance Abuse: A Comprehensive Textbook,* Joyce H. Lowinson, Pedro Ruiz, Robert B. Millman, and John G. Langrod, eds. (New York: Lippincott Williams & Wilkins, 2004), 617.

4. Edward M. Brecher and the Editors of *Consumer Reports* Magazine, "Enter Methadone Maintenance," chap. 14 in *The Consumers Union Report on Licit and Illicit Drugs* (1972). Available at Schaffer Library of Drug Policy, www .druglibrary.org/schaffer/library/studies/cu/CU14.html (accessed January 8, 2009).

5. Peter Conrad and Joseph W. Schneider, *Deviance and Medicalization: From Badness to Sickness* (Philadelphia, Pa.: Temple University Press, 1992), 134.

6. Edward M. Brecher and the editors of *Consumer Reports* magazine, "How Well Does Methadone Maintenance Work?" chap. 15 in *The Consumers Union Report on Licit and Illicit Drugs* (1972). Available at Schaffer Library of Drug Policy, http://druglibrary.org/schaffer/Library/studies/cu/CU15.html (accessed January 8, 2009).

7. Herman Joseph, "Medical Methadone Maintenance: The Further Concealment of a Stigmatized Condition," *Methadone Today,* 1995, www.methadonetoday.org/dole_nys.htm (accessed January 11, 2009).

8. David T. Courtwright, *Dark Paradise: A History of Opiate Addiction in America* (Boston: Harvard University Press, 2001), 172.

9. Colleen O'Donnell and Marcia Trick, *Methadone Maintenance Treatment and the Criminal Justice System* (Washington, D.C.: National Association of State Alcohol/Drug Abuse Directors, 2006). Available at www.nasadad.org/resource.php?base_id=650 (accessed January 11, 2009).

10. World Service Board of Trustees, "Regarding Methadone and Other Drug Replacement Programs," *Narcotics Anonymous,* Bulletin 29 (1996), www.na.org/bulletins/bull29.htm (accessed January 11, 2009).

Chapter 14. Fentanyl

1. European Monitoring Centre for Drugs and Drug Addiction, "Fentanyl," 2008, www.emcdda.europa.eu/publications/drug-profiles/fentanyl (accessed March 10, 2009).

2. Evelyn Pringle, "Fentanyl Deaths—Severe Math Problems at FDA," *Counterpunch,* March 27, 2006, www.counterpunch.org/pringle03282006.html (accessed March 10, 2009).

3. T. Stephen Jones et al., "Nonpharmaceutical Fentanyl-Related Deaths— Multiple States, April 2005–March 2007," *Center for Disease Control Morbidity and Mortality Weekly Report,* July 25, 2008, www.cdc.gov/mmwr/preview/mmwrhtml/mm5729a1.htm (accessed March 10, 2009).

4. William Langston, M.D., interview by Frontline, PBS, January 29, 2009, www.pbs.org/wgbh/pages/frontline/parkinsons/interviews/langston.html (accessed March 10, 2009).

5. Joe Schwarz, "Aim High: Synthetic Opiates Deliver Surprising Side Effects," *Canadian Chemical News,* November 1, 2005, www.accessmylibrary.com/coms2/summary_0286-17674944_ITM (accessed March 10, 2009).

6. National Institute of Health, *The Role of the Environment in Parkinson's Disease* (Research Triangle Park, N.C.: National Institute of Environmental Health Sciences, 2005). Available at www.niehs.nih.gov/health/topics/conditions/parkinson/docs/parkinson.pdf (accessed March 10, 2009).

7. *BBC News World Edition,* "In Quotes: Moscow Hostage Crisis," October 25, 2002, http://news.bbc.co.uk/2/hi/europe/2358667.stm (accessed March 10, 2009).

8. Sabrina Tavernise with Sophia Kishkovsky, "Hostage Drama in Moscow:

The Scene; The Survivors Dribble Out, All with a Story to Tell," *New York Times,* October 28, 2002, http://query.nytimes.com/gst/fullpage.html?res= 9B05E0DD173FF93BA15753C1A9649C8B63 (accessed March 10, 2009).

9. "How Special Forces Ended Siege," BBC News World Edition, October 29, 2002, http://news.bbc.co.uk/2/hi/europe/2363601.stm (accessed March 10, 2009).

10. Ibid.

11. "Russia Names Siege Gas," BBC News World Edition, October 30, 2002, http://news.bbc.co.uk/2/hi/europe/2377563.stm (accessed March 10, 2009).

12. Susan K. Mikota and Donald C. Plumb, "The Elephant Formulary: Carfentanil," Elephant Care, 2006, www.elephantcare.org/Drugs/carfenta.htm (accessed March 10, 2009).

13. ZooPharm, "Drug Information: Carnfentanil Citrate," 2007, www.zoopharm .net/drugs/carfentanil.php (accessed March 10, 2009).

Chapter 15. Samuel Taylor Coleridge

1. Samuel Taylor Coleridge, note published with the poem "Kubla Khan." Available at Norton Anthology of Poetry, www.wwnorton.com/college/english/ nap/Kubla_Khan_Coler.htm (accessed August 7, 2010).

2. Ibid.

3. Samuel Taylor Coleridge, note on a manuscript copy of "Kubla Khan." Available at University of Virginia Electronic Text Center, http://etext.virginia.edu/stc/ Coleridge/poems/notes.html#KublaKhan (accessed March 10, 2009).

4. James Gillman, *The Life of Samuel Taylor Coleridge* (1838). Available at Project Gutenberg, http://infomotions.com/etexts/gutenberg/dirs/etext05/7smtg10 .htm (accessed March 10, 2009).

5. Ibid.

6. Cheryl Bolen, "Sara Coleridge: Wife of an Opium Eater," www.cherylbolen .com/coleridge.htm (accessed March 11, 2009).

7. Ibid.

8. John Keats, letter of John Keats to George and Georgiana Keats, April 25, 1819. Available at University of Virginia Electronic Text Center, http://etext.virginia .edu/stc/Keats/on_STC.html (accessed March 11, 2009).

9. Samuel Taylor Coleridge, "Cologne," 1828. Available at University of Virginia Electronic Text Center, http://etext.virginia.edu/stc/Coleridge/poems/ Cologne.html (accessed March 11, 2009).

10. Bolen, "Sara Coleridge."

Chapter 16. Thomas de Quincey

1. Thomas de Quincey, *Confessions of an English Opium-Eater* (1821). Available at Project Gutenberg, www.gutenberg.org/files/2040/2040-h/2040-h.htm (accessed March 11, 2009).

2. Ibid.

3. Ibid.

4. David Watson Rannie, *Wordsworth and His Circle* (Bethuen, Mich.: University of Michigan Press, 1907), 206.

5. Peter Landry, "The Classical Fiction Writers: Thomas de Quincey," Blupete Biographies, www.blupete.com/Literature/Biographies/Literary/DeQuincey .htm (accessed March 12, 2009).

6. de Quincey, *Confessions*.

7. Ibid.

8. Robert Morrison, "Thomas de Quincey—Chronology," Thomas de Quincey Homepage, September 13, 2008, www.queensu.ca/english/tdq/chron.html (accessed March 11, 2009).

9. David Masson, *De Quincey* (New York: Macmillan & Company, 1902), 81.

Chapter 17. Elizabeth Barrett Browning

1. Louise Foxcroft, *The Making of Addiction* (Surrey, England: Ashgate Publishers, 2007), 46.

2. Elizabeth Barrett Browning, *The Letters of Elizabeth Barrett Browning,* Frederic George Kenyon, ed. (New York: Macmillan, 1897), 288.

3. Richard S. Kennedy and Donald S. Hair, *The Dramatic Imagination of Robert Browning: A Literary Life* (Columbia: University of Missouri Press, 2007), 7.

4. Julia Markus, "Interview," *Ebony* 50, no. 7 (May 1995): 100.

5. Foxcroft, *Making of Addiction,* 47.

6. Ibid.

7. Angela Leighton, *Elizabeth Barrett Browning* (Bloomington: Indiana University Press, 1986), 31.

8. Margaret Foster, *Selected Poems and Letters of Elizabeth Barrett Browning,* 3rd ed. (Baltimore: Johns Hopkins University Press, 1988), xv.

9. Julia Ward Howe, *Words for the Hour* (Boston: Ticknor and Fields, 1857), 146.

10. Foxcroft, *Making of Addiction,* 48.

Chapter 18. Eugene O'Neill

1. Arthur Gelb, Barbara Gelb, and Ric Burns, writers, transcript of "Eugene O'Neill," *American Experience,* PBS, 2006, www.pbs.org/wgbh/amex/oneill/filmmore/pt.html (accessed February 1, 2009).

2. Ibid.

3. Eugene O'Neill, *Long Day's Journey into Night* (New Haven, Conn.: Yale University Press, 1956), 96.

4. Barbara Gelb, "A Second Look, and a Second Chance to Forgive," *New York Times,* March 19, 2000, http://query.nytimes.com/gst/fullpage.html?res=9C0DE4DB113BF93AA25750C0A9669C8B63&sec=&spon=&pagewanted=print (accessed February 2, 2009).

5. O'Neill, *Long Day's Journey,* 75.

6. Nancy J. Herman, *Deviance: A Symbolic Interactionist Approach* (Lanham, Md.: Rowman Altamira, 1995), 207.

7. Stephen R. Kandall, *Substance and Shadow: Women and Addiction in the United States* (Boston: Harvard University Press, 1999), 80.

8. O'Neill, *Long Day's Journey,* 97.

9. Doris Alexander, *Eugene O'Neill's Last Plays: Separating Art from Autobiography* (Athens: University of Georgia Press, 2005), 122.

Chapter 19. Nelson Algren

1. Nelson Algren, "The Art of Fiction No. 11," interview by Alston Anderson and Terry Southern, *Paris Review* 11 (Winter 1955), http://theparisreview.org/media/4987_ALGREN.pdf.

2. "The Motion Picture Production Code of 1930 (Hays Code)." Available at Arts Reformation, www.artsreformation.com/a001/hays-code.html (accessed January 26, 2009).

3. Nelson Algren, "Art of Fiction."

4. Ibid.

5. Nelson Algren, *The Man with the Golden Arm: 50th Anniversary Critical Edition* (New York: Seven Stories Press, 1999), 123.

6. Stephen J. Whitfield, *The Culture of the Cold War* (Baltimore: Johns Hopkins University Press, 1996), 183.

Chapter 20. Charlie Parker

1. Carl Woideck, *Charlie Parker* (Ann Arbor: University of Michigan Press, 1998), 10.

2. Jill Jonnes, *Hep-Cats, Narcs, and Pipe Dreams: A History of America's Romance with Illegal Drugs* (Baltimore: Johns Hopkins University Press, 1999), 120.

3. Daniel Belgrad, *The Culture of Spontaneity* (Chicago: University of Chicago Press, 1999), 182.

4. Geoffrey I. Wills, "Forty Lives in the Bebop Business: Mental Health in a Group of Eminent Jazz Musicians," *The British Journal of Psychiatry* 183 (2003): 255–59.

5. Jack Chambers, *Milestones: the Music and Times of Miles Davis* (Cambridge, Mass: Da Capo Press, 1998), 137.

6. Llew Walker, "Addiction," *Bird Lives,* September 19, 2005, www.birdlives.co.uk/index.php/addiction.html (accessed April 1, 2009).

7. Robert George Reisner, *Bird: The Legend of Charlie Parker* (Cambridge, Mass.: Da Capo Press, 1977), 42.

8. Woideck, *Charlie Parker,* 49.

Chapter 21. William S. Burroughs

1. William S. Burroughs, "William S. Burroughs: The Creem Interviews," interview by Jeffrey Morgan, *Creem Magazine,* www.creemmagazine.com/_site/BeatGoesOn/WilliamSBurroughs/CreemInterviews001.html (accessed February 25, 2009).

2. *Burroughs,* directed by Howard Brookner, 1984. Available at http://video.google.com/videoplay?docid=9198809969200913970 (accessed April 14, 2009).

3. William S. Burroughs, *Junky* (New York: Penguin Books, 1977), xv.

4. William S. Burroughs, *Naked Lunch* (New York: Grove Press, 2003), 10.

5. Appeal of P.O.D. Docket No. 1/150—BIG TABLE Magazine Available at United States Postal Service, www.usps.com/judicial/1959deci/1-150d.htm (accessed April 15, 2009).

6. John C. Kramer, M.D., "William Burroughs: A Sketch," *Journal of Psychoactive Drugs* (January–March 1981). Available at www.erowid.org/culture/characters/burroughs_william/burroughs_william_article1.shtml (accessed April 15, 2009).

7. William S. Burroughs, *Last Words: The Final Journals of William S. Burroughs,* James Rauerholz, ed. (New York: Grove Press, 2001), 252.

Chapter 22. Lou Reed

1. Nicholas Taylor, "The Velvet Underground in New York, New York in the Velvet Underground," *PopMatters,* 2001, www.popmatters.com/music/features/020207-velvetunderground.html (accessed February 2, 2009).

2. Warholstars, "Andy Warhol Chronology, 1966," www.warholstars.org/chron/1966.html (accessed August 3, 2010).

3. Clinton Heylin, ed., *All Yesterdays' Parties: The Velvet Underground in Print, 1966–1971* (Cambridge, Mass.: Da Capo Press, 2006), 12.

4. Marc Masters, "NO! The Origins of No Wave," *Pitchfork Media,* January 15, 2008, www.pitchforkmedia.com/article/feature/47828-no-the-origins-of-no-wave (accessed February 4, 2009).

5. Lou Reed, interview, 1974. Available at YouTube, www.youtube.com/watch?v=mf2pF5oMdP4 (accessed February 4, 2009).

6. Lou Reed, "Lou Reed Forum: Ask Lou," Lou Reed official site, December 13, 2007, http://loureed.com/forum/comments.php?DiscussionID=2&page=1#Item_0 (accessed February 4, 2009).

7. Allison Adato, "Crash and Burn: The Most Untimely Death of a White-Hot Germ," *Los Angeles Times,* December 3, 2000, http://home.earthlink.net/~aladato/darby.html (accessed February 4, 2009).

Chapter 23. Gia Carangi

1. Stephen Fried, *Thing of Beauty: The Tragedy of Supermodel Gia* (New York: Pocket Books, 1993), chapter 1. Available at www.stephenfried.com/gia/giabook_chp1.html (accessed April 2, 2009).

2. The Gia Carangi Project, "Biography," www.giamariecarangi.hpg.com.br/biography1.htm (accessed April 2, 2009).

3. *The Self-Destruction of Gia,* directed by J. J. Martin, 2003.

4. Lawrie Masterson, "Fashion Victim," *Australian Women's Weekly,* April 1998. Available at www.giamariecarangi.hpg.com.br/australian/article8.JPG (accessed April 5, 2009).

5. "History of AIDS up to 1986," AVERT, www.avert.org/aids-history-86.htm (accessed April 5, 2009).

6. Lawrence K. Altman, "Spread of AIDS Virus Is Unabated among Intravenous Drug Takers," *New York Times,* June 4, 1987, www.nytimes.com/1987/06/04/us/spread-of-aids-virus-is-unabated-among-intravenous-drug-takers.html (accessed April 5, 2009).

7. Amy M. Spindler, "The 90s Version of the Decadent Look," *New York Times,* May 7, 1996, www.nytimes.com/1996/05/07/style/the-90-s-version-of-the-decadent-look.html (accessed April 5, 2009).

8. Christopher S. Wren, "Clinton Calls Fashion Ads' 'Heroin Chic' Deplorable," *New York Times,* May 22, 1997, www.nytimes.com/1997/05/22/us/clinton-

calls-fashion-ads-heroin-chic-deplorable.html?scp=2&sq=heroin chic clinton &st=cse (accessed April 5, 2009).

9. Ibid.

10. Richard B. Woodward, "Whither Fashion Photography," *New York Times,* June 22, 1997, www.nytimes.com/1997/06/08/style/whither-fashion-photography .html?scp=5&sq=heroin chic clinton&st=cse&pagewanted=all (accessed April 5, 2009).

Chapter 24. Layne Staley

1. Gene Johnson, "Layne Staley, Lead Singer of Alice in Chains, Found Dead at 34 in Seattle Home," *Associated Press,* April 20, 2002, http://slick.org/ deathwatch/mailarchive/msg00715.html (accessed February 11, 2009).

2. Jon Wiederhorn, "Late Alice in Chains Singer Layne Staley's Last Interview Revealed in New Book," MTV, February 25, 2003, www.mtv.com/news/ articles/1470138/20030225/story.jhtml (accessed February 11, 2009).

3. Charles R. Cross, "The Last Days of Layne Staley," *Rolling Stone,* June 1, 2002, http://aic.gsg2007.de/Artikel/RS%200106.html (accessed February 11, 2009).

4. *Seattle Times* Staff, "'Seattle Scene' and Heroin Use: How Bad Is It?" *Seattle Times,* April 20, 1994, http://community.seattletimes.nwsource.com/archive/ ?date=19940420&slug=1906421 (accessed February 11, 2009).

5. Wiederhorn, "Layne Staley's Last Interview."

6. Ibid.

7. Jon Wiederhorn, "To Hell and Back," *Rolling Stone,* February 8, 1996, www .rollingstone.com/artists/aliceinchains/articles/story/5934699/cover_story_ to_hell_and_back (accessed February 11, 2009).

8. Ibid.

9. Wiederhorn, "Layne Staley's Last Interview."

10. Pat Kearney, "We Left Him Alone," *Blender,* August 2002, www.blender.com/ guide/articles.aspx?id=373 (accessed February 11, 2009).

Chapter 25. Robert Earl "DJ Screw" Davis

1. Bilal Allah, "DJ Screw: Giving It to You Slow," *Rap Pages* (November 1995): 84.

2. Jesse Washington, "Life in the Slow Lane," *Houston Press,* January 18, 2001, www.houstonpress.com/2001-01-18/news/life-in-the-slow-lane (accessed March 15, 2009).

3. Michael Hall, "The Slow Life and Fast Death of DJ Screw," *Texas Monthly* (April 2001), www.texasmonthly.com/2001-04-01/feature.php (accessed March 15, 2009).

4. Wyeth Pharmaceuticals, "Phenergan (Promethazine) Information," RxList, June 2007, www.rxlist.com/phenergan-drug.htm (accessed March 18, 2009).

5. Hall, "Slow Life."

6. Washington, "Life in the Slow Lane."

7. Ibid.

8. YouTube, "DJ Screw: The Untold Story Part 11 of 11," www.youtube.com/watch?v=8PLx9Bb8JkI&feature=PlayList&p=F3119981B1281AE5&index=10 (accessed March 15, 2009).

9. Hall, "Slow Life."

10. Bryan Robinson, "Cough Syrup Abuse in Texas Takes Center Stage," *ABC News,* August 17, 2005, http://abcnews.go.com/Health/LegalCenter/Story?id=1045329 (accessed March 20, 2009).

11. RapSearch, "Bun B Reacts to Pimp C's Death," www.rapsearch.com/news/article/bun-b-reacts-to-pimp-c-s-death (accessed March 20, 2009).

Chapter 26. Cultivation

1. Alexander Cockburn and Jeffrey St. Clair, *Whiteout: The CIA, Drugs, and the Press* (London: Verso, 1998), 230.

2. VOA Afghanistan Service, "The Business of Opium in Afghanistan: Nangahar Poppies," *Voice of America,* May 27, 2008, www.voanews.com/english/archive/2008-05/2008-05-27-voa38.cfm (accessed April 8, 2009).

3. Juan G. Tokatlian, "The United States and Illegal Crops in Colombia: The Tragic Mistake of Futile Fumigation," Center for Latin American Studies (CLAS) Working Papers No. 3 (Berkeley: Center for Latin American Studies, University of California, Berkeley, 2003). Available at http://repositories.cdlib.org/clas/wp/3 (accessed August 3, 2010).

4. Global Exchange, "The Failed Drug War," December 1, 2004, www.globalexchange.org/countries/americas/colombia/failedDrugWar.html (accessed April 8, 2009).

5. Silence Maestas, "Plant and Entheogen FAQ," Firefly Pages, 2006, http://firefly.gydja.com/plantfaq.html (accessed April 8, 2009).

6. Conversation with Christopher Penczak, 2008.

Chapter 27. Poppy Tea

1. David Elliston Allen and Gabrielle Hatfield, *Medicinal Plants in Folk Tradition: An Ethnobotany of Britain & Ireland* (Portland, Ore.: Timber Press, 2004), 77.

2. Dan McDougall, "Afghans Hit Hardest by Biggest Opium Crop," *Guardian,*

May 15, 2007, www.guardian.co.uk/world/2007/may/13/afghanistan.drugstrade (accessed January 30, 2009).

3. Jason Vest and Cynthia Cotts, "DEA to Florists: The Poppies Are Unlovely: Inside the War on Floral Arrangements," *US News and World Report,* March 9, 1997, www.usnews.com/usnews/biztech/articles/970317/archive_006475.htm (accessed January 31, 2009).

4. U.S. Drug Enforcement Administration, "Intelligence Alert—Opium Poppies Sold over the Internet from California," *Microgram Bulletin* 36, no. 5 (May 2003), www.usdoj.gov/dea/programs/forensicsci/microgram/mg0503/mg0503 .html (accessed August 3, 2010).

5. County of Santa Clara Crime Laboratory, "Poppy Tea Analysis," Physical Evidence Examination Report, San Jose, Calif., November 21, 2003. Available at Poppy Seed Tea Can Kill You, www.poppyseedtea.com/Poppy_Tea_Analysis .html (accessed January 31, 2009).

6. "Poppy Tea Is the Fucking Devil!" Bluelight: Other Drugs Forum, www .bluelight.ru/vb/showthread.php?t=368766 (accessed January 31, 2009).

Chapter 28. Pills, Tablets, and Capsules

1. B. Ebbell, trans., *The Ebers Papyrus* (Copenhagen: Levin & Munksgaard, 1937). Available at www.macalester.edu/~cuffel/ebers.htm (accessed August 3, 2010).

2. Rosie Mestel, "The Colorful History of Pills Can Fill Many a Tablet," *Los Angeles Times,* March 25, 2002, http://articles.latimes.com/2002/mar/25/ health/he-booster25 (accessed April 10, 2009).

3. C. J. S. Thomspon, *Mystery and Art of the Apothecary* (Whitefish, Mont.: Kessinger Publishing, 2003), 29.

4. Larry Ausberger, "Hard and Soft Shell Capsules," in *Modern Pharmaceutics,* 4th ed., Gilbert S. Banker and Christopher T. Rhodes, eds. (London: Informa Healthcare, 2002), 336.

Chapter 29. Smoking

1. Keith McMahon, *The Fall of the God of Money: Opium Smoking in Nineteenth-Century China* (Lanham, Md.: Rowman & Littlefield Publishers, 2002), 36.

2. Ellen N. La Motte, "History of the Opium Trade in China," *The Opium Monopoly* (New York: Macmillan, 1920), chapter 15. Available at Schaffer Library of Drug Policy, www.druglibrary.org/schaffer/history/om/om15.htm (accessed April 17, 2009).

3. Jill Jonnes, *Hep-Cats, Narcs, and Pipe Dreams: A History of America's Romance with Illegal Drugs* (Baltimore: Johns Hopkins University Press, 1999), 27.

4. Transcript of episode 5, "Chinese Opium Scale, Butte, Montana," *History Detectives,* PBS, 2006, www.pbs.org/opb/historydetectives/pdf/406_opiumscale.pdf (accessed April 17, 2009).

5. Louise Foxcroft, *The Making of Addiction* (Surrey, England: Ashgate Publishers, 2007), 71.

6. Bob Newhart, transcript of "How Did Sir Walter Raleigh Sell His Tobacco?" *Bob Newhart Show,* NBC, April 18, 1962. Available at Tobacco Documents Online, http://tobaccodocuments.org/pm/1003044449-4450.html (accessed April 20, 2009).

7. Frank Dikötter, "'Patient Zero': China and the Myth of the Opium Plague" (London: School of Oriental and African Studies, Inaugural Lecture Series, October 24, 2003). Available at http://web.mac.com/dikotter/Dikotter/Publications.html (accessed April 19, 2009).

8. John Blatherwick, "Toxic Leukoencephalopathy Continues to Rise among BC Heroin Smokers," *Vancouver Coastal Health,* November 27, 2003, www.vch.ca/news/docs/2003_11_27_toxic_leukoencephalopathy.pdf (accessed April 20, 2009).

Chapter 30. Insufflation

1. Russell Durant and Jo Thakker, *Substance Use and Abuse: Cultural and Historical Perspectives* (Thousand Oaks, Calif.: SAGE, 2003), 87.

2. Chris Bury, "An Innocent Name for a Deadly Drug," *ABC News,* May 24, 2007, http://abcnews.go.com/Nightline/Story?id=3023299 (accessed April 29, 2009).

3. Kent Fischer and Jason Trahan, "New Drug Craze Hits DISD: Tylenol PM-Heroin Combo May Have Caused Dallas Teen's Death," *Dallas Morning News,* April 28, 2006, www.dallasnews.com/sharedcontent/dws/dn/latestnews/stories/042806dnmetnewdrug.13fb8bb3.html (accessed April 21, 2009).

4. Jason Trahan, Sergio Chapa, and Frank Trejo, "Lives Cut Short by Cheese," *Dallas Morning News,* April 16, 2007, www.dallasnews.com/sharedcontent/dws/news/localnews/stories/041507dnmetcheeseprofiles.373a0e5.html (accessed April 29, 2009).

5. John Burnett, "'Cheese' Heroin Hooking Young Users in Dallas," *NPR Morning Edition,* March 26, 2008, www.npr.org/templates/story/story.php?storyId=89070113 (accessed April 29, 2009).

6. Andy Lines, "Cheese-like Heroin Killing Texan Teens," *Observer,* September 9, 2007, www.guardian.co.uk/world/2007/sep/09/usa.drugstrade (accessed April 29, 2009).

7. U.S. Drug Enforcement Administration, "Cheese Heroin Linked to Mexican Drug Cartels, Gangs in Texas," Get Smart about Drugs: A DEA Resource for Parents, www.getsmartaboutdrugs.com/news/cheese_heroin_linked_to_mexican_drug_cartels_gangs_in_texas.html (accessed April 29, 2009).

8. Scott Price, "Local Heroin Use, Deaths Increase: Police Attribute Several Recent Overdoses to the Drug," *Grapevine Courier,* April 3, 2009.

9. Domingo Ramirez Jr., "Certain That Heroin Killed Her Teenage Son, Euless Mom Hopes His Story Helps Other Parents," Dallas *Star-Telegram,* April 17, 2009.

10. John Stewart Milne, *Surgical Instruments in Greek and Roman Times* (Oxford: Clarendon Press, 1907), 109–10.

11. M. J. Paech, C. B. Lim, S. L. Banks, M. W. M. Rucklidge, and D. A. Doherty, "A New Formulation of Nasal Fentanyl Spray for Postoperative Analgesia: A Pilot Study," *Anaesthesia* 58, no. 8 (14 July 2003): 740–44.

12. Javelin Pharmaceuticals, "Rylomine™ (Intranasal Morphine)," www.javelinpharmaceuticals.com/rylomine.html (accessed April 29, 2009).

13. Liz Highleyman, "Further Evidence Shows that Hepatitis C Virus (HCV) Can Be Transmitted through Snorting Drugs," HIV and Hepatitis.com, September 18, 2008, www.hivandhepatitis.com/hep_c/news/2008/091908_a.html (accessed April 30, 2009).

Chapter 31. Injection

1. Gillian R. Hamilton and Thomas F. Baskett, "In the Arms of Morpheus: The Development of Morphine for Postoperative Pain Relief," *Canadian Journal of Anesthesia* 47 (2000): 367–74.

2. Richard P. T. Davenport-Hines, *The Pursuit of Oblivion: A Global History of Narcotics* (New York: W. W. Norton & Co., 2002), 100–101.

3. Christopher Hallam, "Enter the Needle: A Brief History of the Syringe," *Safer Injecting,* 2007, www.saferinjecting.net/stuff-enter-the-needle.htm (accessed April 30, 2009).

4. James A. Incardi, *Handbook of Drug Control in the United States* (Westport, Conn.: Greenwood Publishing Group, 1990), 2.

5. Tom Carnwath and Ian Smith, *Heroin Century* (London: Routledge, 2002), 40–41.

6. Brendan Jensen, "High Life: An Addict Comes Clean on Four Decades of Feeding the Need," *Baltimore City Paper,* August 9, 2000, www.citypaper.com/news/story.asp?id=3576 (accessed April 30, 2009).

7. Carnwath and Smith, *Heroin Century,* 40.

8. Randy Shilts, *And the Band Played On* (New York: St. Martin's/Stonewall Inn Editions, 2000), 97.

9. Sandra D. Lane, "Needle Exchange: A Brief History" (1993). Available at AIDS Education Global Information System, www.aegis.com/law/journals/1993/ HKFNE009.html (accessed May 2, 2009).

10. Jon Zibbell, "Brief History of Needle Exchange in the U.S.," Springfield Users' Council, www.springfielduserscouncil.org/articles/brief-history.html (accessed May 2, 2009).

11. Ibid.

12. Tom Cannell, "The Struggle to Implement Needle Exchange in Three Cities," *Yale Journal of Public Health* 1, no. 2 (2004), www.yaleph.com/archive/ vol1no2/story1.html (accessed May 2, 2004).

13. Rong-gong Lin Ii and Daniel Costello, "Police Presence Puts Chill on Needle Exchange," *Los Angeles Times,* November 4, 2005, http://articles.latimes .com/2005/nov/04/local/me-needle4 (accessed May 2, 2009).

Chapter 32. Dependence, Addiction, and Tolerance

1. Jerry Mandel, "The Mythical Roots of U.S. Drug Policy: Soldier's Disease and Addicts in the Civil War" (2002). Available at Schaffer Library of Drug Policy, www.druglibrary.org/schaffer/History/soldis.htm (accessed February 28, 2009).

2. Ibid.

3. Richard P. T. Davenport-Hines, *The Pursuit of Oblivion: A Global History of Narcotics* (New York: W. W. Norton & Co., 2002), 100.

4. David F. Musto, *The American Disease: Origins of Narcotic Control*, 3rd ed. (New York: Oxford University Press US, 1999), 2.

5. National Institute on Drug Abuse, "Pain and Opiophobia," *Research Report Series—Prescription Drugs: Abuse and Addiction* (2005), www.nida.nih.gov/ researchreports/prescription/prescription6a.html (accessed May 3, 2009).

6. Lance P. Longo and Brian Johnson, "Addiction: Part I. Benzodiazepines—Side Effects, Abuse Risk and Alternatives," *American Family Physician* (April 1, 2000), www.aafp.org/afp/20000401/2121.html (accessed May 3, 2000).

7. Daniel K. Hall-Flavin, M.D., "Antidepressant Withdrawal: Is There Such a Thing?" Mayo Clinic, September 11, 2008, www.mayoclinic.com/health/ antidepressant-withdrawal/AN01425 (accessed May 3, 2009).

8. Nils Bejrot, "Addiction to Pleasure: A Biological and Social-Psychological Theory of Addiction," in *Theories on Drug Abuse: Selected Contemporary Perspectives,* Dan J. Lettieri, Mollie Sayers, and Helen Wallenstein Pearson, eds.

(Washington, D.C.: U.S. Department of Health and Human Services, 1980), 252.

9. Andrew Gasson, "Wilkie Collins and Laudanum," Wilkie Collins Information Pages, www.wilkie-collins.info/wilkie_collins_opium.htm (accessed May 3, 2009).

10. Kelly J. Powell, Noura S. Abul-Husn, Asha Jhamandas, Mary C. Olmstead, Richard J. Beninger, and Khem Jhamandas, "Paradoxical Effects of the Opioid Antagonist Naltrexone on Morphine Analgesia, Tolerance, and Reward in Rats," *The Journal of Pharmacology and Experimental Therapeutics* 300, no. 2 (February 2002): 588–96.

Chapter 33. Getting Clean and Staying Clean

1. George B. Greaves, "An Existential Theory of Drug Dependence," in *Theories on Drug Abuse: Selected Contemporary Perspectives,* Dan J. Lettieri, Mollie Sayers, and Helen Wallenstein Pearson, eds. (Washington, D.C.: U.S. Department of Health and Human Services, 1980), 27.

2. Suboxone.com, "Suboxone: Frequently Asked Questions," 2007, www.suboxone.com/patients/suboxone/faqs.aspx (accessed May 4, 2009).

3. P. Barabe, "The Religion of Iboga or the Bwiti of the Fangs," William J. Gladstone, ed. (1997), originally published as "La religion d'Eboga ou le Bwiti des Fanges," *Med. trop.* 12, no. 3 (May/June 1982): 251–57. Available at the Ibogaine Dossier, www.ibogaine.desk.nl/barabe.html (accessed May 5, 2009).

4. Peter Gorman, "Howard Lotsof: Taking Aim at Addiction," Peter Gorman Archive, http://petergormanarchive.com/at/interviews/howard-lotsof-taking-aim-at-addiction.html (accessed May 5, 2009).

5. Ibid.

6. Brian Vastag, "Addiction Treatment Strives for Legitimacy," *Journal of the American Medical Association* 288, no. 24 (December 25, 2002): 3096–3101. Available at Ibogaine Research Project, www.ibogaine-research.org/Ibogaine-Research-Project/Areas/Media/JAMA.htm (accessed May 5, 2009).

Afterword

1. Kenneth Grant, *The Magical Revival* (London: Skoob Books, 1972), 97.

INDEX